BAD SAMARITANS

Ha-Joon Chang is a Cambridg███████████████████████████
decades, has taught and resea███ **KU-610-360**███████████
development and globalisation. He has also worked as a
consultant for the World Bank, the Asian Development Bank,
various UN agencies and for the governments of Brazil, Canada,
Japan, South Africa, the UK, and Venezuela. He has published
numerous articles and books, including *Kicking Away the Ladder
– Development Strategy in Historical Perspective*, which won the
2003 Myrdal Prize and has been translated into seven languages.
In 2005, he and Richard Nelson of Columbia University received
the Leontief Prize, whose previous winners include John Kenneth
Galbraith and Amartya Sen. He has been on the editorial board
of the *Cambridge Journal of Economics* since 1992.

Praise for *Bad Samaritans*

'Every orthodoxy needs effective critics. Ha-Joon Chang is probably the
world's most effective critic of globalization. He does not deny the
benefits to developing countries of integration into the world economy.
But he draws on the lessons of history to argue that they must be allowed
to integrate on their own terms.' **Martin Wolf,** *Financial Times*

'In this more polemical tract, [Chang] adds the spark of personal
reflection . . . and some mischievous rhetorical set-pieces.' *Economist*

'Lucid, deeply informed, and enlivened with striking illustrations, this
penetrating study could be entitled "Economics in the Real World".'
Noam Chomsky

'Intelligent and provocative . . .' *Glasgow Herald*

'This is an excellent book . . . deploys the logical discipline of economics
and its engagement with quantitative evidence, but does so in jargon-
free prose that sparkles with anecdotes and practical observations.'
International Affairs

HA-JOON CHANG

Bad Samaritans

*The Guilty Secrets of Rich Nations and
the Threat to Global Prosperity*

BUSINESS
BOOKS

Published by Random House Business Books 2008

2 4 6 8 10 9 7 5 3 1

Copyright © Ha-Joon Chang 2007

Ha-Joon Chang has asserted his right under the Copyright, Designs
and Patents Act 1988 to be identified as the author of this work

First published in Great Britain in 2007 by
Random House Business Books
Random House, 20 Vauxhall Bridge Road,
London SW1V 2SA

www.rbooks.co.uk

Addresses for companies within The Random House Group Limited can be found at:
www.randomhouse.co.uk/offices.htm

The Random House Group Limited Reg. No. 954009

A CIP catalogue record for this book is available from the British Library

ISBN 9781905211371

The Random House Group Limited supports The Forest Stewardship
Council (FSC), the leading international forest certification organisation. All our
titles that are printed on Greenpeace approved FSC certified paper carry the FSC logo.
Our paper procurement policy can be found at www.rbooks.co.uk/environment

Typeset by Palimpsest Book Production Limited,
Grangemouth, Stirlingshire

Printed and bound in Great Britain by
CPI Bookmarque, Croydon CR0 4TD

Contents

development?

To Hee-Jeong

Acknowledgements

The idea of writing an accessible book on globalization and development that is critical of the reigning orthodoxy first came from Duncan Green a few years ago. He convinced me that I have some unusual and interesting things to say on these topics and, therefore, that I should put them together for an audience that is much bigger than the one I usually write for. Initially, we were going to write the book together, combining his long-time experience as an NGO activist and my academic research, to produce something that has both a solid academic foundation and campaign flair. In the event, Duncan became the head of research at Oxfam and had to withdraw from the project due to his workload. But later, when I started to write the book on my own, he very kindly read all the chapters of the book (often more than one version of them) and provided me with insightful comments, both substantively and editorially. He also graciously put up with me ringing him up without warning to thrash out my ideas. I deeply thank him for his generosity, wisdom and patience.

When Duncan withdrew, the project lost its propeller and drifted rather aimlessly for a while. I became busy with other things and, more importantly, it was not easy to make the existence of my project known to the relevant publishers. Then Richard Toye kindly introduced me to Ivan Mulcahy, my literary agent. Ivan had a vision how to turn an undeveloped semi-academic treatise into a genuinely accessible book and taught me a lot of things in the art of writing for a wider audience. His colleague Jonathan Conway at Mulcahy & Viney also provided critical input in shaping the project.

In formulating the book, I benefited tremendously from discussions with Chris Cramer. He has always been a generous friend, but the intellectual energy he invested in helping me shape this book was exceptional even by his own high standards. Richard Toye not only introduced me to my literary agent but also provided very helpful comments on overall structure and some of the individual arguments of the book. Deepak Nayyar took time out from his busy schedule to go through my initial proposal and gave me a lot of sagacious comments. In developing the book, I have also benefited from discussions with Dean Baker, Jonathan di John, Barbara Harriss-White, Peter Nolan, Gabriel Palma, Bob Rowthorn, Ajit Singh, Rosemary Thorp, John Toye and Mark Weisbrot.

As I was writing the chapters, I received useful comments from a number of people. My sometime co-author, Ilene Grabel, read all the chapters and gave me very important feedback. Robert Molteno not only read all the chapters and gave me wonderful editorial advice but also provided useful comments. Peter Beattie, Shailaja Fennell, Elias Khalil, Amy Klatzkin, Kangkook Lee, Chris Pallas, Richard Schmale and Sarah Wood read earlier versions of some of the chapters and gave me helpful suggestions.

The book would not have had the richness of information without the help of three very able research assistants. Luba Fakrhutdinova was on call to provide help with all aspects of the book, especially data work. Hassan Akram excavated a lot of wonderful historical material for the culture chapter and also offered helpful comments on some of the other chapters. Ariane McCabe did a great job in finding material for a number of chapters, especially the chapter on intellectual property rights, on which she also provided useful comments. I would also like to thank Luiz de Andrade Filho and Kenia Parsons for their assistance.

Without the first-class input from the Random House editorial team, the book would have looked much poorer. Nigel Wilcockson gave me extremely helpful advice on how to improve both the structure and the narrative of the book. He effectively restrained my tendency to get over-excited with trivia and taught me how to bring out the essential points without becoming too schematic or boring. I would also like to thank Elizabeth Hennessy for her excellent copy-editing job and Emily Rhodes for her able assistance.

My daughter, Yuna, and son, Jin-Gyu – unknowingly – helped me come up with some of the key analogies in the book. They also patiently waited for my return from an emotional exile in the last phase of the book. Finally, I would like to thank my wife, Hee-Jeong, for her emotional and intellectual support. Throughout the whole process of preparing for and writing the book, she had to put up with an obsessed and unpleasant man (yet again!). She also read most of the early draft chapters and made many incisive comments. She used to complain that I was using her as an intellectual guinea pig, but she does not quite realise how many of her comments were crucial in shaping, rather than just improving, my arguments. Without her, the book could not have been written. I dedicate the book to her.

Mozambique's economic miracle

How to escape poverty

Mozambique Takes on the Big Boys

Nuts and volts

June 28th 2061 | MAPUTO

From *The Economist* print edition

Tres Estrelas announces a new breakthrough in fuel cell technology

In a carefully staged event to coincide with the country's independence day on June 25th, Maputo-based Tres Estrelas, the largest African business group outside South Africa, unveiled a breakthrough technology for mass production of hydrogen fuel cells. 'When our new plant goes into production in the autumn of 2063,' Mr Armando Nhumaio, the ebullient chairman of the company announced, 'we will be able to take on the big boys from Japan and the USA by offering consumers much better value for money.' Analysts agree that the new technology from Tres Estrelas means hydrogen fuel is set to replace alcohol as the main source of power for automobiles. 'This is bound to pose a serious challenge to the leading alcohol fuel producers, like Petrobras of Brazil and Alconas of Malaysia,' says Nelson Mbeki-Malan, the head of the prestigious Energy Economics Research Institute at the University of Western Cape, South Africa.

Tres Estrelas has made its own rocket-fuelled journey from humble beginnings. The company started out exporting cashew nuts in 1968, seven years before Mozambique's independence from the Portuguese. It then did well by diversifying into textiles and sugar refining. Subsequently, it made a bolder move into electronics, first as a subcontractor for the Korean electronics giant, Samsung, and later as an

1

independent producer. But an announcement in 2030 that hydrogen fuel cell production was to be its next venture generated considerable scepticism. 'Everyone thought we were crazy,' says Mr Nhumaio. 'The fuel cell division bled money for 17 years. Luckily, in those days, we did not have many outside shareholders requiring instant results. We persisted in our belief that building a world-class firm requires a long period of preparation.'

The company's rise symbolizes the economic miracle that is modern Mozambique. In 1995, three years after the end of its bloody 16-year civil war, Mozambique had a *per capita* income of only $80 and was literally the poorest economy in the world. With deep political divisions, rampant corruption and a sorry 33% literacy rate, its prospects ranged from dire to grim. In 2000, eight years after the end of the civil war, the average Mozambican still earned only $210 a year, just over half that of the average Ghanaian, who was earning $350. However, since then, Mozambique's economic miracle has transformed it into one of the richest economies in Africa and a solid upper-middle-income country. With a bit of luck and sweat, it may even be able to join the ranks of the advanced economies in the next two or three decades.

'We will not rest on our laurels,' says Mr Nhumaio, whose roguish grin is reported to hide a steely determination. 'This is a tough industry where technology changes fast. Product life-cycles are short and no one can expect to last long as the market leader based on only one innovation. Competitors may appear on the horizon out of nowhere any day.' After all, his company has just sprung a nasty surprise on the Americans and the Japanese. Might a relatively unknown fuel cell manufacturer somewhere in Nigeria decide that, if Tres Estrelas was able to move from the darkest shadows to the top of the tree, then perhaps it could too?

Mozambique may or may not succeed in living up to my fantasy. But what would your reaction have been, had you been told in 1961, a century before the Mozambican dream, that South Korea would, in 40 years' time, be one of the world's leading exporters of mobile phones, a strictly science-fiction product at that time? Hydrogen fuel cells do at least exist today.

In 1961, eight years after the end of its fratricidal war with North Korea, South Korea's yearly income stood at $82 per person. The average Korean earned *less than half* the average Ghanaian citizen ($179).[1] The Korean War – which, incidentally, started on June 25, Mozambique's independence day – was one of the bloodiest in human history, claiming four million lives in just over three years (1950–3). Half of South Korea's manufacturing base and more than 75% of its railways were destroyed in the conflict. The country had shown some organizational ability by managing to raise its literacy ratio to 71% by 1961 from the paltry 22% level it had inherited in 1945 from its Japanese colonial masters, who had ruled Korea since 1910. But it was widely considered a basket case of developmental failure. A 1950s internal report from USAID – the main US government aid agency then, as now – called Korea a 'bottomless pit'. At the time, the country's main exports were tungsten, fish and other primary commodities.

As for Samsung,* now one of the world's leading exporters of mobile phones, semiconductors and computers, the company started out as an exporter of fish, vegetables and fruit in 1938, seven years before Korea's independence from Japanese colonial rule. Until the 1970s, its main lines of business were sugar refining and textiles that it had set up in the mid-1950s.[2] When it moved into the semiconductor industry by acquiring a 50% stake in Korea Semiconductor in 1974, no one took it seriously. After all, Samsung did not even manufacture colour TV sets until 1977. When it declared its intention, in 1983, to take on the big boys of the semiconductor industry from the US and Japan by designing its own chips, few were convinced.

Korea, one of the poorest places in the world, was the sorry country I was born into on October 7 1963. Today I am a citizen of one of the wealthier, if not wealthiest, countries in the world. During my lifetime,

---

* Samsung in Korean means Three Stars, as does my fictitious Mozambican firm, Tres Estrelas. The last sentence in my imaginary 2061 *Economist* piece is based on a real *Economist* article about Samsung, 'As good as it gets?' (January 13 2005), whose final sentence reads: 'Might a relatively unknown electronics manufacturer somewhere in China decide that, if Samsung was able to move from the darkest shadows to the top of the tree, then perhaps it could too?' The 17 years during which the fuel cell division of my fictitious Mozambican firm lost money is the same investment period during which the electronics division of Nokia, founded in 1960, lost money.

per capita income in Korea has grown something like 14 times, in purchasing power terms. It took the UK over two centuries (between the late 18th century and today) and the US around one and half centuries (the 1860s to the present day) to achieve the same result.[3] The material progress I have seen in my 40-odd years is as though I had started life as a British pensioner born when George III was on the throne or as an American grandfather born while Abraham Lincoln was president.

The house I was born and lived in until I was six was in what was then the north-western edge of Seoul, Korea's capital city. It was one of the small (two-bedroom) but modern homes that the government built with foreign aid in a programme to upgrade the country's dilapidated housing stock. It was made with cement bricks and was poorly heated, so it was rather cold in winter – the temperature in Korea's winter can sink to 15 or even 20 degrees below zero. There was no flushing toilet, of course: that was only for the very rich.

Yet my family had some great luxuries that many others lacked, thanks to my father, an elite civil servant in the Finance Ministry who had diligently saved his scholarship money while studying at Harvard for a year. We owned a black-and-white TV set, which exerted a magnetic pull on our neighbours. One family friend, an up-and-coming young dentist at St Mary's, one of the biggest hospitals in the country, somehow used to find the time to visit us whenever there was a big sports match on TV – ostensibly for reasons totally unrelated to the match. In today's Korea, he would be contemplating upgrading the second family TV in the bedroom to a plasma screen. A cousin of mine who had just moved from my father's native city of Kwangju to Seoul came to visit on one occasion and quizzed my mother about the strange white cabinet in the living room. It was our refrigerator (the kitchen being too small to accommodate it). My wife, Hee-Jeong, born in Kwangju in 1966, tells me that her neighbours would regularly 'deposit' their precious meat in the refrigerator of her mother, the wife of a prosperous doctor, as if she was the manager of an exclusive Swiss private bank.

A small cement-brick house with a black-and-white TV and a refrigerator may not sound much, but it was a dream come true for my parents' generation, who had lived through the most turbulent and deprived times: Japanese colonial rule (1910–45), the Second World War, the division of the country into North and South Korea (1948) and the Korean War. Whenever I and my sister, Yonhee, and brother, Hasok, complained about food, my mother would tell us how spoilt we were. She would remind us that, when they were our age, people of her generation would count themselves lucky if they had an egg. Many families could not afford them; even those who could reserved them for fathers and working older brothers. She used to recall her heartbreak when her little brother, starving during the Korean War at the age of five, said that he would feel better if he could only hold a rice bowl in his hands, even if it was empty. For his part, my father, a man with a healthy appetite who loves his beef, had to survive as a secondary school student during the Korean War on little more than rice, black-market margarine from the US army, soy sauce and chilli paste. At the age of ten, he had to watch helplessly as his seven-year-old younger brother died of dysentery, a killer disease then that is all but unknown in Korea today.

Years later, in 2003, when I was on leave from Cambridge and staying in Korea, I was showing my friend and mentor, Joseph Stiglitz, the Nobel Laureate economist, around the National Museum in Seoul. We came across an exhibition of beautiful black-and-white photographs showing people going about their business in Seoul's middle-class neighbourhoods during the late 1950s and the early 1960s. It was exactly how I remembered my childhood. Standing behind me and Joe were two young women in their early twenties. One screamed, 'How can that be Korea? It looks like Vietnam!' There was less than 20 years' age gap between us, but scenes that were familiar to me were totally alien to her. I turned to Joe and told him how 'privileged' I was as a development economist to have lived through such a change. I felt like an historian of mediaeval England who has actually witnessed the Battle of Hastings or an astronomer who has voyaged back in time to the Big Bang.

Our next family house, where I lived between 1969 and 1981, at the height of Korean economic miracle, not only had a flushing toilet but also boasted a central heating system. The boiler, unfortunately, caught fire soon after we moved in and almost burned the house down. I don't tell you this in complaint; we were lucky to have one – most houses were heated with coal briquettes, which killed thousands of people every winter with carbon monoxide poisoning. But the story does offer an insight into the state of Korean technology in that far-off, yet really so recent, era.

In 1970 I started primary school. It was a second-rate private school that had 65 children in each class. We were very proud because the state school next door had 90 children per class. Years later, in a seminar at Cambridge, a speaker said that because of budget cuts imposed by the International Monetary Fund (more on this later), the average number of pupils per classroom in several African countries rose from 30-something to 40-something in the 1980s. Then it hit me just how bad things had been in the Korean schools of my childhood. When I was in primary school, the poshest school in the country had 40 children in a class, and everyone wondered, 'how do they do that?' State schools in some rapidly expanding urban areas were stretched to the limit, with up to 100 pupils per class and teachers running double, sometimes triple, shifts. Given the conditions, it was little wonder that education involved beating the children liberally and teaching everything by rote. The method has obvious drawbacks, but at least Korea has managed to provide at least six years' education to virtually every child since the 1960s.

In 1972, when I was in Year 3 (US third grade), my school playground suddenly became a campsite for soldiers. They were there to pre-empt any student demonstrations against the martial law being imposed by the president of the country, (former) General Park Chung-Hee. Thankfully, they were not there to take on me and my friends. We Korean kids may be known for our academic precocity, but constitutional politics were frankly a little bit beyond us nine-year-olds. My primary school was attached to a university, whose rebellious students were the soldiers' target. Indeed, Korean university students were the nation's conscience throughout the political dark age of the military dictatorship and they also played the leading role in putting an end to it in 1987.

After he had come to power in a military coup in 1961, General

Park turned 'civilian' and won three successive elections. His electoral victories were propelled by his success in launching the country's economic 'miracle' through his Five Year Plans for Economic Development. But the victories were also ensured by election rigging and political dirty tricks. His third and supposedly final term as president was due to end in 1974, but Park just could not let go. Halfway through his third term, he staged what Latin Americans call an 'auto-coup'. This involved dissolving the parliament and establishing a rigged electoral system to guarantee him the presidency for life. His excuse was that the country could ill afford the chaos of democracy. It had to defend itself against North Korean communism, the people were told, and accelerate its economic development. His proclaimed goal of raising the country's *per capita* income to 1,000 US dollars by 1981 was considered overly ambitious, bordering on delusional.

President Park launched the ambitious Heavy and Chemical Industrialization (HCI) programme in 1973. The first steel mill and the first modern shipyard went into production, and the first locally designed cars (made mostly from imported parts) rolled off the production lines. New firms were set up in electronics, machinery, chemicals and other advanced industries. During this period, the country's *per capita* income grew phenomenally by more than five times, in US dollar terms, between 1972 and 1979. Park's apparently delusional goal of $1,000 *per capita* income by 1981 was actually achieved four years ahead of schedule. Exports grew even faster, increasing nine times, in US dollar terms, between 1972 and 1979.[4]

The country's obsession with economic development was fully reflected in our education. We learned that it was our patriotic duty to report anyone seen smoking foreign cigarettes. The country needed to use every bit of the foreign exchange earned from its exports in order to import machines and other inputs to develop better industries. Valuable foreign currencies were really the blood and sweat of our 'industrial soldiers' fighting the export war in the country's factories. Those squandering them on frivolous things, like illegal foreign cigarettes, were 'traitors'. I don't believe any of my friends actually went as far as reporting such 'acts of treason'. But it did feed the gossip mill when kids saw foreign cigarettes in a friend's house. The friend's father

– it was almost invariably men who smoked – would be darkly commented on as an unpatriotic and therefore immoral, if not exactly criminal, individual.

Spending foreign exchange on anything not essential for industrial development was prohibited or strongly discouraged through import bans, high tariffs and excise taxes (which were called luxury consumption taxes). 'Luxury' items included even relatively simple things, like small cars, whisky or cookies. I remember the minor national euphoria when a consignment of Danish cookies was imported under special government permission in the late 1970s. For the same reason, foreign travel was banned unless you had explicit government permission to do business or study abroad. As a result, despite having quite a few relatives living in the US, I had never been outside Korea until I travelled to Cambridge at the age of 23 to start as a graduate student there in 1986.

This is not to say that no one smoked foreign cigarettes or ate illicit cookies. A considerable quantity of illegal and semi-legal foreign goods was in circulation. There was some smuggling, especially from Japan, but most of the goods involved were things brought in – illegally or semi-legally – from the numerous American army bases in the country. Those American soldiers who fought in the Korean War may still remember malnourished Korean children running after them begging for chewing gum or chocolates. Even in the Korea of the 1970s, American army goods were still considered luxuries. Increasingly affluent middle class families could afford to buy m&m chocolates and Tang juice powders from shops and itinerant pedlars. Less affluent people might go to restaurants that served *boodae chige*, literally 'army base stew'. This was a cheaper version of the classic Korean stew, *kimchee chige*, using *kimchee* (cabbages pickled in garlic and chilli) but substituting the other key ingredient, pork belly, with cheaper meats, like surplus bacon, sausages and spam smuggled out of American army bases.

I longed for the chance to sample the tins of spam, corned beef, chocolates, biscuits and countless other things whose names I did not even know, from the boxes of the American Army's 'C Ration' (the canned and dried food ration for the battlefield). A maternal uncle, who was a general in the Korean army, used to accumulate supplies during joint field exercises with his American colleagues and gave them to me as an occasional treat. American soldiers cursed the wretched quality of their field rations. For me they were like a Fortnum & Mason picnic hamper. But, then, I was living in a country where vanilla ice cream had so little vanilla in it that I thought vanilla meant 'no flavour', until I learnt English in secondary school. If that was the case with a well-fed upper-middle-class child like me, you can imagine what it must have been like for the rest.

When I went to secondary school, my father gave me a Casio electronic calculator, a gift beyond my wildest dreams. Then it was probably worth half a month's wages for a garment factory worker, and was a huge expense even for my father, who spared nothing on our education. Some 20 years later, a combination of rapid development in electronics technologies and the rise in Korea's living standards meant that electronic calculators were so abundant that they were given out as free gifts in department stores. Many of them ended up as toys for toddlers (no, I don't believe this is why Korean kids are good at maths!).

Korea's economic 'miracle' was not, of course, without its dark sides. Many girls from poor families in the countryside were forced to find a job as soon as they left primary school at the age of 12 – to 'get rid of an extra mouth' and to earn money so that at least one brother could receive higher education. Many ended up as housemaids in urban middle-class families, working for room and board and, if they were lucky, a tiny amount of pocket money. The other girls, and the less fortunate boys, were exploited in factories where conditions were reminiscent of 19th-century 'dark satanic mills' or today's sweatshops in China. In the textile and garment industries, which were the main export industries, workers often worked 12 hours or more in very hazardous and unhealthy conditions for low pay. Some factories refused to serve soup in the canteen, lest the workers should require an extra toilet break that might wipe out their wafer-thin profit margins. Conditions were better in the newly emerging heavy industries – cars, steel, chemicals, machinery and so on – but, overall, Korean workers, with their average 53–4 hour working week, put in longer hours than just about anyone else in the world at the time.

Urban slums emerged. Because they were usually up in the low mountains that comprise a great deal of the Korean landscape, they were nicknamed 'Moon Neighbourhoods', after a popular TV sitcom series of the 1970s. Families of five or six would be squashed into a tiny room and hundreds of people would share one toilet and a single standpipe for running water. Many of these slums would ultimately be cleared forcefully by the police and the residents dumped in far-flung neighbourhoods, with even worse sanitation and poorer road access, to make way for new apartment blocks for the ever-growing middle class. If the poor could not get out of the new slums fast enough (but getting out of the slums was at least possible, given the rapid growth of the economy and the creation of new jobs), the urban sprawl would catch up with them and see them rounded up once again and dumped in an even more remote place. Some people ended up scavenging in the city's main rubbish dump, Nanji Island. Few people outside Korea were aware that the beautiful public parks surrounding the impressive Seoul Football Stadium they saw during the 2002 World Cup were built literally on top of the old rubbish dump on the island (which nowadays has an ultra-modern eco-friendly methane-burning power station, which taps into the organic material dumped there).

In October 1979, when I was still a secondary school student, President Park was unexpectedly assassinated by the chief of his own Intelligence Service, amid mounting popular discontent with his dictatorship and the economic turmoil following the Second Oil Shock. A brief 'Spring of Seoul' followed, with hopes of democracy welling up. But it was brutally ended by the next military government of General Chun Doo-Hwan, which seized power after the two-week armed popular uprising that was crushed in the Kwangju Massacre of May 1980.

Despite this grave political setback, by the early 1980s, Korea had become a solid middle-income country, on a par with Ecuador, Mauritius and Costa Rica. But it was still far removed from the prosperous nation we know today. One of the slang expressions common among us high-school students was 'I've been to Hong Kong', which meant 'I have had an experience out of this world'. Even today, Hong

Kong is still considerably richer than Korea, but the expression reflects the fact that, in the 1960s or the 1970s, Hong Kong's *per capita* income was three to four times greater than my country's.

When I went to university in 1982, I became interested in the issue of intellectual property rights, something that is even more hotly debated today. By that time, Korea had become competent enough to copy advanced products and rich enough to want the finer things in life (music, fashion goods, books). But it was still not sophisticated enough to come up with original ideas and to develop and own international patents, copyrights and trademarks.

Today, Korea is one of the most 'inventive' nations in the world – it ranks among the top five nations in terms of the number of patents granted annually by the US Patent Office. But until the mid-1980s it lived on 'reverse engineering'. My friends would buy 'copy' computers that were made by small workshops, which would take apart IBM machines, copy the parts, and put them together. It was the same with trademarks. At the time, the country was one of the 'pirate capitals' of the world, churning out fake Nike shoes and Louis Vuitton bags in huge quantities. Those who had more delicate consciences would settle for near-counterfeits. There were shoes that looked like Nike but were called Nice, or shoes that had the Nike swoosh but with an extra prong. Counterfeit goods were rarely sold as the genuine article. Those who bought them were perfectly aware that they were buying fakes; the point was to make a fashion statement, rather than to mislead. Copyrighted items were treated in the same way. Today, Korea exports a large and increasing quantity of copyrighted materials (movies, TV soaps, popular songs), but at the time imported music (LP records) or films (videos) were so expensive that few people could afford the real thing. We grew up listening to pirate rock'n' roll records, which we called '*tempura* shop records', because their sound quality was so bad it sounded as if someone was deep-frying in the background. As for foreign books, they were still beyond the means of most students. Coming from a well-off family that was willing to invest in education, I did have some imported books. But most of my books in English were pirated. I could never have entered and survived Cambridge without those illegal books.

By the time I was finishing my graduate studies at Cambridge in the late 1980s, Korea had become a solid upper-middle-income country. The surest proof of this was that European countries stopped demanding that Koreans get an entry visa. Most of us by then had no reason to want to emigrate illegally anyway. In 1996, the country even joined the OECD (Organisation for Economic Co-operation and Development) – the club of the rich countries – and declared itself to have 'arrived', although that euphoria was badly deflated by the financial crisis that engulfed Korea in 1997. Since that financial crisis, the country has not been doing as well by its own high standards, mainly because it has over-enthusiastically embraced the 'free market rules' model. But that is a story for later.

Whatever its recent problems have been, Korea's economic growth and the resulting social transformation over the last four and a half decades have been truly spectacular. It has gone from being one of the poorest countries in the world to a country on a par with Portugal and Slovenia in terms of *per capita* income.[5] A country whose main exports included tungsten ore, fish and wigs made with human hair has become a high-tech powerhouse, exporting stylish mobile phones and flat-screen TVs coveted all over the world. Better nutrition and health care mean that a child born in Korea today can expect to live 24 years longer than someone born in the early 1960s (77 years instead of 53 years). Instead of 78 babies out of 1,000, only five babies will die within a year of birth, breaking far fewer parents' hearts. In terms of these life-chance indicators, Korea's progress is as if Haiti had turned into Switzerland.[6] How has this 'miracle' been possible?

For most economists, the answer is a very simple one. Korea has succeeded because it has followed the dictates of the free market. It has embraced the principles of sound money (low inflation), small government, private enterprise, free trade and friendliness towards foreign investment. The view is known as neo-liberal economics.

Neo-liberal economics is an updated version of the liberal economics of the 18th-century economist Adam Smith and his followers. It first emerged in the 1960s and has been the dominant economic view since the 1980s. Liberal economists of the 18th and the

19th centuries believed that unlimited competition in the free market was the best way to organise an economy, because it forces everyone to perform with maximum efficiency. Government intervention was judged harmful because it reduces competitive pressure by restricting the entry of the potential competitors, whether through import controls or the creation of monopolies. Neo-liberal economists support certain things that the old liberals did not – most notably certain forms of monopoly (such as patents or the central bank's monopoly over the issue of bank notes) and political democracy. But in general they share the old liberals' enthusiasm for the free market. And despite a few 'tweaks' in the wake of a whole series of disappointing results of neo-liberal policies applied to developing nations during the past quarter of a century, the core neo-liberal agenda of deregulation, privatization and opening up of international trade and investment has remained the same since the 1980s.

In relation to the developing countries, the neo-liberal agenda has been pushed by an alliance of rich country governments led by the US and mediated by the 'Unholy Trinity' of international economic organizations that they largely control – the International Monetary Fund (IMF), the World Bank and the World Trade Organisation (WTO). The rich governments use their aid budgets and access to their home markets as carrots to induce the developing countries to adopt neo-liberal policies. This is sometimes to benefit specific firms that lobby, but usually to create an environment in the developing country concerned that is friendly to foreign goods and investment in general. The IMF and the World Bank play their part by attaching to their loans the condition that the recipient countries adopt neo-liberal policies. The WTO contributes by making trading rules that favour free trade in areas where the rich countries are stronger but not where they are weak (e.g., agriculture or textiles). These governments and international organizations are supported by an army of ideologues. Some of these people are highly trained academics who should know the limits of their free-market economics but tend to ignore them when it comes to giving policy advice (as happened especially when they advised the former communist economies in the 1990s). Together, these various bodies and individuals form a powerful propaganda machine, a financial-intellectual complex backed by money and power.

This neo-liberal establishment would have us believe that, during its miracle years between the 1960s and the 1980s, Korea pursued a neo-liberal economic development strategy.[7] The reality, however, was very different indeed. What Korea actually did during these decades was to nurture certain new industries, selected by the government in consultation with the private sector, through tariff protection, subsidies and other forms of government support (e.g., overseas marketing information services provided by the state export agency) until they 'grew up' enough to withstand international competition. The government owned all the banks, so it could direct the life blood of business – credit. Some big projects were undertaken directly by state-owned enterprises – the steel maker, POSCO, being the best example – although the country had a pragmatic, rather than ideo-logical, attitude to the issue of state ownership. If private enterprises worked well, that was fine; if they did not invest in important areas, the government had no qualms about setting up state-owned enter-prises (SOEs); and if some private enterprises were mismanaged, the government often took them over, restructured them, and usually (but not always) sold them off again.

The Korean government also had absolute control over scarce foreign exchange (violation of foreign exchange controls could be punished with the death penalty). When combined with a carefully designed list of priorities in the use of foreign exchange, it ensured that hard-earned foreign currencies were used for importing vital machinery and industrial inputs. The Korean government heavily controlled foreign investment as well, welcoming it with open arms in certain sectors while shutting it out completely in others, according to the evolving national development plan. It also had a lax attitude towards foreign patents, encouraging 'reverse engineering' and over-looking 'pirating' of patented products.

The popular impression of Korea as a free-trade economy was created by its export success. But export success does not require free trade, as Japan and China have also shown. Korean exports in the earlier period – things like simple garments and cheap electronics –

were all means to earn the hard currencies needed to pay for the advanced technologies and expensive machines that were necessary for the new, more difficult industries, which were protected through tariffs and subsidies. At the same time, tariff protection and subsidies were not there to shield industries from international competition forever, but to give them the time to absorb new technologies and establish new organizational capabilities until they could compete in the world market.

The Korean economic miracle was the result of a clever and pragmatic mixture of market incentives and state direction. The Korean government did not vanquish the market as the communist states did. However, it did not have blind faith in the free market either. While it took markets seriously, the Korean strategy recognized that they often need to be corrected through policy intervention.

Now, if it was just Korea that became rich through such 'heretical' policies, the free-market gurus might be able to dismiss it as merely the exception that proves the rule. However, Korea is no exception. As I shall show later, practically *all* of today's developed countries, including Britain and the US, the supposed homes of the free market and free trade, have become rich on the basis of policy recipes that go against neo-liberal economics.

Today's rich countries used protection and subsidies, while discriminating against foreign investors – all anathema to today's economic orthodoxy and now severely restricted by multilateral treaties, like the WTO Agreements, and proscribed by aid donors and international financial organizations (notably the IMF and the World Bank). There are a few countries that did not use much protection, such as the Netherlands and (until the First World War) Switzerland. But they deviated from the orthodoxy in other ways, such as their refusal to protect patents (more on this in later chapters). The records of today's rich countries on policies regarding foreign investment, state-owned enterprises, macroeconomic management and political institutions also show significant deviations from today's orthodoxy regarding these matters.

But, if this is the case, why don't the rich countries recommend to today's developing countries the strategies that served them so well? Why do they instead hand out a fiction about the history of capitalism, and a bad one at that?

In 1841, a German economist, Friedrich List, criticized Britain for preaching free trade to other countries, while having achieved its economic supremacy through high tariffs and extensive subsidies. He accused the British of 'kicking away the ladder' that they had climbed to reach the world's top economic position: '[i]t is a very common clever device that when anyone has attained the summit of greatness, he *kicks away the ladder* by which he has climbed up, in order to deprive others of the means of climbing up after him [italics added]'.[8]

Today, there are certainly some people in the rich countries who preach free market and free trade to the poor countries in order to capture larger shares of the latter's markets and to pre-empt the emergence of possible competitors. They are saying 'do as we say, not as we did' and act as 'Bad Samaritans', taking advantage of others who are in trouble.* But what is more worrying is that many of today's Bad Samaritans do not even realize that they are hurting the developing countries with their policies. The history of capitalism has been so totally re-written that many people in the rich world do not perceive the historical double standards involved in recommending free trade and free market to developing countries.

I am not suggesting that there is a sinister secret committee somewhere that systematically air-brushes undesirable people out of photographs and re-writes historical accounts. However, history is written by the victors and it is human nature to re-interpret the past from the point of view of the present. As a result, the rich countries have, over time, gradually, if often sub-consciously, re-written their own histories to make them more consistent with how they see themselves today, rather than as they really were – in much the same way that today people write about Renaissance 'Italy' (a country that did not exist until 1871) or include the French-speaking Scandinavians (Norman conqueror kings) in the list of 'English' kings and queens.

---

* The original story is that of the 'Good Samaritan' from the Bible. In that parable, a man who was robbed by highwaymen was helped by a 'Good Samaritan', despite the fact that the Samaritans were stereotyped as being callous and not above taking advantage of the others in trouble.

The result is that many Bad Samaritans may be recommending free-trade, free-market policies to the poor countries in the honest but mistaken belief that those are the routes their own countries took in the past to become rich. But they are in fact making the lives of those whom they are trying to help more difficult. Sometimes these Bad Samaritans may be more of a problem than those knowingly engaged in 'kicking away the ladder', because self-righteousness is often more stubborn than self-interest.

So how do we dissuade the Bad Samaritans from hurting the poor countries, whatever their intentions are? What else should they do instead? This book offers some answers through a mix of history, analysis of the world today, some future predictions and suggestions for change.

The place to start is with a true history of capitalism and globalization, which I examine in the next two chapters (chapters 1 and 2). In these chapters, I will show how many things that the reader may have accepted as 'historical facts' are either wrong or partial truths. Britain and the US are *not* the homes of free trade; in fact, for a long time they were the most protectionist countries in the world. Not all countries have succeeded through protection and subsidies, but few without them. For developing countries, free trade has rarely been a matter of choice; it was often an imposition from outside, sometimes even through military power. Most of them did very poorly under free trade; they did much better when they used protection and subsidies. The best-performing economies have been those that opened up their economies selectively and gradually. Neo-liberal free-trade free-market policy claims to sacrifice equity for growth, but in fact it achieves neither; growth has slowed down in the past two and a half decades when markets were freed and borders opened.

In the main chapters of the book that follow the historical chapters (chapters 3 to 9), I deploy a mixture of economic theory, history and contemporary evidence to turn much of the conventional wisdom about development on its head. Free trade reduces freedom of choice for poor countries. Keeping foreign companies out may be good for them in the long run. Investing in a company that is going to make a loss for 17 years may be an excellent proposition. Some of the world's best firms are owned and run by the state. 'Borrowing' ideas from more productive foreigners is essential for economic development. Low inflation and government prudence may be harmful for economic development. Corruption exists because there is too much, not too little, market. Free market and democracy are not natural partners. Countries are poor not because their people are lazy; their people are 'lazy' because they are poor.

Like this opening chapter, the closing chapter of the book opens with an alternative 'future history' – but this time a very bleak one. The scenario is deliberately pessimistic, but it is firmly rooted in reality, showing how close we are to such a future, should we continue with the neo-liberal policies propagated by the Bad Samaritans. In the rest of the chapter, I present some key principles, distilled from the detailed policy alternatives that I discuss throughout the book, which should guide our action if we are to enable developing countries to advance their economies. Despite the bleak opening, the chapter – and therefore the book – closes with a note of optimism, explaining why I believe most Bad Samaritans can be changed and really made to help developing countries improve their economic situations.

CHAPTER 1

The Lexus and the olive
tree revisited

Myths and facts about globalization

Once upon a time, the leading car maker of a developing country exported its first passenger cars to the US. Up to that day, the little company had only made shoddy products – poor copies of quality items made by richer countries. The car was nothing too sophisticated – just a cheap subcompact (one could have called it 'four wheels and an ashtray'). But it was a big moment for the country and its exporters felt proud.

Unfortunately, the product failed. Most thought the little car looked lousy and savvy buyers were reluctant to spend serious money on a family car that came from a place where only second-rate products were made. The car had to be withdrawn from the US market. This disaster led to a major debate among the country's citizens.

Many argued that the company should have stuck to its original business of making simple textile machinery. After all, the country's biggest export item was silk. If the company could not make good cars after 25 years of trying, there was no future for it. The government had given the car maker every opportunity to succeed. It had ensured high profits for it at home through high tariffs and draconian controls on foreign investment in the car industry. Fewer than ten years ago, it even gave public money to save the company from imminent bankruptcy. So, the critics argued, foreign cars should now be let in freely and foreign car makers, who had been kicked out 20 years before, allowed to set up shop again.

Others disagreed. They argued that no country had got anywhere without developing 'serious' industries like automobile production.

They just needed more time to make cars that appealed to everyone.

The year was 1958 and the country was, in fact, Japan. The company was Toyota, and the car was called the Toyopet. Toyota started out as a manufacturer of textile machinery (Toyoda Automatic Loom) and moved into car production in 1933. The Japanese government kicked out General Motors and Ford in 1939 and bailed out Toyota with money from the central bank (Bank of Japan) in 1949. Today, Japanese cars are considered as 'natural' as Scottish salmon or French wine, but fewer than 50 years ago, most people, including many Japanese, thought the Japanese car industry simply should not exist.

Half a century after the Toyopet debacle, Toyota's luxury brand Lexus has become something of an icon for globalization, thanks to the American journalist Thomas Friedman's book, *The Lexus and the Olive Tree*. The book owes its title to an epiphany that Friedman had on the Shinkansen bullet train during his trip to Japan in 1992. He had paid a visit to a Lexus factory, which mightily impressed him. On his train back from the car factory in Toyota City to Tokyo, he came across yet another newspaper article about the troubles in the Middle East where he had been a long-time correspondent. Then it hit him. He realized that that 'half the world seemed to be . . . intent on building a better Lexus, dedicated to modernizing, streamlining, and privatizing their economies in order to thrive in the system of globalization. And half of the world – sometimes half the same country, sometimes half the same person – was still caught up in the fight over who owns which olive tree'.[1]

According to Friedman, unless they fit themselves into a particular set of economic policies that he calls the Golden Straitjacket, countries in the olive-tree world will not be able to join the Lexus world. In describing the Golden Straitjacket, he pretty much sums up today's neo-liberal economic orthodoxy: in order to fit into it, a country needs to privatize state-owned enterprises, maintain low inflation, reduce the size of government bureaucracy, balance the budget (if not running a surplus), liberalize trade, deregulate foreign investment, deregulate capital markets, make the currency convertible, reduce corruption and privatize pensions.[2] According to him, this is the only path to success in the new global economy. His Straitjacket is the only gear suitable for the harsh but exhilarating game of global-ization. Friedman is categorical: 'Unfortunately, this Golden Straitjacket is pretty much "one-size fits all" . . . It is not always pretty or gentle or comfortable. But it's here and it's the only model on the rack this historical season.'[3]

However, the fact is that, had the Japanese government followed the free-trade economists back in the early 1960s, there would have been no Lexus. Toyota today would, at best, be a junior partner to some western car manufacturer, or worse, have been wiped out. The same would have been true for the entire Japanese economy. Had the country donned Friedman's Golden Straitjacket early on, Japan would have remained the third-rate industrial power that it was in the 1960s, with its income level on a par with Chile, Argentina and South Africa[4] – it was then a country whose prime minister was insultingly dismissed as 'a transistor-radio salesman' by the French president, Charles De Gaulle.[5] In other words, had they followed Friedman's advice, the Japanese would now not be exporting the Lexus but still be fighting over who owns which mulberry tree (that feeds the silkworms).

The official history of globalization

Our Toyota fable suggests that there is something spectacularly jarring in the story of globalization promoted by Thomas Friedman and his colleagues. In order to tell you what it is exactly, I need to tell you what I call the 'official history of globalization' and discuss its limitations.

According to this history, globalization has progressed over the last three centuries in the following way.[6] Britain adopted free-market and free-trade policies in the 18th century, well ahead of other countries. By the middle of the 19th century, the superiority of these policies became so obvious, thanks to Britain's spectacular economic success, that other countries started liberalizing their trade and deregulating their domestic economies. This liberal world order, perfected around 1870 under British hegemony, was based on: *laissez-faire* industrial poli-cies at home; low barriers to the international flows of goods, capital and labour; and macroeconomic stability, both nationally and internationally, guaranteed by the principles of sound money (low inflation) and balanced budgets. A period of unprecedented prosperity followed.

Unfortunately, things started to go wrong after the First World War. In response to the ensuing instability of the world economy, countries unwisely began to erect trade barriers again. In 1930, the US abandoned free trade and enacted the infamous Smoot-Hawley tariff. Countries like Germany and Japan abandoned liberal policies and erected high trade barriers and created cartels, which were intimately associated with their fascism and external aggression. The world free trade system finally ended in 1932, when Britain, hitherto the champion of free trade, succumbed to temptation and itself re-introduced tariffs. The resulting contraction and instability in the world economy, and then, finally, the Second World War, destroyed the last remnants of the first liberal world order.

After the Second World War, the world economy was re-organized on a more liberal line, this time under American hegemony. In particular, some significant progress was made in trade liberalization among the rich countries through the early GATT (General Agreement on Trade and Tariffs) talks. But protectionism and state intervention still persisted in most developing countries and, needless to say, in the communist countries.

Fortunately, illiberal policies have been largely abandoned across the world since the 1980s following the rise of neo-liberalism. By the late 1970s, the failures of so-called import substitution industrialization (ISI) in developing countries – based on protection, subsidies and regulation – had become too obvious to ignore.* The economic 'miracle' in

---

* The idea behind import substitution industrialization is that a backward country starts producing industrial products that it used to import, thereby 'substituting' imported industrial products with domestically produced equivalents. This is achieved by making imports artificially expensive by means of tariffs and quotas against imports, or subsidies to domestic producers. The strategy was adopted by many Latin American countries in the 1930s. At the time, most other developing countries were not in a position to practise the ISI strategy, as they were either colonies or subject to 'unequal treaties' that deprived them of the right to set their own tariffs (see below). The ISI strategy was adopted by most other developing countries after they gained independence between the mid-1940s and the mid-1960s.

East Asia, which was already practising free trade and welcoming foreign investment, was a wake-up call for the other developing countries. After the 1982 Third World debt crisis, many developing countries abandoned interventionism and protectionism, and embraced neo-liberalism. The crowning glory of this trend towards global integration was the fall of communism in 1989.

These national policy changes were made all the more necessary by the unprecedented acceleration in the development of transport and communications technologies. With these developments, the possibilities of entering mutually beneficial economic arrangements with partners in faraway countries – through international trade and investment – increased dramatically. This has made openness an even more crucial determinant of a country's prosperity than before.

Reflecting the deepening global economic integration, the global governance system has recently been strengthened. Most importantly, in 1995 the GATT was upgraded to the WTO (World Trade Organisation), a powerful agency pushing for liberalization not just in trade but also in other areas, like foreign investment regulation and intellectual property rights. The WTO now forms the core of the global economic governance system, together with the IMF (International Monetary Fund) – in charge of access to short-term finance – and the World Bank – in charge of longer-term investments.

The result of all these developments, according to the official history, is a globalized world economy comparable in its liberality and potential for prosperity only to the earlier 'golden age' of liberalism (1870–1913). Renato Ruggiero, the first director-general of the WTO, solemnly declared that, as a consequence of this new world order, we now have 'the potential for eradicating global poverty in the early part of the next [21st] century – a Utopian notion even a few decades ago, but a real possibility today.'[7]

This version of the history of globalization is widely accepted. It is supposed to be the route map for policy makers in steering their countries towards prosperity. Unfortunately, it paints a fundamentally misleading picture, distorting our understanding of where we have come from, where we are now and where we may be heading for. Let's see how.

The real history of globalization

On 30 June 1997, Hong Kong was officially handed back to China by its last British governor, Christopher Patten. Many British commentators fretted about the fate of Hong Kong's democracy under the Chinese Communist Party, although democratic elections in Hong Kong had only been permitted as late as 1994, 152 years after the start of British rule and only three years before the planned hand-over. But no one seems to remember how Hong Kong came to be a British possession in the first place.

Hong Kong became a British colony after the Treaty of Nanking in 1842, the result of the Opium War. This was a particularly shameful episode, even by the standards of 19th-century imperialism. The growing British taste for tea had created a huge trade deficit with China. In a desperate attempt to plug the gap, Britain started exporting opium produced in India to China. The mere detail that selling opium was illegal in China could not possibly be allowed to obstruct the noble cause of balancing the books. When a Chinese official seized an illicit cargo of opium in 1841, the British government used it as an excuse to fix the problem once and for all by declaring war. China was heavily defeated in the war and forced to sign the Treaty of Nanking, which made China 'lease' Hong Kong to Britain and give up its right to set its own tariffs.

So there it was – the self-proclaimed leader of the 'liberal' world declaring war on another country because the latter was getting in the way of its illegal trade in narcotics. The truth is that the free movement of goods, people, and money that developed under British hegemony between 1870 and 1913 – the first episode of globalization – was made possible, in large part, by military might, rather than market forces. Apart from Britain itself, the practitioners of free trade during this period were mostly weaker countries that had been forced into, rather than had voluntarily adopted, it as a result of colonial rule or 'unequal treaties' (like the Nanking Treaty), which, among other things, deprived them of the right to set tariffs and imposed externally determined low, flat-rate tariffs (3–5%) on them.[8]

Despite their key role in promoting 'free' trade in the late 19th and early 20th centuries, colonialism and unequal treaties hardly get any mention in the hordes of pro-globalisation books.[9] Even when they are explicitly discussed, their role is seen as positive on the whole. For example, in his acclaimed book, *Empire*, the British historian Niall Ferguson honestly notes many of the misdeeds of the British empire, including the Opium War, but contends that the British empire was a good thing overall – it was arguably the cheapest way to guarantee free trade, which benefits everyone.[10] However, the countries under colonial rule and unequal treaties did very poorly. Between 1870 and 1913, *per capita* income in Asia (excluding Japan) grew at 0.4% per year, while that in Africa grew at 0.6% per year.[11] The corresponding figures were 1.3% for Western Europe and 1.8% per year for the USA.[12] It is particularly interesting to note that the Latin American countries, which by that time had regained tariff autonomy and were boasting some of the highest tariffs in the world, grew as fast as the US did during this period.[13]

While they were imposing free trade on weaker nations through colonialism and unequal treaties, rich countries maintained rather high tariffs, especially industrial tariffs, for themselves, as we will see in greater detail in the next chapter. To begin with, Britain, the supposed home of free trade, was one of the most protectionist countries until it converted to free trade in the mid-19th century. There was a brief period during the 1860s and the 1870s when something approaching free trade did exist in Europe, especially with zero tariffs in Britain. However, this proved short-lived. From the 1880s, most European countries raised protective barriers again, partly to protect their farmers from cheap food imported from the New World and partly to promote their newly emerging 'heavy and chemical' industries, such as steel, chemicals and machinery.[14] Finally, even Britain, as I have noted, the chief architect of the first wave of globalization, abandoned free trade and re-introduced tariffs in 1932. The official history describes this event as Britain 'succumbing to the temptation' of protectionism. But it typically fails to mention that this was due to the decline in British economic supremacy, which in turn was the result of the success of protectionism on the part of competitor countries, especially the USA, in developing their own new industries.

Thus, the history of the first globalization in the late 19th and early 20th centuries has been rewritten today in order to fit the current neo-liberal orthodoxy. The history of protectionism in today's rich countries is vastly underplayed, while the imperialist origin of the high degree of global integration on the part of today's developing countries is hardly ever mentioned. The final curtain coming down on the episode – that is, Britain's abandonment of free trade – is also presented in a biased way. It is rarely mentioned that what really made Britain abandon free trade was precisely the successful use of protectionism by its competitors.

Neo-liberals vs neo-idiotics?

In the official history of globalization, the early post-Second-World-War period is portrayed as a period of incomplete globalization. While there was a significant increase in integration among the rich countries, accelerating their growth, it is said, most developing countries refused to fully participate in the global economy until the 1980s, thus holding themselves back from economic progress.

This story misrepresents the process of globalization among the rich countries during this period. These countries did significantly lower their tariff barriers between the 1950s and the 1970s. But during this period, they also used many other nationalistic policies to promote their own economic development – subsidies (especially for research and development, or R&D), state-owned enterprises, government direction of banking credits, capital controls and so on. When they started implementing neo-liberal programmes, their growth decelerated. In the 1960s and the 1970s, *per capita* income in the rich countries grew by 3.2% a year, but its growth rate fell substantially to 2.1% in the next two decades.[15]

But more misleading is the portrayal of the experiences of developing countries. The postwar period is described by the official historians of globalization as an era of economic disasters in these countries. This was because, they argue, these countries believed in 'wrong' economic theories that made them think they could defy market logic. As a result, they suppressed activities which they were good at (agriculture, mineral extraction and labour-intensive manufacturing) and promoted 'white elephant' projects that made them feel proud but were economic nonsense – the most notorious example of this is Indonesia producing heavily subsidized jet aeroplanes.

The right to 'asymmetric protection' that the developing countries secured in 1964 at the GATT is portrayed as 'the proverbial rope on which to hang one's own economy!', in a well-known article by Jeffrey Sachs and Andrew Warner.[16] Gustavo Franco, a former president of the Brazilian central bank (1997–99), made the same point more succinctly, if more crudely, when he said his policy objective was 'to undo forty years of stupidity' and that the only choice was 'to be neo-liberal or neo-idiotic'.[17]

The problem with this interpretation is that the 'bad old days' in the developing countries weren't so bad at all. During the 1960s and the 1970s, when they were pursuing the 'wrong' policies of protectionism and state intervention, *per capita* income in the developing countries grew by 3.0% annually.[18] As my esteemed colleague Professor Ajit Singh once pointed out, this was the period of 'Industrial Revolution in the Third World'.[19] This growth rate is a huge improvement over what they achieved under free trade during the 'age of imperialism' (see above) and compares favourably with the 1–1.5% achieved by the rich countries during the Industrial Revolution in the 19th century. It also remains the best that they have ever recorded. Since the 1980s, after they implemented neo-liberal policies, they grew at only about half the speed seen in the 1960s and the 1970s (1.7%). Growth slowed down in the rich countries too, but the slowdown was less marked (from 3.2% to 2.1%), not least because they did not introduce neo-liberal policies to the same extent as the developing countries did. The average growth rate of developing countries in this period would be even lower if we exclude China and India. These two countries, which accounted for 12% of total developing country income in 1980 and 30% in 2000, have so far refused to put on Thomas Friedman's Golden Straitjacket.[20]

Growth failure has been particularly noticeable in Latin America and Africa, where neo-liberal programmes were implemented more thoroughly than in Asia. In the 1960s and the 1970s, *per capita* income in Latin America was growing at 3.1% per year, slightly faster than the developing country average. Brazil, especially, was growing almost as fast as the East Asian 'miracle' economies. Since the 1980s, however, when the continent embraced neo-liberalism, Latin America has been growing at less than one-third of the rate of the 'bad old days'. Even if we discount the 1980s as a decade of adjustment and take it out of the equation, *per capita* income in the region during the 1990s grew at basically half the rate of the 'bad old days' (3.1% vs 1.7%). Between 2000 and 2005, the region has done even worse; it virtually stood still, with *per capita* income growing at only 0.6% per year.[21] As for Africa, its *per capita* income grew relatively slowly even in the 1960s and the 1970s (1–2% a year). But since the 1980s, the region has seen a *fall* in living standards. This record is a damning indictment of the neo-liberal orthodoxy, because most of the African economies have been practically run by the IMF and the World Bank over the past quarter of a century.

The poor *growth* record of neo-liberal globalization since the 1980s is particularly embarrassing. Accelerating growth – if necessary at the cost of increasing inequality and possibly some increase in poverty – was the proclaimed goal of neo-liberal reform. We have been repeatedly told that we first have to 'create more wealth' before we can distribute it more widely and that neo-liberalism was the way to do that. As a result of neo-liberal policies, income inequality has increased in most countries as predicted, but growth has actually slowed down significantly.[22]

Moreover, economic instability has markedly increased during the period of neo-liberal dominance. The world, especially the developing world, has seen more frequent and larger-scale financial crises since the 1980s. In other words, neo-liberal globalization has failed to deliver on all fronts of economic life – growth, equality and stability. Despite this, we are constantly told how neo-liberal globalization has brought unprecedented benefits.

The distortion of facts in the official history of globalization is also evident at country level. Contrary to what the orthodoxy would have us believe, virtually all the successful developing countries since the

Second World War initially succeeded through nationalistic policies, using protection, subsidies and other forms of government intervention.

I have already discussed the case of my native Korea in some detail in the Prologue, but other 'miracle' economies of East Asia have also succeeded through a strategic approach to integration with the global economy. Taiwan used a strategy that is very similar to that of Korea, although it used state-owned enterprises more extensively while being somewhat friendlier to foreign investors than Korea was. Singapore has had free trade and relied heavily on foreign investment, but, even so, it does not conform in other respects to the neo-liberal ideal. Though it welcomed foreign investors, it used considerable subsidies in order to attract transnational corporations in industries it considered strategic, especially in the form of government investment in infrastructure and education targeted at particular industries. Moreover, it has one of the largest state-owned enterprise sectors in the world, including the Housing Development Board, which supplies 85% of all housing (almost all land is owned by the government).

Hong Kong is the exception that proves the rule. It became rich despite having free trade and a *laissez-faire* industrial policy. But it never was an independent state (not even a city state like Singapore) but a city within a bigger entity. Until 1997, it was a British colony used as a platform for Britain's trading and financial interests in Asia. Today, it is the financial centre of the Chinese economy. These facts made it less necessary for Hong Kong to have an independent industrial base, although, even so, it was producing twice as much manufacturing output *per capita* as that of Korea until the mid-1980s, when it started its full absorption into China. But even Hong Kong was not a total free market economy. Most importantly, all land was owned by the government in order to control the housing situation.

The more recent economic success stories of China, and increasingly India, are also examples that show the importance of strategic, rather than unconditional, integration with the global economy based on a nationalistic vision. Like the US in the mid-19th century, or Japan and Korea in the mid-20th century, China used high tariffs to build up its industrial base. Right up to the 1990s, China's average tariff was

over 30%. Admittedly, it has been more welcoming to foreign investment than Japan or Korea were. But it still imposed foreign ownership ceilings and local contents requirements (the requirements that
the foreign firms buy at least a certain proportion of their inputs from
local suppliers).

India's recent economic success is often attributed by the pro-
globalizers to its trade and financial liberalization in the early 1990s.
As some recent research reveals, however, India's growth acceleration
really began in the 1980s, discrediting the simple 'greater openness
accelerates growth' story.[23] Moreover, even after the early 1990s trade
liberalization, India's average manufacturing tariffs remained at above
30% (it is still 25% today). India's protectionism before the 1990s was
certainly over-done in some sectors. But this is not to say that India
would have been even more successful had it adopted free trade at
independence in 1947. India has also imposed severe restrictions on
foreign direct investment – entry restrictions, ownership restrictions and
various performance requirements (e.g., local contents requirements).

The one country that seems to have succeeded in the postwar
globalization period by using the neo-liberal strategy is Chile. Indeed,
Chile adopted the strategy before anyone else, including the US and
Britain, following the *coup d'état* by General Augusto Pinochet back
in 1973. Since then, Chile has grown quite well – although nowhere
nearly as fast as the East Asian 'miracle' economies.[24] And the country
has been constantly cited as a neo-liberal success story. Its good growth
performance is undeniable. But even Chile's story is more complex
than the orthodoxy suggests.

Chile's early experiment with neo-liberalism, led by the so-called
Chicago Boys (a group of Chilean economists trained at the University
of Chicago, one of the centres of neo-liberal economics), was a disaster.
It ended in a terrible financial crash in 1982, which had to be resolved
by the nationalization of the whole banking sector. Thanks to this crash,
the country recovered the pre-Pinochet level of income only in the late
1980s.[25] It was only when Chile's neo-liberalism got more pragmatic
after the crash that the country started doing well. For example, the
government provided exporters with a lot of help in overseas marketing
and R&D.[26] It also used capital controls in the 1990s to successfully

reduce the inflow of short-term speculative funds, although its recent free trade agreement with the US has forced it to promise never to use them again. More importantly, there is a lot of doubt about the sustainability of Chile's development. Over the past three decades, the country has lost a lot of manufacturing industries and become excessively dependent on natural-resources-based exports. Not having the technological capabilities to move into higher-productivity activities, Chile faces a clear limit to the level of prosperity it can attain in the long run.

To sum up, the truth of post-1945 globalization is almost the polar opposite of the official history. During the period of controlled globalization underpinned by nationalistic policies between the 1950s and the 1970s, the world economy, especially in the developing world, was growing faster, was more stable and had more equitable income distribution than in the past two and a half decades of rapid and uncontrolled neo-liberal globalization. Nevertheless, this period is portrayed in the official history as one of unmitigated disaster of nationalistic policies, especially in developing countries. This distortion of the historical record is peddled in order to mask the failure of neo-liberal policies.

Who's running the world economy?

Much of what happens in the global economy is determined by the rich countries, without even trying. They account for 80% of world output, conduct 70% of international trade and make 70–90% (depending on the year) of all foreign direct investments.[27] This means that their national policies can strongly influence the world economy.

But more important than their sheer weight is the rich countries' willingness to throw that very weight about in shaping the rules of the global economy. For example, developed countries induce poorer countries to adopt particular policies by making them a condition for their foreign aid or by offering them preferential trade agreements in return for 'good behaviour' (adoption of neo-liberal policies). Even more important in shaping options for developing countries are, however, what I call the 'Unholy Trinity' of multilateral organizations

– namely the IMF, the World Bank and the WTO (World Trade Organisation). Though they are not puppets of the rich countries, the Unholy Trinity are largely controlled by the rich countries, so they devise and implement Bad Samaritan policies that those countries want.

The IMF and the World Bank were originally set up in 1944 at a conference between the Allied forces (essentially the US and Britain), which worked out the shape of postwar international economic governance. This conference was held in the New Hampshire resort of Bretton Woods, so these agencies are sometimes collectively called the Bretton Woods Institutions (BWIs). The IMF was set up to lend money to countries in balance of payments crises so that they can reduce their balance of payments deficits without having to resort to deflation. The World Bank was set up to help the reconstruction of war-torn countries in Europe and the economic development of the post-colonial societies that were about to emerge – which is why it is officially called the International Bank for Reconstruction and Development. This was supposed to be done by financing projects in infrastructure development (e.g., roads, bridges, dams).

Following the Third World debt crisis of 1982, the roles of both the IMF and the World Bank changed dramatically. They started to exert a much stronger policy influence on developing countries through their joint operation of so-called structural adjustment programmes (SAPs). These programmes covered a much wider range of policies than what the Bretton Woods Institutions had originally been mandated to do. The BWIs now got deeply involved in virtually all areas of economic policy in the developing world. They branched out into areas like government budgets, industrial regulation, agricultural pricing, labour market regulation, privatization and so on. In the 1990s, there was a further advance in this 'mission creep' as they started attaching so-called governance conditionalities to their loans. These involved intervention in hitherto unthinkable areas, like democracy, government decentralization, central bank independence and corporate governance.

This mission creep raises a serious issue. The World Bank and the IMF initially started with rather limited mandates. Subsequently, they argued that they have to intervene in new areas outside their original mandates, as they, too, affect economic performance, a failure in which has driven countries to borrow money from them. However, on this reasoning, there is no area of our life in which the BWIs cannot intervene. Everything that goes on in a country has implications for its economic performance. By this logic, the IMF and the World Bank should be able to impose conditionalities on everything from fertility decisions, ethnic integration and gender equality, to cultural values.

Don't get me wrong. I am not one of those people who are against loan conditionalities on principle. It is reasonable for the lender to attach conditions. But conditions should be confined to only those aspects that are most relevant to the repayment of the loan. Otherwise, the lender may intrude in all aspects of the borrower's life.

Suppose I am a small businessman trying to borrow money from my bank in order to expand my factory. It would be natural for my bank manager to impose a unilateral condition on how I am going to repay. It might even be reasonable for him to impose conditions on what kind of construction materials I can use and what kind of machinery I can buy in expanding my factory. But, if he attaches the condition that I cut down on my fat intake on the (not totally irrelevant) grounds that a fatty diet reduces my ability to repay the loan by making me unhealthy, I would find this unreasonably intrusive. Of course, if I am really desperate, I may swallow my pride and agree even to this unreasonable condition. But when he makes it a further condition that I spend less than an hour a day at home (on the grounds that spending less time with the family will increase my time available for business and therefore reduce the chance of loan default), I would probably punch him in the face and storm out of the bank. It is not that my diet and family life have no bearings whatsoever on my ability to manage my business. As my bank manager reasons, they *are* relevant. But the point is that their relevance is indirect and marginal.

In the beginning, the IMF only imposed conditions closely related to the borrower country's management of its balance of payments, such as currency devaluation. But then it started putting conditions on government budgets on the grounds that budget deficits are a key cause of balance of payments problems. This led to the imposition of conditions like the privatization of state-owned enterprises, because it was argued that the losses made by those enterprises were an important source of budget deficits in many developing countries. Once such an extension of logic began, there was no stopping. Since everything is related to everything else, anything could be a condition. In 1997, in Korea, for example, the IMF laid down conditions on the amount of debt that *private sector* companies could have, on the grounds that over-borrowing by these companies was the main reason for Korea's financial crisis.

To add insult to injury, the Bad Samaritan rich nations often demand, as a condition for their financial contribution to IMF packages, that the borrowing country be made to adopt policies that have little to do with fixing its economy but that serve the interests of the rich countries lending the money. For example, on seeing Korea's 1997 agreement with the IMF, one outraged observer commented: 'Several features of the IMF plan are replays of the policies that Japan and the United States have long been trying to get Korea to adopt. These included accelerating the . . . reductions of trade barriers to specific Japanese products and opening capital markets so that foreign investors can have majority ownership of Korean firms, engage in hostile takeovers . . . , and expand direct participation in banking and other financial services. Although greater competition from manufactured imports and more foreign ownership could . . . help the Korean economy, Koreans and others saw this . . . as an abuse of IMF power to force Korea at a time of weakness to accept trade and investment policies it had previously rejected'.[28] This was said not by some anticapitalist anarchist but by Martin Feldstein, the conservative Harvard economist who was the key economic advisor to Ronald Reagan in the 1980s.

The IMF-World Bank mission creep, combined with the abuse of conditionalities by the Bad Samaritan nations, is particularly unacceptable when the policies of the Bretton Woods Institutions have produced slower growth, more unequal income distribution and greater economic instability in most developing countries, as I pointed out earlier in this chapter.

But how on earth can the IMF and the World Bank persist for so long in pursuing the wrong policies that produce such poor outcomes? This is because their governance structure severely biases them towards the interests of the rich countries. Their decisions are made basically according to the share capital that a country has (in other words, they have a one-dollar-one-vote system). This means that the rich countries, which collectively control 60% of the voting shares, have an absolute control over their policies, while the US has a *de facto* veto in relation to decisions in the 18 most important areas.[29]

One result of this governance structure is that the World Bank and the IMF have imposed on developing countries standard policy packages that are considered to be universally valid by the rich countries, rather than policies that are carefully designed for each particular developing country, predictably producing poor results as a consequence. Another result is that, even when their policies may be appropriate, they have often failed because they are resisted by the locals as impositions from outside.

In response to mounting criticisms, the World Bank and the IMF have recently reacted in a number of ways. On the one hand, there have been some window-dressing moves. Thus the IMF now calls the Structural Adjustment Programme the Poverty Reduction and Growth Facility Programme, in order to show that it cares about poverty issues, though the contents of the programme have hardly changed from before. On the other hand, there have been some genuine efforts to open dialogues with a wider constituency, especially the World Bank's engagement with NGOs (non-governmental organizations). But the impacts of such consultation are at best marginal. Moreover, when increasing numbers of NGOs in developing countries are indirectly funded by the World Bank, the value of such an exercise is becoming more doubtful.

The IMF and the World Bank have also tried to increase the 'local ownership' of their programmes by involving local people in their design. However, this has borne few fruits. Many developing countries lack the intellectual resources to argue against powerful international organizations with an army of highly trained economists and a lot of financial clout behind them. Moreover, the World Bank and the IMF have taken what I call the 'Henry Ford approach to diversity' (he famously said that customers could have a car painted 'any colour so long as it's black'). The range of local variation in policies that they find acceptable is very narrow. Also, with the increasing tendency for developing countries to elect or appoint ex-World Bank or ex-IMF officials to key economic posts, 'local' solutions are increasingly resembling the solutions provided by the Bretton Woods Institutions.

Completing the Unholy Trinity, the World Trade Organisation was launched in 1995, following the conclusion of the so-called Uruguay Round of the GATT talks. I will discuss the substance of what the WTO does in greater detail in later chapters, so here let me focus just on its governance structure.

The World Trade Organisation has been criticized on a number of grounds. Many believe that it is little more than a tool with which the developed countries pry open developing markets. Others argue that it has become a vehicle for furthering the interests of transnational corporations. There are elements of truth in both of these criticisms, as I will show in later chapters.

But, despite these criticisms, the World Trade Organisation is an international organization in whose running the developing countries have the greatest say. Unlike the IMF or the World Bank, it is 'democratic' – in the sense of allowing one country one vote (of course, we can debate whether giving China, with 1.3 billion people, and Luxembourg, with fewer than half a million people, one vote each is really 'democratic'). And, unlike in the UN, where the five permanent members of the Security Council have veto power, no country has a veto in the WTO. Since they have the numerical advantage, the developing countries count far more in the WTO than they do in the IMF or the World Bank.

Unfortunately, in practice, votes are never taken, and the organization is essentially run by an oligarchy comprising a small number of rich countries. It is reported that, in various ministerial meetings (Geneva 1998, Seattle 1999, Doha 2001, Cancun 2003), all the important negotiations were held in the so-called Green Rooms on a 'by-invitation-only' basis. Only the rich countries and some large developing countries that they cannot ignore (e.g., India and Brazil) were invited. Especially during the 1999 Seattle meeting, it was reported that some developing country delegates who tried to get into Green Rooms without invitation were physically thrown out.

But even without such extreme measures, the decisions are likely to be biased towards the rich countries. They can threaten and bribe developing countries by means of their foreign aid budgets or using their influence on the loan decisions by the IMF, the World Bank and 'regional' multilateral financial institutions.*

Moreover, there exists a vast gap in intellectual and negotiation resources between the two groups of countries. A former student of mine, who has just left the diplomatic service of his native country in Africa, once told me that his country had only three people, including himself, to attend all the meetings at the WTO in Geneva. The meetings often numbered more than a dozen a day, so he and his colleagues dropped a few meetings altogether and divided up the rest between the three of them. This meant that they could allocate only two to three hours to each meeting. Sometimes they went in at the right moment and made some useful contributions. Some other times, they were not so lucky and got completely lost. In contrast, the US – to take the example at the other extreme – had dozens of people working on intellectual property rights alone. But my former student said his country was lucky – more than 20 developing countries do not have a single person based in Geneva, and many have to get by with only one or two people. Many more stories like this can be told, but they all suggest that international trade negotiations are a highly lopsided affair; it is like a war where some people fight with pistols while the others engage in aerial bombardment.

Are the Bad Samaritans winning?

Margaret Thatcher, the British prime minister who spearheaded the neo-liberal counter-revolution, once famously dismissed her critics saying

---

* These include the Asian Development Bank (ADB), the Inter-American Development Bank (IDB), the African Development Bank (AFDB) and the European Bank for Reconstruction and Development (EBRD), which deals with the former communist economies.

that 'There is no alternative'. The spirit of this argument – known as TINA (There Is No Alternative) – permeates the way globalization is portrayed by the Bad Samaritans.

The Bad Samaritans like to present globalization as an inevitable result of relentless developments in the technologies of communication and transportation. They like to portray their critics as backward-looking 'modern-day Luddites'[30] who 'fight over who owns which olive tree'. Going against this historical tide only produces disasters, it is argued, as evidenced by the collapse of the world economy during the inter-war period and by the failures of state-led industrialization in the developing countries in the 1960s and the 1970s. It is argued that there is only one way to survive the historic tidal force that is globalization, and that is to put on the one-size-fits-all Golden Straitjacket which virtually all the successful economies have allegedly worn on their way to prosperity. There is no alternative.

In this chapter, I have shown that the TINA conclusion stems from a fundamentally defective understanding of the forces driving globalization and a distortion of history to fit the theory. Free trade was often imposed on, rather than chosen by, weaker countries. Most countries that had the choice did not choose free trade for more than brief periods. Virtually all successful economies, developed and developing, got where they are through selective, strategic integration with the world economy, rather than through unconditional global integration. The performance of the developing countries was much better when they had a large amount of policy autonomy during the 'bad old days' of state-led industrialization than when they were totally deprived of it during the first globalization (in the era of colonial rule and unequal treaties) or when they had much less policy autonomy (as in the past quarter of a century).

There is nothing inevitable about globalization, because it is driven more by politics (that is, human will and decision) than technology, as the Bad Samaritans claim. If it were technology that determined the extent of globalization, it would be impossible to explain how the world was much less globalized in the 1970s (when we had all the modern technologies of transport and communication except the internet) than in the 1870s (when we relied on steamships and wired telegraphy). Technology only defines the outer boundaries of globalization. Exactly what shape it takes depends on what we do with national policies and what international agreements we make. If that is the case, the TINA thesis is wrong. There is an alternative, or rather there are many alternatives, to the neo-liberal globalization that is happening today. The rest of this book is going to explore those alternatives.

CHAPTER 2

The double life of Daniel Defoe

How did the rich countries become rich?

Daniel Defoe, the author of *Robinson Crusoe*, had a colourful life. Before writing novels, he was a businessman, importing woollen goods, hosiery, wine and tobacco. He also worked in the government in the royal lotteries and in the Glass Duty Office that collected the notorious 'window tax', a property tax levied according to the number of a house's windows. He was also an influential author of political pamphlets and led a double life as a government spy. First he spied for Robert Harley, the Tory speaker of the House of Commons. Later, he complicated his life even further by spying for the Whig government of Robert Walpole, Harley's political arch-enemy.

As if being a businessman, novelist, tax collector, political commentator and spy wasn't providing sufficient stimulus, Defoe was also an economist. This aspect of his life is even less well known than his spying. Unlike his novels, which include *Robinson Crusoe* and *Moll Flanders*, Defoe's main economic work, *A Plan of the English Commerce* (1728), is almost forgotten now. The popular biography of Defoe by Richard West does not mention the book at all, while the award-winning biography by Paula Backscheider mentions it largely in relation to marginal subjects, such as Defoe's view on native Americans.[1] However, the book was a thorough and insightful account of Tudor industrial policy that has much to teach us today.

In the book (henceforth *A Plan*), Defoe describes how the Tudor monarchs, especially Henry VII and Elizabeth I, used protectionism, subsidies, distribution of monopoly rights, government-sponsored industrial espionage and other means of government intervention to develop England's woollen manufacturing industry, Europe's high-tech industry at the time. Until Tudor times, Britain had been a relatively backward economy, relying on exports of raw wool to finance imports. The woollen manufacturing industry was centred in the Low Countries (today Belgium and the Netherlands), especially the cities of Bruges, Ghent and Ypres in Flanders. Britain exported its raw wool and made a reasonable profit. But those foreigners who knew how to convert the wool into clothes were generating much greater profits. It is a law of competition that people who can do difficult things which other cannot will earn more profit. This is the situation that Henry VII wanted to change in the late 15th century.[2]

According to Defoe, Henry VII sent royal missions to identify locations suited to woollen manufacturing.[3] Like Edward III before him, he poached skilled workers from the Low Countries.[4] He also increased the tax on the export of raw wool, and even temporarily banned its export, in order to encourage further processing of the raw material at home. In 1489, he also banned the export of unfinished cloth, save for coarse pieces below a certain market value, in order to promote further processing at home.[5] His son, Henry VIII, continued the policy and banned the export of unfinished cloth in 1512, 1513 and 1536.

As Defoe emphasizes, Henry VII did not have any illusions as to how quickly the English producers could catch up with their sophisticated competitors in the Low Countries.[6] The King raised export duties on raw wool only when the English industry was established enough to handle the volume of wool to be processed. Henry then quickly withdrew his ban on raw wool exports when it became clear that Britain simply did not have the capacity to process all the raw wool it produced.[7] Indeed, according to A Plan, it was not until 1578, in the middle of Elizabeth I's reign (1558–1603) – nearly 100 years after Henry VII had started his 'import substitution industrialization' policy in 1489 – that Britain had sufficient processing capacity to ban raw wool exports totally.[8] Once in place, however, the export ban drove the competing manufacturers in the Low Countries, who were now deprived of their raw materials, to ruin.

Without the policies put in place by Henry VII and further pursued by his successors, it would have been very difficult, if not impossible, for Britain to have transformed itself from a raw-material exporter into the European centre of the then high-tech industry. Wool manufacture became Britain's most important export industry. It provided most of the export earnings to finance the massive import of raw materials and food that fed the Industrial Revolution.[9] *A Plan* shatters the foundation myth of capitalism that Britain succeeded because it figured out the true path to prosperity before other countries – free market and free trade.

Daniel Defoe's fictional hero, Robinson Crusoe, is often used by economics teachers as the pure example of 'rational economic man', the hero of neo-liberal free-market economics. They claim that, even though he lives alone, Crusoe has to make 'economic' decisions all the time. He has to decide how much to work in order to satisfy his desire for material consumption and leisure. Being a rational man, he puts in precisely the minimum amount of work to achieve the goal. Suppose Crusoe then discovers another man living alone on a nearby island. How should they trade with each other? The free-market theory says that introducing a market (exchange) does not fundamentally alter the nature of Crusoe's situation. Life goes on much as before, with the additional consideration that he now needs to establish the rate of exchange between his product and his neighbour's. Being a rational man, he will continue to make the right decisions. According to free-market economics, it is precisely because we are like Crusoe that free markets work. We know exactly what we want and how best to achieve it. Consequently, leaving people to do what they desire and know to be good for themselves is the best way to run the economy. Government just gets in the way.

The kind of economics that underpins Defoe's *Plan* is exactly the opposite of Robinson Crusoe economics. In *A Plan*, Defoe clearly shows that it was not the free market but government protection and subsidies that developed British woollen manufacturing. Defying signals from the market that his country was an efficient raw wool producer and should remain so, Henry VII introduced policies that deliberately distorted such unwelcome truths. By doing so, he started the process that eventually transformed Britain into a leading manufacturing nation. Economic development requires people like Henry VII, who build a new future, rather than people like Robinson Crusoe, who live for today.

Thus, in addition to his double life as a spy, Defoe also led a double life as an economist – without realizing it, he created the central character in free market economics in his fictional work, yet his own economic analysis clearly illustrated the limits of free market and free trade.

Britain takes on the world

Defoe started his double life as a spy for the Tory government, but later, as I mentioned, he spied for the Whig government of Robert Walpole. Walpole is commonly known as the first British prime minister, although he was never called that by his contemporaries.[10]

Walpole was notorious for his venality – he is said to have 'reduced corruption to a regular system'. He deftly juggled the disbursement of aristocratic titles, government offices and perks in order to maintain his power base, which enabled him to remain the prime minister for a staggering 21 years (1721–42). His political skills were immortalized by Jonathan Swift in his novel, *Gulliver's Travels*, in the character of Flimnap. Flimnap is the prime minister of the empire of Lilliput and champion of Dance of the Rope, the frivolous method by which the holders of high offices in Lilliput are selected.[11]

Yet Walpole was a highly competent economic manager. During his time as chancellor of the exchequer, he enhanced the creditworthiness of his government by creating a 'sinking fund' dedicated to repaying the debts. He became prime minister in 1721 because he was considered the only person who had the ability to manage the financial mess left behind by the infamous South Sea Bubble.*

Upon becoming prime minister, Walpole launched a policy reform that dramatically shifted the focus of British industrial and trade policies. Prior to Walpole, the British government's policies were, in general,

* The South Sea Company was set up in 1711 by Robert Harley, Defoe's first spymaster, and was granted exclusive trading rights in Spanish South America. It made little actual profit, but talked up its stock with the most extravagant rumours of the value of its potential trade. A speculative frenzy developed around its shares in 1720, with its stock price rising by ten times in seven months between January and August 1720. The stock price then started falling and, by early 1721, was back where it had been in January 1720.

aimed at capturing trade through colonization and the Navigation Act (which required that all trade with Britain should be conducted in British ships) and at generating government revenue. The promotion of woollen manufacturing was the most important exception, but even that was partly motivated by the desire to generate more government revenue. In contrast, the policies introduced by Walpole after 1721 were deliberately aimed at promoting manufacturing industries. Introducing the new law, Walpole stated, through the King's address to Parliament: 'it is evident that nothing so much contributes to promote the public well-being as the exportation of manufactured goods and the importation of foreign raw matrial'.[12]

Walpole's 1721 legislation essentially aimed to protect British manufacturing industries from foreign competition, subsidize them and encourage them to export.[13] Tariffs on imported foreign manufactured goods were significantly raised, while tariffs on raw materials used for manufacture were lowered, or even dropped altogether. Manufacturing exports were encouraged by a series of measures, including export subsidies.[14] Finally, regulation was introduced to control the quality of manufactured products, especially textile products, so that unscrupulous manufacturers could not damage the reputation of British products in foreign markets.[15]

These policies are strikingly similar to those used with such success by the 'miracle' economies of East Asia, such as Japan, Korea and Taiwan, after the Second World War. Policies that many believe, as I myself used to, to have been invented by Japanese policy-makers in the 1950s – such as 'duty drawbacks on inputs for exported manufactured products* and the imposition of export product quality standards by the government† – were actually early British inventions.[16]

Walpole's protectionist policies remained in place for the next

* This is a practice where a manufacturer exporting a product is paid back the tariff that it has paid for the imported inputs used in producing the product. This is a way of encouraging exports.
† This is a practice where the government sets the minimum quality standards for export products and punishes those exporters who do not meet them. This is intended to prevent substandard export products tarnishing the image of the exporting country. It is particularly useful when products do not have well-recognized brand names and, therefore, are identified by their national origin.

century, helping British manufacturing industries catch up with and then finally forge ahead of their counterparts on the Continent. Britain remained a highly protectionist country until the mid-19th century. In 1820, Britain's average tariff rate on manufacturing imports was 45–55%, compared to 6–8% in the Low Countries, 8–12% in Germany and Switzerland and around 20% in France.[17]

Tariffs were, however, not the only weapon in the arsenal of British trade policy. When it came to its colonies, Britain was quite happy to impose an outright ban on advanced manufacturing activities that it did not want developed. Walpole banned the construction of new rolling and slitting steel mills in America, forcing the Americans to specialize in low value-added pig and bar iron, rather than high value-added steel products.

Britain also banned exports from its colonies that competed with its own products, home and abroad. It banned cotton textile imports from India ('calicoes'), which were then superior to the British ones. In 1699 it banned the export of woollen cloth from its colonies to other countries (the Wool Act), destroying the Irish woollen industry and stifling the emergence of woollen manufacture in America.

Finally, policies were deployed to encourage primary commodity production in the colonies. Walpole provided export subsidies to (on the American side) and abolished import taxes on (on the British side) raw materials produced in the American colonies (such as hemp, wood and timber). He wanted to make absolutely sure that the colonists stuck to producing primary commodities and never emerged as competitors to British manufacturers. Thus they were compelled to leave the most profitable 'high-tech' industries in the hands of Britain – which ensured that Britain would enjoy the benefits of being on the cutting edge of world development.[18]

The double life of the British economy

The world's first famous free-market economist, Adam Smith, vehemently attacked what he called the 'mercantile system' whose chief architect was Walpole. Adam Smith's masterpiece, *The Wealth of*

Nations, was published in 1776, at the height of the British mercantile system. He argued that the restrictions on competition that the system was producing through protection, subsidies and granting of monopoly rights were bad for the British economy.*

Adam Smith understood that Walpole's policies were becoming obsolete. Without them, many British industries would have been wiped out before they had had the chance to catch up with their superior rivals abroad. But once British industries had become internationally competitive, protection became less necessary and even counter-productive. Protecting industries that do not need protection any more is likely to make them complacent and inefficient, as Smith observed. Therefore, adopting free trade was now increasingly in Britain's interest. However, Smith was somewhat ahead of his time. Another generation would pass before his views became truly influential, and it was not until 84 years after *The Wealth of Nations* was published that Britain became a genuine free trading nation.

By the end of the Napeolenic Wars in 1815, four decades after the publication of *The Wealth of Nations*, British manufacturers were firmly established as the most efficient in the world, except in a few limited areas where countries like Belgium and Switzerland possessed technological leads. British manufacturers correctly perceived that free trade was now in their interest and started campaigning for it (having said that, they naturally remained quite happy to restrict trade when it suited them, as the cotton manufacturers did when it came to the export of textile machinery that might help foreign competitors). In particular, the manufacturers agitated for the abolition of the Corn Laws that limited the country's ability to import cheap grains. Cheaper food was important to them because it could lower wages and raise profits.

The anti-Corn Law campaign was crucially helped by the economist, politician and stock-market player, David Ricardo. Ricardo came up with the theory of comparative advantage that still forms the core

---

* However, Smith was a patriot even more than he was a free market economist. He supported free market and free trade only because he thought they were good for Britain, as we can see from his praise of the Navigation Acts – the most blatant kind of 'market-distorting' regulation – as 'the wisest of all the commercial regulations of England'.

of free trade theory. Before Ricardo, people thought foreign trade makes sense only when a country can make something more cheaply than its trading partner. Ricardo, in a brilliant inversion of this commonsensical observation, argued that trade between two countries makes sense even when one country can produce everything more cheaply than another. Although this country is more efficient in producing everything than the other, it can still gain by specializing in things in which it has the greatest cost advantage over its trading partner. Conversely, even a country that has no cost advantage over its trading partner in producing any product can gain from trade if it specializes in products in which it has the least cost disadvantage. With this theory, Ricardo provided the 19th-century free traders with a simple but powerful tool to argue that free trade benefits every country.

Ricardo's theory is absolutely right – within its narrow confines. His theory correctly says that, *accepting their current levels of technology as given*, it is better for countries to specialize in things that they are relatively better at. One cannot argue with that.

His theory fails when a country wants to acquire more advanced technologies so that it can do more difficult things that few others can do – that is, when it wants to develop its economy. It takes time and experience to absorb new technologies, so technologically backward producers need a period of protection from international competition during this period of learning. Such protection is costly, because the country is giving up the chance to import better and cheaper products. However, it is a price that has to be paid if it wants to develop advanced industries. Ricardo's theory is, thus seen, for those who accept the *status quo* but not for those who want to change it.

The big change in British trade policy came in 1846, when the Corn Laws were repealed and tariffs on many manufacturing goods were abolished. Free trade economists today like to portray the repeal of the Corn Laws as the ultimate victory of Adam Smith's and David Ricardo's wisdom over wrong-headed mercantilism.[19] The leading free trade economist of our time, Jagdish Bhagwati of Columbia University, calls this a 'historic transition'.[20]

However, many historians familiar with the period point out that making food cheaper was only one aim of the anti-Corn Law campaigners. It was also an act of 'free trade imperialism' intended to 'halt the move to industrialisation on the Continent by enlarging the market for agricultural produce and primary materials'.[21] By opening its domestic agricultural market wider, Britain wanted to lure its competitors back into agriculture. Indeed, the leader of the anti-Corn Law movement, Richard Cobden, argued that, without the Corn Laws: 'The factory system would, in all probability, not have taken place in America and Germany. It most certainly could not have flourished, as it has done, both in these states, and in France, Belgium and Switzerland, through the fostering bounties which the high-priced food of the British artisan has offered to the cheaper fed manufacturer of those countries'.[22] In the same spirit, in 1840, John Bowring of the Board of Trade, a key member of the anti-Corn Law League, explicitly advised the member states of the German *Zollverein* (Customs Union) to specialize in growing wheat and sell the wheat to buy British manufactures.[23] Moreover, it was not until 1860 that tariffs were completely abolished. In other words, Britain adopted free trade only when it had acquired a technological lead over its competitors 'behind high and long-lasting tariff barriers', as the eminent economic historian Paul Bairoch once put it.[24] No wonder Friedrich List talked about 'kicking away the ladder'.

America enters the fray

The best critique of Britain's hypocrisy may have been written by a German, but the country that best resisted Britain's ladder-kicking in terms of policy was not Germany. Nor was it France, commonly known as the protectionist counterpoint to free-trading Britain. In fact, the counterbalance was provided by the US, Britain's former colony and today's champion of free trade.

Under British rule, America was given the full British colonial treatment. It was naturally denied the use of tariffs to protect its new industries. It was prohibited from exporting products that competed with British products. It was given subsidies to produce raw materials. Moreover, outright restrictions were imposed on what Americans could manufacture. The spirit behind this policy is best summed up by a remark William Pitt the Elder made in 1770. Hearing that new industries were emerging in the American colonies, he famously said: '[The New England] colonies should not be permitted to manufacture so much as a horseshoe nail'.[25] In reality, British policies were a little more lenient than this may imply: some industrial activities were permitted. But the manufacture of high-technology products was banned.

Not all Britons were as hard-hearted as Pitt. In recommending free trade to the Americans, some were convinced that they were helping them. In his *Wealth of Nations*, Adam Smith, the Scottish father of free market economics, solemnly advised the Americans not to develop manufacturing. He argued that any attempt to 'stop the importation of European manufactures' would 'obstruct instead of promoting the progress of their country towards real wealth and greatness'.[26]

Many Americans agreed, including Thomas Jefferson, the first secretary of state and the third president. But others fiercely disagreed. They argued that the country needed to develop manufacturing industries and use government protection and subsidies to that end, as Britain had done before them. The intellectual leader of this movement was a half-Scottish upstart called Alexander Hamilton.

Hamilton was born on the Caribbean island of Nevis, the illegitimate child of a Scottish pedlar (who dubiously claimed an aristocratic lineage) and a woman of French descent. He climbed to power thanks to his sheer brilliance and boundless energy. At 22, he was an aide-de-camp to George Washington in the War of Independence. In 1789, at the outrageously early age of 33, he became the country's first finance minister (treasury secretary).

In 1791, Hamilton submitted his *Report on the Subject of Manufactures* (henceforth the *Report*) to the US Congress. In it, he expounded his view that the country needed a big programme to develop its industries. The core of his idea was that a backward country like the US should protect its 'industries in their infancy' from foreign competition and nurture them to the point where they could stand on their own feet. In recommending such a course of action for his young country, the impudent 35-year-old finance minister with only a liberal arts degree from a then second-rate college (King's College of New York, now Columbia University) was openly going against the advice of the world's most famous economist, Adam Smith.

The practice of protecting 'infant industries' had existed before, as I have shown, but it was Hamilton who first turned it into a theory and gave it a name (the term 'infant industry' was invented by him). The theory was later further developed by Friedrich List, who is today often mistakenly known as its father. List actually started out as a free-trader; he was one of the leading promoters of one of world's first free trade agreements – the German *Zollverein*, or Customs Union. He learned the infant industry argument from the Americans during his political exile in the US in the 1820s. Hamilton's infant industry argument inspired many countries' economic development programmes and became the *bête noire* of free trade economists for generations to come.

In the *Report*, Hamilton proposed a series of measures to achieve the industrial development of his country, including protective tariffs and import bans; subsidies; export ban on key raw materials; import liberalization of and tariff rebates on industrial inputs; prizes and patents for inventions; regulation of product standards; and development of financial and transportation infrastructures.[27] Although Hamilton rightly cautioned against taking these policies too far, they are, nevertheless, a pretty potent and 'heretical' set of policy prescriptions. Were he the finance minister of a developing country today, the IMF and the World Bank would certainly have refused to lend money to his country and would be lobbying for his removal from office.

Congress's action following Hamilton's *Report* fell far short of his recommendations, largely because US politics at the time were dominated by Southern plantation owners with no interest in developing American manufacturing industries. Quite understandably, they wanted to be able to import higher-quality manufactured products from Europe at the lowest possible price with the proceeds they earned from exporting agricultural products. Following Hamilton's *Report*, the average tariff on foreign manufactured goods was raised from around 5% to around 12.5%, but it was far too low to induce those buying manufactured goods to support the nascent American industries.

Hamilton resigned as treasurey secretary in 1795, following the scandal surrounding his extra-marital affair with a married woman, without the chance to further advance his programme. The life of this brilliant if caustic man was cut short in his 50th year (1804) in a pistol duel in New York, to which he was challenged by his friend-turned-political rival, Aaron Burr, the then vice president under Thomas Jefferson.[28] Had he lived for another decade or so, however, Hamilton would have been able to see his programme adopted in full.

When the Anglo-American War broke out in 1812, the US Congress immediately doubled tariffs from the average of 12.5% to 25%. The war also made the space for new industries to emerge by interrupting the manufactured imports from Britain and the rest of Europe. The new group of industrialists who had now arisen naturally wanted the protection to continue, and, indeed, to be increased, after the war.[29] In 1816, tariffs were raised further, bringing up the average to 35%. By 1820, the average tariff rose further to 40%, firmly establishing Hamilton's programme.

Hamilton provided the blueprint for US economic policy until the end of the Second World War. His infant industry programme created the condition for a rapid industrial development. He also set up the government bond market and promoted the development of the banking system (once again, against opposition from Thomas Jefferson and his followers).[30] It is no hyperbole for the New York Historical Society to have called him 'The Man Who Made Modern America' in a recent exhibition.[31] Had the US rejected Hamilton's vision and accepted that of his archrival, Thomas Jefferson, for whom the ideal society was an agrarian economy made up of self-governing yeoman farmers (although this slave-owner had to sweep the slaves who supported this lifestyle under the carpet), it would never have been able to propel itself from being a minor agrarian power rebelling against its powerful colonial master to the world's greatest super-power.

Abraham Lincoln and America's bid for supremacy

Although Hamilton's trade policy was well established by the 1820s, tariffs were an ever-present source of tension in US politics for the following three decades. The Southern agrarian states constantly attempted to lower industrial tariffs, while the Northern manufacturing states argued the case for keeping them high or even raising them further. In 1832, pro-free trade South Carolina even refused to accept the new federal tariff law, causing a political crisis. The so-called Nullification Crisis was resolved by President Andrew Jackson, who offered some tariff reduction (though not a lot, despite his image as the folk hero of American free market capitalism), while threatening South Carolina with military action. This served to patch things up temporarily, but the festering conflict eventually came to a violent resolution in the Civil War that was fought under the presidency of Abraham Lincoln.

Many Americans call Abraham Lincoln, the 16th president (1861–5), the Great Emancipator – of the American slaves. But he might equally be labelled the Great Protector – of American manufacturing. Lincoln was a strong advocate of infant industry protection. He cut his political teeth under Henry Clay of the Whig Party, who advocated the building of the 'American System', which consisted of infant industry protection ('Protection for Home Industries', in Clay's words) and investment in infrastructure such as canals ('Internal Improvements').[32] Lincoln, born in the same state of Kentucky as Clay, entered politics as a Whig state lawmaker of Illinois in 1834 at the age of 25, and was Clay's trusted lieutenant in the early days of his political career.

The charismatic Clay stood out from early on in his career. Almost as soon as he was elected to Congress in 1810, he became the Speaker of the House (from 1811 until 1820 and then again in 1823–5). As a politician from the West, he wanted to persuade the Western states to join forces with the Northern states, in the development of whose manufacturing industries Clay saw the future of his country. Traditionally, the Western states, without much industry, had been advocates of free trade and thus allied themselves with the pro-free trade Southern states. Clay argued that they should switch sides to back a protectionist programme of industrial development in return for federal investments in infrastructure to develop the region. Clay ran for the presidency three times (1824, 1832 and 1844) without success, although he came very close to winning the popular vote in the 1844 election. The Whig candidates who did manage to become presidents – William Harrison (1841–4) and Zachary Taylor (1849–51) – were generals with no clear political or economic views.

In the end, what made it possible for the protectionists to win the presidency with Lincoln as their candidate was the formation of the Republican Party. Today the Republican Party calls itself the GOP (Grand Old Party), but it is actually younger than the Democratic Party, which has existed in one form or another since the days of Thomas Jefferson (when it was called, somewhat confusingly to the modern observer, the Democratic Republicans). The Republican Party was a mid-19th-century invention, based on a new vision that befitted a country that was rapidly moving outward (into the West) and forward (through industrialization), rather than harking back to an increasingly unsustainable agrarian economy based on slavery.

The winning formula that the Republican Party came up with was to combine the American System of the Whigs with the free distribution of (often already illegally occupied) public land so strongly wanted by the Western states. This call for free distribution of public land was naturally anathema to the Southern landlords, who saw it as the start of a slippery slope towards a comprehensive land reform. The legislation for such distribution had been constantly thwarted by the Southern Congressmen. The Republican Party undertook to pass the Homestead Act, which promised to give 160 acres of land to any settler who would farm it for five years. This act was passed during the Civil War in 1862, by which time the Southern Congressmen had withdrawn.

Slavery was *not* as divisive an issue in pre-Civil-War US politics as most of us today believe it to have been. Abolitionists had a strong influence in some Northern states, especially Massachusetts, but the mainstream Northern view was not abolitionist. Many people who were opposed to slavery thought that black people were racially inferior and thus were against giving them full citizenship, including the right to vote. They believed the proposal by radicals for an immediate abolition of slavery to be highly unrealistic. The Great Emancipator himself shared these views. In response to a newspaper editorial urging immediate slave emancipation, Lincoln wrote: 'If I could save the Union without freeing any slave, I would do it; and if I could save it by freeing all the slaves, I would do it; and if I could do it by freeing some and leaving others alone, I would also do that'.[33] Historians of the period agree that his abolition of slavery in 1862 was more of a strategic move to win the war than an act of moral conviction. Disagreement over trade policy, in fact, was at least as important as, and possibly more important than, slavery in bringing about the Civil War.

During the 1860 election campaign, the Republicans in some protectionist states assailed the Democrats as a 'Southern-*British*-Antitariff-Disunion party [my italics]', playing on Clay's idea of the *American* system which implied that free trade was in the British, not American, interest.[34] However, Lincoln tried to keep quiet on the tariff issue during the election campaign, not just to avoid attacks from the Democrats but also to keep the fragile new party united, as there were some free-traders in the party (mostly former Democrats who were anti-slavery).

But, once elected, Lincoln raised industrial tariffs to their highest level so far in US history.[35] The expenditure for the Civil War was given as an excuse – in the same way in which the first significant rise in US tariffs came about during the Anglo-American War (1812–16). However, after the war, tariffs stayed at wartime levels or above. Tariffs on manufactured imports remained at 40–50% until the First World War, and were the highest of any country in the world.[36]

In 1913, following the Democratic electoral victory, the Underwood Tariff bill was passed, reducing the average tariff on manufactured goods from 44% to 25%.[37] But tariffs were raised again very soon afterwards, thanks to American participation in the First World War. After the Republican return to power in 1921, tariffs went up again, although they did not go back to the heights of the 1861–1913 period. By 1925, the average manufacturing tariff had climbed back up to 37%. Following the onset of the Great Depression, there came the 1930 Smooth-Hawley tariff, which raised tariffs even higher.

Along with the much-trumpeted wisdom of the Anti-Corn Law movement, the stupidity of the Smoot-Hawley tariff has become a key fable in free trade mythology. The free trade economist Jagdish Bhagwati called it 'the most visible and dramatic act of anti-trade folly'.[38] But this view is misleading. The Smoot-Hawley tariff may have provoked an international tariff war, thanks to bad timing, especially given the new status of the US as the world's largest creditor nation after the First World War. But it was simply not the radical departure from the country's traditional trade policy stance that free trade economists claim it to have been. Following the bill, the average industrial tariff rate rose to 48%. The rise from 37% (1925) to 48% (1930) is not exactly small but it is hardly a seismic shift. Moreover, the 48% obtained after the bill comfortably falls within the range of the rates that had prevailed in the country ever since the Civil War, albeit in the upper region thereof.

Despite being the most protectionist country in the world throughout the 19th century and right up to the 1920s, the US was also the fastest growing economy. The eminent Swiss economic historian, Paul Bairoch, points out that there is no evidence that the only significant reduction of protectionism in the US economy (between 1846 and 1861) had any noticeable positive impact on the country's rate of economic growth.[39] Some free trade economists argue that the US grew quickly during this period *despite* protectionism, because it had so many other favourable conditions for growth, particularly its abundant natural resources, large domestic market and high literacy rate.[40] The force of this counter-argument is diminished by the fact that, as we shall see, many other countries with few of those conditions also grew rapidly behind protective barriers. Germany, Sweden, France, Finland, Austria, Japan, Taiwan and Korea come to mind.

It was only after the Second World War that the US – with its industrial supremacy now unchallenged – liberalized its trade and started championing the cause of free trade. But the US has never practised free trade to the same degree as Britain did during its free trade period (1860 to 1932). It has never had a zero-tariff regime like Britain. It has also been much more aggressive in using non-tariff protectionist measures when necessary.[41] Moreover, even when it shifted to freer (if not absolutely free) trade, the US government promoted key industries by another means, namely, public funding of R&D. Between the 1950s and the mid-1990s, US federal government funding accounted for 50–70% of the country's total R&D funding, which is way above the figures, around 20%, found in such 'government-led' countries as Japan and Korea. Without federal government funding for R&D, the US would not have been able to maintain its technological lead over the rest of the world in key industries like computers, semiconductors, life sciences, the internet and aerospace.

Other countries, guilty secrets

Given that protectionism is bad for economic growth, how can the two most successful economies in history have been so protectionist? One possible answer is that, while Britain and the US were protectionist, they were economically more successful than other countries because they were less protectionist than others. Indeed, it seems likely that other rich countries known for their protectionist tendencies – such as France, Germany and Japan – had even higher tariff walls than those of Britain and the US.

This is not true. None of the other countries among today's wealthy nations were ever as protectionist as Britain or the US, with the brief exception of Spain in the 1930s.[42] France, Germany and Japan – the three countries that are usually considered to be the homes of protectionism – always had lower tariffs than Britain or the US (until the latter two countries converted to free trade following their economic ascendancy).

France is often presented as the protectionist counterpoint to free-trade Britain. But, between 1821 and 1875, especially up until the early 1860s, France had lower tariffs than Britain.[43] Even when it became protectionist – between the 1920s and the 1950s – its average industrial tariff rate was never over 30%. The average industrial tariff rates in Britain and the US were 50–55% at their heights.

Tariffs were always relatively low in Germany. Throughout the 19th and in the early 20th century (until the First World War), the average manufacturing tariff rate in Germany was 5–15%, way below the American and the British (before the 1860s) rates of 35–50%. Even in the 1920s, when it became more protective of its industries, Germany's average industrial tariff rate stayed around 20%. The frequent equation of fascism with protectionism in free trade mythology is highly misleading in this sense.

As for Japan, in the very early days of its industrial development, it actually practised free trade. But this was not out of choice but due to a series of unequal treaties that it was forced by Western countries to sign upon its opening in 1853. These treaties bound Japan's tariff rate below 5% until 1911. But, even after it regained tariff autonomy and raised manufacturing tariffs, the average industrial tariff rate was only about 30%.

It was only after the Second World War, when the US became top dog and liberalized its trade, that countries like France came to look protectionist. But, even then, the difference was not that great. In 1962, the average industrial tariff in the US was still 13%. With only 7% average industrial tariff rates, the Netherlands and West Germany were considerably less protectionist than the US. Tariff rates in Belgium, Japan, Italy, Austria and Finland were only slightly higher, ranging from 14% to 20%. France, with a tariff rate of 30% in 1959, was the one exception.[44] By the early 1970s, the US could not claim to be the leading practitioner of free trade any more. By then, other rich countries had caught up with it economically and found themselves able to lower their industrial tariffs. In 1973, the US average industrial tariff rate was 12%, compared to Finland's 13%, Austria's 11% and Japan's 10%. The average tariff rate of the EEC (European Economic Community) countries was considerably lower than the US rate, at only 8%.[45]

So the two champions of free trade, Britain and the US, were not only not free trade economies, but had been the two most protectionist economies among rich countries – that is, until they each became the world's dominant industrial power.*

* The average tariff rate, of course, does not tell us the full story. A country may have a relatively low average tariff rate, but this could be the result of the heavy protection of certain sectors counterbalanced by very low or zero tariffs in other sectors. For example, during the late 19th and the early 20th century, while maintaining a relatively moderate *average* industrial tariff rate (5–15%), Germany accorded strong tariff protection to strategic industries like iron and steel. During the same period, Sweden also provided high protection to its newly emerging engineering industries, although its average tariff rate was 15–20%. In the first half of the 20th century, Belgium maintained moderate levels of overall protection (around 10% average industrial tariff rate), but heavily protected key textile sectors (30–60%) and the iron industry (85%).

Of course, tariffs are only one of the many tools that a country can use to promote its infant industries. After all, Hamilton's original recommendation listed eleven types of measures to promote infant industry, including patents, product quality standards and public investment in infrastructure. Britain and the US may have used tariffs most aggressively, but other countries often used other means of policy intervention – for example, state-owned enterprises, subsidies or export marketing support – more intensively.

In the early days of their industrialization, when there were not enough private sector entrepreneurs who could take on risky, large-scale ventures, most of today's rich country governments (except the US and the British) set up state-owned enterprises. In some case, they provided so many subsidies and other help (e.g., poaching skilled workers from abroad) to some private-sector enterprises that they were effectively public-private joint ventures. In the 18th century, Prussia, the leader of German industrialization, promoted industries like linen, iron and steel by means of these methods. Japan started steel, shipbuilding and railway industries through state ownership and targeted subsidies (more on this in chapter 5). In the late 19th century, the Swedish government took the lead in developing the railways. As of 1913, it owned one-third of the railways in terms of mileage and 60% in terms of goods transported – this at a time when the leaders in railway development, namely Britain and the US, relied almost entirely on the private sector. Public-private co-operation in Sweden continued in the development of the telegraph, telephone and hydro-electric sectors. The Swedish government also subsidised R&D from early on.

After the Second World War, state efforts to promote industry were intensified in most rich countries. The biggest shift was in France. Contrary to the popular image, the French state has not always been interventionist. There certainly had been a tradition of state activism, represented by Jean-Baptiste Colbert, Louis XIV's long-time finance minister (1865–83), but it was rejected after the French Revolution. So, between the end of Napoleon's rule and the Second World War, except during the rule of Napoleon III, the French state took an extreme *laissez-faire* approach to economic policy. One major historical account of French economic policy points out that, during this period, the industrial promotion strategy of the French government 'consisted largely of organising exhibitions, looking after the Chambers of Commerce, gathering economic statistics, and distributing decorations to businessmen'.[46] After 1945, acknowledging that its conservative, hands-off policies were responsible for its relative economic decline and thus defeats in two world wars, the French state took a much more active role in the economy. It launched 'indicative' (as opposed to communism's 'compulsory') planning, took over key industries through nationalization, and channelled investment into strategic industries through state-owned banks. To create the breathing space for new industries to grow, industrial tariffs were maintained at a relatively high level until the 1960s. The strategy worked very well. By the 1980s, France had transformed itself into a technological leader in many areas.

In Japan, the famous MITI (Ministry of International Trade and Industry) orchestrated an industrial development programme that has now become a legend. Japan's industrial tariffs were not particularly high after the Second World War, but imports were tightly controlled through government control over foreign exchange. Exports were promoted in order to maximize the supply of foreign currency needed to buy up better technology (either by buying machinery or by paying for technology licences). This involved direct and indirect export subsidies as well as information and marketing help from JETRO (Japan External Trade Organisation), the state trading agency. There were other measures to create the space needed for the accumulation of new productive capabilities by infant industries. The Japanese government channelled subsidized credits into key sectors through 'directed credit progammes'. It also heavily regulated foreign investment by transnational corporations (TNCs). Foreign investment was simply banned in most key industries. Even when it was allowed, there were strict ceilings on foreign ownership, usually a maximum of 49%. Foreign companies were required to transfer technology and buy at least specified proportions of their inputs locally (the so-called local contents requirement). The Japanese government also regulated the inflow of technologies, to make sure that overly obsolete or over-priced technologies were not imported. However, unlike in the 19th century, the Japanese government did not use SOEs in key manufacturing industries.

Countries like Finland, Norway, Italy and Austria – which were all relatively backward at the end of the Second World War and saw the need for rapid industrial development – also used strategies similar to those used by France and Japan to promote their industries. All of them had relatively high tariffs until the 1960s. They all actively used SOEs to upgrade their industries. This was particularly successful in Finland and Norway. In Finland, Norway and Austria, the government was very much involved in directing the flow of bank credit to strategic industries. Finland heavily controlled foreign investment. In many parts of Italy, local government provided support for marketing and R&D to small and medium-sized firms in the locality.

Thus practically all of today's rich countries used nationalistic policies (e.g., tariffs, subsidies, restrictions on foreign investment) to promote their infant industries, though the exact mix of policies used, as well as their timing and duration, differed across countries. There were some exceptions: notably the Netherlands (which has had the best free-trade credentials since the 19th century) and Switzerland (until the First World War) consistently practised free trade. But even they do not conform to today's neo-liberal ideal, as they did not protect patents until the early 20th century. The Netherlands introduced a patent law in 1817, but abolished it in 1869 and did not re-introduce it until 1912. The Swiss introduced their first patent law in 1888, but it protected only mechanical inventions. It introduced a full patent law only in 1907 (more on these cases in chapter 6).

Against the kind of historical evidence that I have presented in this chapter, free trade economists have argued that the mere co-existence of protectionism and economic development does not prove that the former caused the latter.[47] This is true. But I am at least trying to explain something (economic development) with another that co-existed with it (protectionism); free trade economists have to explain how free trade can be an explanation for the economic success of today's rich countries, when it simply had not been practised very much before they became rich.

Learning the right lessons from history

The Roman politician and philosopher Cicero once said: 'Not to know what has been transacted in former times is to be always a child. If no use is made of the labours of past ages, the world must remain always in the infancy of knowledge.'

Nowhere else is the observation more relevant than in the design of development policy, but nowhere is it more ignored. Though we have a wealth of historical experiences to draw upon, we do not bother to learn them and unquestioningly accept the prevailing myth that today's rich countries developed through free-trade, free-market policy.

But history tells us that, in the early stage of their development, virtually all successful countries used some mixture of protection, subsidies and regulation in order to develop their economies. The history of the successful developing countries that I discussed in chapter 1 shows that. More importantly, the history of today's rich countries also confirms that, as I have discussed in this chapter.

Unfortunately, another lesson of history is that rich countries have 'kicked away the ladder' by forcing free-market, free-trade policies on poor countries. Already established countries do not want more competitors emerging through the nationalistic policies they themselves successfully used in the past. Even the newest member of the club of rich countries, my native Korea, has not been an exception to this pattern. Despite once having been one of the most protectionist countries in the world, it now advocates steep cuts in industrial tariffs, if not total free trade, in the WTO. Despite once having been the world piracy capital, it gets upset that the Chinese and the Vietnamese are producing pirate CDs of Korean pop music and pirate DVDs of Korean movies. Worse, these Korean free-marketeers are often the same people who, not so long ago, actually drafted and implemented interventionist, protectionist policies in their earlier jobs. Most of them probably learned their free market economics from pirate-copied American economics textbooks, while listening to pirate-copied rock and roll music and watching pirate-copied videos of Hollywood films in their spare time.

Even more prevalent and important than 'ladder-kicking', however, is historical amnesia. In the Prologue, I explained the gradual and subtle process in which history is re-written to fit a country's present self-image. As a result, many rich country people recommend free-trade, free-market policies in the honest belief that these are policies that their own ancestors used in order to make their countries rich. When the poor countries protest that those policies hurt, those protests are dismissed as being intellectually misguided[48] or as serving the interests of their corrupt leaders.[49] It never occurs to those Bad Samaritans that the policies they recommend are fundamentally at odds with what history teaches us to be the best development policies. The intention behind their policy recommendations may be honourable, but their effects are no less harmful than those from policy recommendations motivated by deliberate ladder-kicking.

Fortunately, history also shows that it is not inevitable that successful countries act as Bad Samaritans and, more importantly, that it is in their enlightened self-interest not to act as one. The most recent and important episode of this kind occurred between the launch of the Marshall Plan in 1947 and the rise of neo-liberalism in the 1980s.

In June 1947, the US abandoned its previous policy of deliberately weakening the German economy and launched the Marshall Plan, which channelled a large amount of money into European post-war reconstruction.* Even though the sum involved in this was not huge,

* The Marshall Plan was announced by George Marshall, the then US secretary of state, in his address at Harvard University on 5 June 1947. Its details were negotiated in a meeting held in Paris from 12 July 1947. It was started in 1948 and ended in 1951, channelling some $13 billion (equivalent to $130 billion today) into the war-torn economies of Europe. The Marshall Plan replaced the Morgenthau Plan that had dictated postwar American foreign policy until then. The Morgenthau Plan, named after the treasury secretary of the time (1934–45), focused on putting an end to Germany's expansionist ambition by 'pastoralizing' it. When combined with the Soviet Union's desire to seize advanced German machinery, it was very effective in destroying the German economy. However, it soon became obvious that such a plan was unviable. After his visit to Germany in 1947, the former US president Herbert Hoover denounced the Morgenthau Plan as 'illusory', and argued that it would not work unless the German population was reduced by 25 million, from 65 million to 40 million. For an enlightening discussion on the subject, see E. Reinert (2003), 'Increasing Poverty in a Globalised World: *Marshall Plans* and *Morgenthau Plans* as Mechanisms of Polarisation of World Incomes' in H-J. Chang (ed.), *Rethinking Development Economics* (Anthem Press, London).

the Marshall Plan played an important role in kickstarting the war-torn European economies by financing essential import bills and financing the re-building of infrastructure. More importantly, it was a political signal that the US saw it in its interest that other nations, even its former enemies, prosper. The US also led other rich countries in helping, or at least allowing, poor countries develop their economies through nationalistic policies. Through the GATT (General Agreement on Tariffs and Trade), also set up in 1947, the US and other rich countries allowed developing countries to protect and subsidize their producers more actively than the rich countries. This was a huge contrast to the days of colonialism and unequal treaties, when developing countries were forced into free trade. This was partly down to the sense of colonial guilt in countries like Britain and France, but it was mostly because of the more enlightened attitude of the then new hegemon of the global economy, the US, towards the economic development of poorer nations.

The result of this enlightened strategy was spectacular. The rich countries experienced the so-called 'Golden Age of Capitalism' (1950–73).[50] *Per capita* income growth rate shot up from 1.3% in the liberal golden age (1870–1913) to 4.1% in Europe. It rose from 1.8% to 2.5% in the US, while it skyrocketed from 1.5% to 8.1% in Japan. These spectacular growth performances were combined with low income inequality and economic stability. More importantly, developing countries also performed very well during this period. As I pointed out in chapter 1, during the 1960s and the 1970s, when they used nationalistic policies under the 'permissive' international system, they grew at 3% in *per capita* terms. This is way above what they had achieved under old liberal policies during 'first globalization' (1870–1913) and twice the rate they have recorded since the 1980s under neo-liberal policies.

Some have discounted the generosity of the US during the 1947–1979 period on the grounds that it was being nice to poor countries only because of the rivalry with the USSR in the Cold War. It would be silly to deny that the Cold War had an important influence on US foreign policy, but that should not stop us from giving credit where it is due. During the 'age of imperialism' in the late 19th and the early

20th century, the powerful countries behaved abominably towards the weaker countries *despite* the intense rivalry amongst themselves.

The history – recent and more distant – that I have discussed in the last two chapters will inform my discussion in the following chapters, where I explain how exactly today's Bad Samaritans are wrong in relation to the key areas of economic policy – international trade, foreign investment regulation, privatisation, protection of intellectual property rights, like patents, and macroeconomic policy – and suggest how their behaviour should be changed if we are to promote economic development in poor countries.

CHAPTER 3

My six-year-old son should get a job

Is free trade always the answer?

I have a six-year-old son. His name is Jin-Gyu. He lives off me, yet he is quite capable of making a living. I pay for his lodging, food, education and health care. But millions of children of his age already have jobs. Daniel Defoe, in the 18th century, thought that children could earn a living from the age of four.

Moreover, working might do Jin-Gyu's character a world of good. Right now he lives in an economic bubble with no sense of the value of money. He has zero appreciation of the efforts his mother and I make on his behalf, subsidizing his idle existence and cocooning him from harsh reality. He is over-protected and needs to be exposed to competition, so that he can become a more productive person. Thinking about it, the more competition he is exposed to and the sooner this is done, the better it will be for his future development. It will whip him into a mentality that is ready for hard work. I should make him quit school and get a job. Perhaps I could move to a country where child labour is still tolerated, if not legal, to give him more choice in employment.

I can hear you say I must be mad. Myopic. Cruel. You tell me that I need to protect and nurture the child. If I drive Jin-Gyu into the labour market at the age of six, he may become a savvy shoeshine boy or even a prosperous street hawker, but he will never become a brain surgeon or a nuclear physicist – that would require at least another dozen years of my protection and investment. You argue that, even from a purely materialistic viewpoint, I would be wiser to invest in my son's education than gloat over the money I save by not sending him to school. After all, if I were right, Oliver Twist would have been better off pick-pocketing for Fagin, rather than being rescued by the misguided Good Samaritan Mr Brownlow, who deprived the boy of his chance to remain competitive in the labour market.

Yet this absurd line of argument is in essence how free-trade economists justify rapid, large-scale trade liberalization in developing countries. They claim that developing country producers need to be exposed to as much competition as possible right now, so that they have the incentive to raise their productivity in order to survive. Protection, by contrast, only creates complacency and sloth. The earlier the exposure, the argument goes, the better it is for economic development.

Incentives, however, are only half the story. The other is capability. Even if Jin-Gyu were to be offered a £20m reward or, alternatively, threatened with a bullet in his head, he would not be able to rise to the challenge of brain surgery had he quit school at the age of six. Likewise, industries in developing countries will not survive if they are exposed to international competition too early. They need time to improve their capabilities by mastering advanced technologies and building effective organizations. This is the essence of the infant industry argument, first theorized by Alexander Hamilton, first treasury secretary of the US, and used by generations of policy-makers before and after him, as I have just shown in the previous chapter.

Naturally, the protection I provide to Jin-Gyu (as the infant industry argument itself says) should not be used to shelter him from competition forever. Making him work at the age of six is wrong, but so is subsidizing him at the age of 40. Eventually he should go out into the big wide world, get a job and live an independent life. He only needs protection while he is accumulating the capabilities to take on a satisfying and well-paid job.

Of course, as happens with parents bringing up their children, infant industry protection can go wrong. Just as some parents are over-protective, governments can cosset infant industries too much. Some children are unwilling to prepare themselves for adult life, just as infant industry support is wasted on some firms. In the way that some children manipulate their parents into supporting them beyond childhood, there are industries that prolong government protection through clever lobbying. But the existence of dysfunctional families is hardly an argument against parenting itself. Likewise, cases of failures in infant industry protection cannot discredit the strategy *per se*. The examples of bad protectionism merely tell us that the policy needs to be used wisely.

Free trade isn't working

Free trade is good – this is the doctrine at the heart of the neo-liberal orthodoxy. To the neo-liberals, there cannot be a more self-evident proposition than this. Professor Willem Buiter, my distinguished former colleague at Cambridge and a former chief economist of the EBRD (European Bank for Reconstruction and Development), once expressed this succinctly: 'Remember: unilateral trade liberalization is not a "concession" or a "sacrifice" that one should be compensated for. It is an act of enlightened self-interest. Reciprocal trade liberalization enhances the gains but is not necessary for gains to be present. The economics is all there'.[1] Belief in the virtue of free trade is so central to the neo-liberal orthodoxy that it is effectively what defines a neo-liberal economist. You may question (if not totally reject) any other element of the neo-liberal agenda – open capital markets, strong patents or even privatisation – and still stay in the neo-liberal church. However, once you object to free trade, you are effectively inviting ex-communication.

Based on such convictions, the Bad Samaritans have done their utmost to push developing countries into free trade – or, at least, much freer trade. During the past quarter of a century, most developing countries have liberalized trade to a huge degree. They were first pushed by the IMF and the World Bank in the aftermath of the Third World debt crisis of 1982. There was a further decisive impetus towards trade liberalization following the launch of the WTO in 1995. During the last decade or so, bilateral and regional free trade agreements (FTAs) have also proliferated. Unfortunately, during this period, developing countries have not done well at all, despite (or because of, in my view) massive trade liberalization, as I showed in chapter 1.

The story of Mexico – poster boy of the free-trade camp – is particularly telling. If any developing country can succeed with free trade, it should be Mexico. It borders on the largest market in the world (the US) and has had a free trade agreement with it since 1995 (the North American Free Trade Agreement or NAFTA). It also has a large diaspora living in the US, which can provide important informal business links.[2] Unlike many other poorer developing countries, it has a decent pool of skilled workers, competent managers and relatively developed physical infrastructure (roads, ports and so on).

Free trade economists argue that free trade benefited Mexico by accelerating growth. Indeed, following NAFTA, between 1994 and 2002, Mexico's *per capita* GDP grew at 1.8% per year, a big improvement over the 0.1% rate recorded between 1985 and 1995.[3] But the decade before NAFTA was also a decade of extensive trade liberalisation for Mexico, following its conversion to neo-liberalism in the mid-1980s. So trade liberalization was also responsible for the 0.1% growth rate.

Wide-ranging trade liberalization in the 1980s and the 1990s wiped out whole swathes of Mexican industry that had been painstakingly built up during the period of import substitution industrialization (ISI). The result was, predictably, a slowdown in economic growth, lost jobs and falls in wages (as better-paying manufacturing jobs disappeared). Its agricultural sector was also hard hit by subsidized US products, especially maize, the staple diet of most Mexicans. On top of that, NAFTA's positive impact (in terms of increasing exports to the US market) has run out of steam in the last few years. During 2001–2005, Mexico's growth performance has been miserable, with an annual growth rate of *per capita* income at 0.3% (or a paltry 1.7% increase in total over five years).[4] By contrast, during the 'bad old days' of ISI (1955–82), Mexico's *per capita* income had grown much faster than during the NAFTA period – at an average of 3.1% per year.[5]

Mexico is a particularly striking example of the failure of premature wholesale trade liberalization, but there are other examples.[6] In Ivory Coast, following tariff cuts of 40% in 1986, the chemical, textile, shoe and automobile industries virtually collapsed. Unemployment soared. In Zimbabwe, following trade liberalization in 1990, the unemployment rate jumped from 10% to 20%. It had been hoped that the capital and labour resources released from the enterprises that went bankrupt due to trade liberalization would be absorbed by new businesses. This simply did not happen on a sufficient scale. It is not surprising that growth evaporated and unemployment soared.

Trade liberalization has created other problems, too. It has increased the pressures on government budgets, as it reduced tariff revenues. This has been a particularly serious problem for the poorer countries. Because they lack tax collection capabilities and because tariffs are the easiest tax to collect, they rely heavily on tariffs (which sometimes account for over 50% of total government revenue).[7] As a result, the fiscal adjustment that has had to be made following large-scale trade liberalization has been huge in many developing countries – even a recent IMF study shows that, in low-income countries that have limited abilities to collect other taxes, *less than 30%* of the revenue lost due to trade liberalization over the last 25 years has been made up by other taxes.[8] Moreover, lower levels of business activity and higher unemployment resulting from trade liberalization have also reduced income tax revenue. When countries were already under considerable pressure from the IMF to reduce their budget deficits, falling revenue meant severe cuts in spending, often eating into vital areas like education, health and physical infrastructure, damaging long-term growth.

It is perfectly possible that *some* degree of *gradual* trade liberalization may have been beneficial, and even necessary, for certain developing countries in the 1980s – India and China come to mind. But what has happened during the past quarter of a century has been a rapid, unplanned and blanket trade liberalization. Just to remind the reader, during the 'bad old days' of protectionist import substitution industrialization (ISI), developing countries used to grow, on average, at double the rate that they are doing today under free trade. Free trade simply isn't working for developing countries.

Poor theory, poor results

Free trade economists find all this quite mysterious. How can countries do badly when they are using such theoretically well-proven ('the economics is all there', as Professor Buiter says) policy as free trade? But they should not be surprised. For their theory has some serious limitations.

Modern free trade argument is based on the so-called Heckscher-Ohlin-Samuelson theory (or the HOS theory).* The HOS theory derives from David Ricardo's theory, which I outlined in chapter 2, but it differs from Ricardo's theory in one crucial respect. It assumes that comparative advantage arises from international differences in the relative endowments of 'factors of production' (capital and labour), rather than international differences in technology, as in Ricardian theory.[9]

According to free trade theory, be it Ricardian or the HOS version, every country has a comparative advantage in some products, as it is, by definition, *relatively* better at producing some things than others.[†] In the HOS theory, a country has comparative advantage in products that more intensively use the factor of production with which it is relatively more richly endowed. So even if Germany, a country relatively richer in capital than labour, can produce *both* automobiles *and* stuffed toys more cheaply than Guatemala, it pays for it to specialize in automobiles, as their production uses capital more intensively. Guatemala, even if it is less efficient in producing both automobiles and stuffed toys than Germany, should still specialize in stuffed toys, whose production uses more labour than capital.

* The HOS theory is named after the two Swedish economists, Eli Heckscher and Bertil Ohlin, who pioneered it in the early 20th century, and Paul Saumelson, the American economist who perfected it in the mid-20th century. In this version of free trade theory, for each product there is only one 'best practice' (i.e., most efficient) technology, which all countries will use if they are producing it. If each product has one best production technology for its production, a country's comparative advantage can *not* be determined by its technologies, as in Ricardo's theory. It is determined by how suitable the technology used for each product is for the country. In the HOS theory, the suitability of a particular technology for a country depends on how intensively it uses the factor of production (i.e., labour or capital) with which the country is relatively abundantly endowed.

† So, 'comparative' in the term 'comparative advantage' is not about comparison between countries but about comparison between products. It is because people mix these two up that they sometimes believe that poor countries do not have comparative advantage in anything – which is a logical impossibility.

The more closely a country conforms to its underlying pattern of comparative advantage, the more it can consume. This is possible due to the increase in its own production (of the goods for which it has comparative advantage), and, more importantly, due to increased trading with other countries that specialize in different products. How can the country achieve this? By leaving things as they are. When they are free to choose, firms will rationally (like Robinson Crusoe) specialize in things that they are relatively good at and trade with foreigners. From this follows the propositions that free trade is best and that trade liberalization, even when it is unilateral, is beneficial.

But the conclusion of the HOS theory critically depends on the assumption that productive resources can move freely across economic activities. This assumption means that capital and labour released from any one activity can immediately and without cost be absorbed by other activities. With this assumption – known as the assumption of 'perfect factor mobility' among economists – adjustments to changing trade patterns pose no problem. If a steel mill shuts down due to an increase in imports because, say, the government reduces tariffs, the resources employed in the industry (the workers, the buildings, the blast furnaces) will be employed (at the same or higher levels of productivity and thus higher returns) by another industry that has become relatively more profitable, say, the computer industry. No one loses from the process.

In reality, this is not the case: factors of production cannot take any form as it becomes necessary. They are usually fixed in their physical qualities and there are few 'general use' machines or workers with a 'general skill' that can be used across industries. Blast furnaces from a bankrupt steel mill cannot be re-moulded into a machine making computers; steel workers do not have the right skills for the computer industry. Unless they are retrained, the steel workers will remain unemployed. At best, they will end up working in low-skill jobs, where their existing skills are totally wasted. This point is poignantly made by the British hit comedy film of 1997, *The Full Monty*, where six unemployed steel workers from Sheffield struggle to rebuild their lives as male strippers. There are clearly winners and losers involved in changing trade patterns, whether it is due to trade liberalization or to the rise of new, more productive foreign producers.

Most free trade economists would accept that there are winners and losers from trade liberalization but argue that their existence cannot be an argument against trade liberalization. Trade liberalization brings overall gains. As the winners gain more than what is lost by the losers, the winners can make up all the latter's losses and still have something left for themselves. This is known as the 'compensation principle' – if the winners from an economic change can fully compensate the losers and still have something left, the change is worth making.

The first problem with this line of argument is that trade liberalization does *not* necessarily bring overall gain. Even if there are winners from the process, their gains may not be as large as the losses suffered by the losers – for example, when trade liberalization reduces the growth rate or even make the economy shrink, as has happened in many developing countries in the past two decades.

Moreover, even if the winners gain more than the losers lose, the compensation is not automatically made through the workings of the market, which means that some people will be worse off than before. Trade liberalization will benefit everyone only when the displaced workers can get better (or at least equally good) jobs quickly, and when the discharged machines can be re-shaped into new machines – which is rarely.

This is a more serious problem in developing countries, where the compensation mechanism is weak, if not non-existent. In developed countries, the welfare state works as a mechanism to partially compensate the losers from the trade adjustment process through unemployment benefits, guarantees of health care and education, and even guarantees of a minimum income. In some countries, such as Sweden and other Scandinavian countries, there are also highly effective retraining schemes for unemployed workers so that they can be equipped with new skills. In most developing countries, however, the welfare state is very weak and sometimes virtually non-existent. As a result, the victims of trade adjustment in these countries do not get even partially compensated for the sacrifice that they have made for the rest of society.

As a result, the gains from trade liberalization in poor countries are likely to be more unevenly distributed than in rich countries. Especially when considering that many people in developing countries are already very poor and close to the subsistence level, large-scale trade liberalization carried out in a short period of time will mean that some people have their livelihoods wrecked. In developed countries, unemployment due to trade adjustment may not be a matter of life and death, but in developing countries it often is. This is why we need to be more cautious with trade liberalization in poorer economies.

The short-run trade adjustment problem arising from the immobility of economic resources and the weakness of compensating mechanisms is, although serious, only a secondary problem with free trade theory. The more serious problem – at least for an economist like myself – is that the theory is about efficiency in the short-run use of given resources, and *not* about increasing available resources through economic development in the long run; contrary to what their proponents would have us believe, free trade theory does *not* tell us that free trade is good for *economic development*.

The problem is this – producers in developing countries entering new industries need a period of (partial) insulation from international competition (through protection, subsidies and other measures) before they can build up their capabilities to compete with superior foreign producers. Of course, when the infant producers 'grow up' and are able to compete with the more advanced producers, the insulation should go. But this has to be done gradually. If they are exposed to too much international competition too soon, they are bound to disappear. That is the essence of the infant industry argument that I set out at the beginning of the chapter with a little help from my son, Jin-Gyu.

In recommending free trade to developing countries, the Bad Samaritans point out that all the rich countries have free(ish) trade. This is, however, like people advising the parents of a six-year-old boy to make him get a job, arguing that successful adults don't live off their parents and, therefore, that being independent must be the reason for their successes. They do not realize that those adults are independent *because* they are successful, and not the other way around.

In fact, most successful people are those who have been well supported, financially and emotionally, by their parents when they were children. Likewise, as I discussed in chapter 2, the rich countries liberalized their trade only when their producers were ready, and usually only gradually even then. In other words, historically, trade liberalization has been the *outcome* rather than the *cause* of economic development.

Free trade may often – although not always – be the best trade policy *in the short run*, as it is likely to maximize a country's current consumption. But it is definitely not the best way to develop an economy. In the long run, free trade is a policy that is likely to condemn developing countries to specialize in sectors that offer low productivity growth and thus low growth in living standards. This is why so few countries have succeeded with free trade, while most successful countries have used infant industry protection to one degree or another. Low income that results from lack of economic development severely restricts the freedom that the poor countries have in deciding their future. Paradoxically, therefore, 'free' trade policy reduces the 'freedom' of the developing countries that practise it.

International trading system and its discontents

Never mind that free trade works neither in practice nor in theory. Despite its abysmal record, the Bad Samaritan rich countries have strongly promoted trade liberalization in developing since the 1980s.

As I discussed in the earlier chapters, the rich countries had been quite willing to let poor countries use more protection and subsidies until the late 1970s. However, this began to change in the 1980s. The change was most palpable in the US, whose enlightened approach to international trade with economically lesser nations rapidly gave way to a system similar to 19th-century British 'free trade imperialism'. This new direction was clearly expressed by the then US president Ronald Reagan in 1986, as the Uruguay Round of GATT talks was starting, when he called for 'new and more liberal agreements with our trading partners – agreement under which they would fully open their markets and treat American products as they treat their own'.[10] Such agreement was realized through the Uruguay Round of GATT trade talks, which started in the Uruguayan city of Punta del Este in 1986 and was concluded in the Moroccan city of Marrakech in 1994. The result was the World Trade Organisation regime – a new international trade regime that was much more biased against the developing countries than the GATT regime.

On the surface, the WTO simply created a 'level playing field' among its member countries, requiring that everyone plays by the same rule – how can we argue against that? Critical to the process was the adoption of the principle of a 'single undertaking', which meant that all members had to sign up to all agreements. In the GATT regime, countries could pick and choose the agreements that they signed up to and many developing countries could stay out of agreements that they did not want – for example, the agreement restricting the use of subsidies. With the single undertaking, all members had to abide by the same rules. All of them had to reduce their tariffs. They were made to give up import quotas, export subsidies (allowed only for the poorest countries) and most domestic subsidies. But, when we look at the detail, we realize that the field is not level at all.

To begin with, even though the rich countries have low average protection, they tend to disproportionately protect products that poor countries export, especially garments and textiles. This means that, when exporting to a rich country market, poor countries face higher tariffs than other rich countries. An Oxfam report points out that: 'The overall import tax rate for the USA is 1.6 per cent. That rate rises steeply for a large number of developing countries: average import taxes range from around four per cent for India and Peru, to seven per cent for Nicaragua, and as much as 14–15 per cent for Bangladesh, Cambodia and Nepal.'[11] As a result, in 2002, India paid more tariffs to the US government than Britain did, despite the fact that the size of its economy was less than one-third that of the UK. Even more strikingly, in the same year, Bangladesh paid almost as much in tariffs to the US government as France, despite the fact that the size of its economy was only 3% that of France.[12]

There are also structural reasons that make what looks like 'levelling the playing field' actually favour developed countries. Tariffs are the best example. The Uruguay Round resulted in all countries, except for the poorest ones, reducing tariffs quite a lot in proportional terms. But the developing countries ended up reducing their tariffs a lot more in absolute terms, for the simple reason that they started with higher tariffs. For example, before the WTO agreement, India had an average tariff rate of 71%. It was cut to 32%. The US average tariff rate fell from 7% to 3%. Both are similar in proportional terms (each representing around a 55% cut), but the absolute impact is very different. In the Indian case, an imported good that formerly cost $171 would now cost only $132 – a significant fall in what the consumer pays (about 23%) that would dramatically alter consumer behaviour. In the American case, the price the consumer pays would have fallen from $107 to $103 – a price difference that most consumers will hardly notice (less than 4%). In other words, the impact of tariff cuts of the same proportion is disproportionately larger for the country whose initial tariff rate is higher.

In addition, there were areas where 'levelling the playing field' meant a one-sided benefit to rich countries. The most important example is the TRIPS (Trade-related Intellectual Property Rights) agreement, which strengthened the protection of patents and other intellectual property rights (more on this in chapter 6). Unlike trade in goods and services, where everyone has something to sell, this is an area where developed countries are almost always sellers and developing countries buyers. Therefore, increasing the protection for intellectual property rights means that the cost is mainly borne by the developing nations. The same problem applies to the TRIMS (Trade-related Investment Measures) agreement, which restricts the WTO member countries' ability to regulate foreign investors (more on this in chapter 4). Once again, most poor countries only receive, and do not make, foreign investment. So, while their ability to regulate foreign companies is reduced, they do not get 'compensated' by any reduction in the regulations that their national firms operating abroad are subject to, as they simply do not have such firms.

Many of the exceptions to the rules were created in areas where the developed countries needed them. For example, while most domestic subsidies are banned, subsidies are allowed in relation to agriculture, basic (as opposed to commercial) R&D (research and development), and reduction of regional disparities. These are all subsidies that happen to be extensively used by the rich countries. The rich nations give out an estimated $100 billion worth of agricultural subsidies every year; these include the $4 billion given to 25,000 American peanut farmers and EU subsidies that allow Finland to produce sugar (from beets).[13] All rich country governments, especially the US government, heavily subsidize basic R&D, which then increases their competitiveness in related industries. Moreover, this is not a subsidy that developing nations can use, even if they are allowed to – they simply do not do much basic R&D, so there is little for them to subsidize. As for regional subsides, which have been extensively used by the European Union, this is another case of apparent neutrality really serving the interests mainly of rich countries. In the name of redressing regional imbalances, they have subsidized firms to induce them to locate in 'depressed' regions. Within the nation, this may be contributing to a reduction in regional inequality. But, when viewed from an international perspective, there is little difference between these subsidies and subsidies given to promote particular industries.

Against these accusations of 'levelling the playing field' only where it suits them, the rich countries often argue that they still give the developing countries 'special and differential treatment' (SDT). But special and differential treatment is now a pale shadow of what it used to be under the GATT regime. While some exceptions are made for the developing countries, especially the poorest ones ('the least developed countries' in WTO jargon), many of these exceptions were in the form of a slightly longer 'transition period' (five to ten years) before they reach the same final goal as the rich countries, rather than the offer of permanent asymmetrical arrangements.[14]

So, in the name of 'levelling the playing field', the Bad Samaritan rich nations have created a new international trading system that is rigged in their favour. They are preventing the poorer countries from using the tools of trade and industrial policies that they had themselves so effectively used in the past in order to promote their own economic development – not just tariffs and subsidies, but also regulation of foreign investment and 'violation' of foreign intellectual property rights, as I will show in subsequent chapters.

Industry for agriculture?

Not satisfied with the result of the Uruguay Round, the rich countries have been pushing for further liberalization by developing economies. There has been a push to tighten restrictions on controls over foreign investment, over and above what was accepted in the TRIMS agreement. This was attempted first through the OECD (in 1998) and then through the World Trade Organisation (in 2003).[15] The move was thwarted both times, so the developed countries have shifted their focus and are now concentrating on a proposal to drastically reduce industrial tariffs in the developing countries.

This proposal, dubbed NAMA (non-agricultural market access), was first launched in the Doha ministerial meeting of the World Trade Organisation in 2001. It got a critical impetus when, in December 2002, the US government dramatically upped the ante by calling for the abolition of all industrial tariffs by 2015. There are various proposals floating around, but, if the rich countries have their way in the NAMA negotiations, the tariff ceiling for developing economies could fall from the current 10–70% to 5–10% – a level that has not been seen since the days of the 'unequal treaties' in the 19th and early 20th centuries, when the weaker countries were deprived of tariff autonomy and forced to set a low, uniform tariff rate, typically 3–5%.

In return for developing countries cutting industrial tariffs, the rich countries promise that they will lower their agricultural tariffs and subsidies, so that the poor countries can increase their exports. This was sold as a win-win deal, even though unilateral trade liberalization should be its own reward, according to free trade theory.

The proposal was debated in the December 2005 Hong Kong ministerial meeting of the World Trade Organisation. As no agreement could be reached, the negotiation was extended until the following summer, where it was finally put into a state of suspended animation – Mr Kamal Nath, the Indian commerce minister, famously described the negotiation to be 'between intensive care and crematorium'. The rich countries said that the developing countries were not offering sufficient industrial tariff cuts, while the developing countries argued that the rich countries were demanding excessively steep industrial tariff cuts and not offering enough reduction in agricultural tariffs and subsidies. The negotiation is stalled for the moment, but this 'industry-agriculture swap' is basically seen as the way forward by many people, even including some traditional critics of the WTO.

In the short run, greater opening of agricultural markets in the rich countries may benefit developing countries – but only a few of them. Many developing countries are in fact net agricultural importers and thus unlikely to benefit from it. They may even get hurt, if they happen to be importers of those agricultural products that are heavily subsidized by the rich countries. Eliminating those subsidies would increase these developing countries' import bills.

Overall, the main beneficiaries of the opening up of agricultural markets in the rich world will be those rich countries with strong agriculture – the US, Canada, Australia and New Zealand.[16] Developed countries do not protect many agricultural products exported by poor countries (e.g., coffee, tea, cocoa) for the simple reason that they do not have any domestic producer to protect. So, where protection and subsidies are going to come down is mainly in 'temperate zone' agricultural products like wheat, beef and dairy. Only two developing countries, Brazil and Argentina, are major exporters of these products. Moreover, some (although obviously not all) of the prospective 'losers' from agricultural trade liberalization within rich countries will be the least well-off people by their national standards (e.g., hard-pressed farmers in Norway, Japan or Switzerland), while some of the beneficiaries in developing countries are already rich even by international standards (e.g., agricultural capitalists in Brazil or Argentina). In this sense, the popular image that agricultural liberalization in rich countries is helping poor peasant farmers in developing countries is misleading.*

* The other main beneficiaries of agricultural liberalization in rich countries, that is, their consumers, do not gain very much. As a proportion of income, their spending on agricultural products is already pretty low (around 13% for food and 4% for alcohol and tobacco, of which only a fraction is the cost of the agricultural produce itself). Moreover, the trade in many agricultural products they buy is already liberalized (e.g., coffee, tea, cocoa).

More importantly, those who see agricultural liberalization in the rich countries as an important way to help poor countries develop often fail to pay enough attention to the fact that it does not come for free. In return, the poor countries will have to make concessions. The problem is that these concessions – reducing industrial tariffs, dismantling foreign investment controls and abandoning 'permissive' intellectual property rights – will make their economic development more difficult in the long run. These are policy tools that are crucial for economic development, as I document throughout this book.

Given this, the current debate surrounding the liberalization of agriculture in rich countries is getting its priorities wrong. It may be valuable for some developing countries to get access to agricultural markets in developed economies.* But it is far more important that we allow developing countries to use protection, subsidies and regulation of foreign investment adequately in order to develop their own economies, rather than giving them bigger agricultural markets overseas. Especially if agricultural liberalization by the rich countries can only be 'bought' by the developing countries giving up their use of the tools of infant industry promotion, the price is not worth paying. Developing countries should not be forced to sell their future for small immediate gains.

More trade, fewer ideologies

It is hard to believe today, but North Korea used to be richer than South Korea. It was the part of Korea that Japan had developed

---

* In the earlier stages of development, most people live on agriculture, so developing agriculture is crucial in reducing poverty. Higher agricultural productivity also creates a pool of healthy and productive workers that can be used later for industrial development. In the early stages of development, agricultural products are also likely to account for a high share of exports, as the country may have little else to sell. Given the importance of export earnings for economic development that I discussed earlier, agricultural exports should be increased as much as possible (although the scope may not be large). And, for this, greater opening of agricultural markets in the rich countries is helpful. But increased agricultural productivity and agricultural exports often require state intervention along the line of 'infant industry promotion'. Agricultural producers, especially the smaller ones, need government investment and support in infrastructure (especially irrigation for production and roads for exports), international marketing and R&D.

industrially when it ruled the country from 1910 until 1945. The Japanese colonial rulers saw the northern part of Korea as the ideal base from which to launch their imperialist plan to take over China. It is close to China, and has considerable mineral resources, especially coal. Even after the Japanese left, their industrial legacy enabled North Korea to maintain its economic lead over South Korea well into the 1960s.

Today, South Korea is one of the world's industrial powerhouses, while North Korea languishes in poverty. Much of this is thanks to the fact that South Korea aggressively traded with the outside world and actively absorbed foreign technologies while North Korea pursued its doctrine of self-sufficiency. Through trade, South Korea learned about the existence of better technologies and earned the foreign currency that it needed in order to buy them. In its own way, North Korea has managed some technological feats. For example, it has figured out a way to mass-produce Vinalon, a synthetic fibre made out of – of all things – limestone, invented by a Korean scientist in 1939. Despite being the second-ever man-made fibre after Nylon, Vinalon did not catch on elsewhere because it did not make a comfortable fabric, but it has allowed North Koreans to be self-sufficient in clothes. But there is a limit to what a single developing country can invent on its own without continuous importation of advanced technologies. Thus, North Korea is technologically stuck in the past, with 1940s Japanese and 1950s Soviet technologies, while South Korea is one of the most technologically dynamic economies in the world. Do we need any better proof that trade is good for economic development?

In the end, economic development is about acquiring and mastering advanced technologies. In theory, a country can develop such technologies on its own, but such a strategy of technological self-sufficiency quickly hits the wall, as seen in the North Korean case. This is why all successful cases of economic development have involved serious attempts to get hold of and master advanced foreign technologies (more on this in chapter 6). But in order to be able to import technologies from developed countries, developing nations need foreign currency to pay for them – whether they want to buy directly (e.g., technology licences, technology consultancy services) or indirectly (e.g., better machines). Some of the necessary foreign currency may be provided through gifts from rich countries (foreign aid), but most has to be earned through exports. Without trade, therefore, there will be little technological progress and thus little economic development.

But there is a huge difference between saying that trade is essential for economic development and saying that free trade is best (or, at least, that freer trade is better) for economic development, as the Bad Samaritans do. It is this sleight of hand that free trade economists have so effectively deployed in cowing their opponents – if you are against free trade, they insinuate, you must be against progress.

As South Korea shows, active participation in international trade does not require free trade. Indeed, had South Korea pursued free trade and not promoted infant industries, it would not have become a major trading nation. It would still be exporting raw materials (e.g., tungsten ore, fish, seaweed) or low-technology, low-price products (e.g., textiles, garments, wigs made with human hair) that used to be its main export items in the 1960s. To go back to the imagery of chapter 1, had they followed free trade policy from the 1960s, Koreans might still be fighting over who owns which tuft of hair, so to speak. The secret of its success lay in a judicious mix of protection and open trade, with the areas of protection constantly changing as new infant industries were developed and old infant industries became internationally competitive. In a way, this is not much of a 'secret'. As I have shown in the earlier chapters, this is how almost all of today's rich countries became rich and this is at the root of almost all recent success stories in the developing world. Protection does not guarantee development, but development without it is very difficult.

Therefore, if they are genuinely to help developing countries develop through trade, wealthy countries need to accept asymmetric protectionism, as they used to between the 1950s and the 1970s. They should acknowledge that they need to have much lower protection for themselves than the developing countries have. The global trading system should support the developmental efforts of developing countries by allowing them to use more freely the tools of infant industry promotion – such as tariff protection, subsidies and foreign investment regulation. At the moment, the system allows protection and subsidies much more readily in areas where the developed countries need them. But it should be the other way around – protection and subsidies should be easier to use where the developing countries need them more.

Here, it is particularly important to get our perspective right about agricultural liberalization in the rich countries. Lowering agricultural protection in those countries may help some developing countries, especially Brazil and Argentina, but not most. Above all, agricultural liberalization in the rich world should not be conditional upon further restrictions on the use of the tools of infant industry promotion by developing nations, as is currently being demanded by the rich countries.

The importance of international trade for economic development cannot be overemphasized. But free trade is *not* the best path to economic development. Trade helps economic development only when the country employs a mixture of protection and open trade, constantly adjusting it according to its changing needs and capabilities. Trade is simply too important for economic development to be left to free trade economists.

CHAPTER 4

The Finn and the elephant

Should we regulate foreign investment?

The Finns like to tell a joke about themselves. What would a German, a Frenchman, an American and a Finn do if they were each asked to write a book on the elephant? The German, with his characteristic thoroughness, would write a thick two-volume, fully annotated study entitled, *Everything That There is to Know About the Elephant*. The Frenchman, with his penchant for philosophical musings and existential anguish, would write a book entitled *The Life and Philosophy of the Elephant*. The American, with his famous nose for good business opportunities, would naturally write a book entitled, *How to Make Money with an Elephant*. The Finn would write a book entitled *What Does the Elephant Think of the Finns?*

The Finns are laughing at their excessive self-consciousness. Their preoccupation with their own identity is understandable. They speak a language that is more related to Korean and Japanese than to the language of their Swedish or Russian neighbours. Finland was a Swedish colony for around six hundred years and a Russian colony for about a hundred. As a Korean, whose country has been pushed around for thousands of years by every neighbour in sight – the Chinese, the Huns, the Mongolians, the Manchurians, the Japanese, the Americans, the Russians, you name it – I know the feeling.

So, it was unsurprising that, after gaining independence from Russia in 1918, Finland tried its best to keep foreigners out. The country introduced a series of laws in the 1930s that officially classified all the enterprises with more than 20% foreign ownership as – hold your breath – 'dangerous'. The Finns may not be the subtlest people in the world, but this is heavy stuff even for them. Finland got, as it had wanted, very little foreign investment.[1] When Monty Python sang in 1980, 'Finland, Finland, Finland ... You are so sadly neglected, and often ignored' ('The Finland Song'), they did not perhaps guess that the Finns *had sought* to be neglected and ignored.

The Finnish law was eventually relaxed in 1987, and the foreign ownership ceiling was raised to 40%, but all foreign investments still had to be approved by the Ministry of Trade and Industry. General liberalization of foreign investment did not come until 1993, as part of the preparations for the country's accession to the EU in 1995.

According to the neo-liberal orthodoxy, this sort of extreme anti-foreign strategy, especially if sustained for over half a century, should have severely damaged Finland's economic prospects. However, since the mid-1990s, Finland has been touted as the paragon of successful global integration. In particular, Nokia, its mobile phone company, has been, figuratively speaking, inducted into the Globalization Hall of Fame. A country that did not want to be a part of the global economy has suddenly become an icon of globalization. How was this possible? We shall answer that later, but first let us examine the arguments for and against foreign investment.

Is foreign capital essential?

Many developing countries find it difficult to generate enough savings to satisfy their own investment demands. Given this, it seems uncontroversial that any additional money they can get from other countries that have surplus savings should be good. Developing countries should open their capital markets, it is argued by the Bad Samaritans, so that such money can flow in freely.

The benefit of having free international movement of capital, neo-liberal economists argue, does not stop at plugging such a 'savings gap'. It improves economic efficiency by allowing capital to flow into projects with the highest possible returns on a global scale. Free cross-border capital flows are also seen as spreading 'best practice' in government policy and corporate governance. Foreign investors would simply pull out, the reasoning goes, if companies and countries were not well run.[2] Some even, controversially, argue that these 'collateral benefits' are even more important than the direct benefits that come from the more efficient allocation of capital.[3]

Foreign capital flows into developing countries consist of three main elements – grants, debts and investments. Grants are money given away (but often with strings attached) by another country and are called foreign aid or official development assistance (ODA). Debts consist of bank loans and bonds (government bonds and corporate bonds).[4] Investments are made up of 'portfolio equity investment', which is equity (share) ownership seeking financial returns rather than managerial influence, and foreign direct investment (FDI), which involves the purchase of equity with a view to influence the management of the firm on a regular basis.[5]

There is an increasingly popular view among neo-liberal econo-mists that foreign aid does not work, although others argue that the 'right' kind of aid (that is, aid that is not primarily motivated by geo-politics) works.[6] Debts and portfolio equity investment have also come under attack for their volatility.[7] Bank loans are notoriously volatile. For example, in 1998, total net bank loans to developing countries were $50 billion; following a series of financial crises that engulfed the developing world (Asia in 1997, Russia and Brazil in 1998, Argentina in 2002), they turned *negative* for the next four years (-$6.5 billion per year on average); by 2005, however, they were 30% higher than in 1998 ($67 billion). Although not as volatile as bank loans, capital inflows through bonds fluctuate a lot.[8] Portfolio equity investment is even more volatile than bonds, although not as volatile as bank loans.[9]

These flows are not just volatile, they tend to come in and go out exactly at the wrong time. When economic prospects in a developing country are *considered* good, too much foreign financial capital may enter. This can temporarily raise asset prices (e.g., prices of stocks, real estate prices) beyond their real value, creating asset bubbles. When things get bad, often because of the bursting of the very same asset bubble, foreign capital tends to leave all at the same time, making the economic downturn even worse. Such 'herd behaviour' was most vividly demonstrated in the 1997 Asian crises, when foreign capital flowed out on a massive scale, despite the good long-term prospects of the economies concerned (Korea, Hong Kong, Malaysia, Thailand and Indonesia).[10]

Of course, this kind of behaviour – known as 'pro-cyclical' behaviour – also exists among domestic investors. Indeed, when things go bad, these investors, using their insider information, often leave the country *before* the foreigners do. But the impact of herd behaviour by foreign investors is much greater for the simple reason that developing country financial markets are tiny relative to the amounts of money sloshing around the international financial system. The Indian stock market, the largest stock market in the developing world, is less than one-thirtieth the size of the US stock market.[11] The Nigerian stock market, the second largest in Sub-Saharan Africa, is worth less than one five-thousandth of the US stock market. Ghana's stock market is worth only 0.006% of the US market.[12] What is a mere drop in the ocean of rich country assets will be a flood that can sweep away financial markets in developing countries.

Given this, it is no coincidence that developing countries have experienced more frequent financial crises since many of them opened their capital markets at the urge of the Bad Samaritans in the 1980s and the 1990s. According to a study by two leading economic historians, between 1945 and 1971, when global finance was not liberalized, developing countries suffered no banking crisis, 16 currency crises and one 'twin crisis' (simultaneous currency and banking crises). Between 1973 and 1997, however, there were 17 banking crises, 57 currency crises and 21 twin crises in the developing world.[13] This is not even counting some of the biggest financial crises that occurred after 1998 (Brazil, Russia and Argentina being the most prominent cases).

The volatility and the pro-cyclicality of international financial flows are what make even some globalization enthusiasts, such as Professor Jagdish Bhagwati, warn against what he calls 'the perils of gung-ho international financial capitalism'.[14] Even the IMF, which used to push strongly for capital market opening during the 1980s and especially the 1990s, has recently changed its stance on this matter, becoming a lot more muted in its support of capital market opening in developing countries.[15] Now it accepts that 'premature opening of the capital account . . . can hurt a country by making the structure of the inflows unfavourable and by making the country vulnerable to sudden stops or reversals of flows.'[16]

The Mother Teresa of foreign capital?

The behaviour of international *financial* flows (debt and portfolio equity investment) is in stark contrast with that of foreign direct investment. Net FDI flows into developing countries were $169 billion in 1997.[17] Despite the financial turmoil in the developing world, it was still $172 billion per year on average between 1998 and 2002.[18] In addition to its stability, foreign direct investment is thought to bring in not just money but a lot of other things that help economic development. Sir Leon Brittan, a former British commissioner of the European Union, sums it up: foreign direct investment is 'a source of extra capital, a contribution to a healthy external balance, a basis for increased productivity, additional employment, effective competition, rational production, technology transfer, and a source of managerial knowhow.'[19]

The case for welcoming foreign direct investment, then, seems overwhelming. FDI is stable, unlike other forms of foreign capital inflows. Moreover, it brings not just money but also enhances the host country's productive capabilities by bringing in more advanced organization, skills and technology. No wonder that foreign direct investment is fêted as if it were 'the Mother Teresa of foreign capital', as Gabriel Palma, the distinguished Chilean economist who is my former teacher and now a colleague at Cambridge, once ironically observed. But foreign direct investment has its limitations and problems.

First, foreign direct investment flows may have been very stable during the financial turmoil in developing countries in the late 1990s and the early 2000s, but it has not always been the case for all countries.[20] When a country has an open capital market, FDI can be made 'liquid' and shipped out rather quickly. As even an IMF publication points out, the foreign subsidiary can use its assets to borrow from domestic banks, change the money into foreign currency and send the money out; or the parent company may recall the intra-company loan it has lent to the subsidiary (this counts as FDI).[21] In the extreme case, most foreign direct investment that came in can go out again through such channels, adding little to the host country's foreign exchange reserve position.[22]

Not only is FDI not necessarily a stable source of foreign currency, it may have negative impacts on the foreign exchange position of the host country. FDI may bring in foreign currency, but it can also generate additional demands for it (e.g., importing inputs, contracting foreign loans). Of course, it can (but may not) also generate additional foreign currency through exporting, but whether it will earn more foreign exchange than it uses is not a foregone conclusion. This is why many countries have imposed controls on the foreign exchange earnings and spending by the foreign companies making the invest-ment (e.g., how much they should export, how much inputs they have to buy locally).[23]

Another drawback with foreign direct investment is that it creates the opportunity for 'transfer pricing' by transnational corporations (TNCs) with operations in more than one country. This refers to the practice where the subsidiaries of a TNC are overcharging or under-charging each other so that profits are highest in those subsidiaries operating in countries with the lowest corporate tax rates. And when I say overcharging or undercharging, I really mean it. A Christian Aid report documents cases of underpriced exports like TV antennas from China at $0.40 apiece, rocket launchers from Bolivia at $40 and US bulldozers at $528, and overpriced imports such as German hacksaw blades at $5,485 each, Japanese tweezers at $4,896, and French wrenches at $1,089.[24] This is a classic problem with TNCs, but today the problem has become more severe because of the proliferation of tax havens that have no or minimal corporate income taxes. Companies can vastly reduce their tax obligations by shifting most of their profits to a paper company registered in a tax haven.

It may be argued that the host country should not complain about transfer pricing, because, without the foreign direct investment in question, the taxable income would not have been generated in the first place. But this is a disingenuous argument. All firms need to use productive resources provided by government with taxpayers' money (e.g., roads, the telecommunications network, workers who have received publicly funded education and training). So, if the TNC subsidiary is not paying its 'fair share' of tax, it is effectively free-riding on the host country.

Even for the technologies, skills and management know-how that foreign direct investment is supposed to bring with it, the evidence is ambiguous: '[d]espite the theoretical presumption that, of the different types of [capital] inflows, FDI has the strongest benefits, it has not proven easy to document these benefits' – and that's what an IMF publication is saying.[25] Why is this? It is because different types of FDI have different productive impacts.

When we think of foreign direct investment, most of us think about Intel building a new microchip factory in Costa Rica or Volkswagen laying down a new assembly line in China – this is known as 'green-field' investment. But a lot of foreign direct investment is made by foreigners buying into an existing local company – or 'brownfield' investment.[26] Brownfield investment has accounted for over half of total world FDI since the 1990s, although the share is lower for developing countries, for the obvious reason that they have relatively fewer firms that foreigners want to take over. At its height in 2001, it accounted for as much as 80% of total world FDI.[27]

Brownfield investment does not add any new production facilities – when General Motors bought up the Korean car maker Daewoo in the wake of the 1997 financial crisis, it just took over the existing factories and produced the same cars, designed by Koreans, under different names. However, brownfield investment can still lead to an increase in productive capabilities. This is because it can bring with it new management techniques or higher quality engineers. The trouble is that there is no guarantee that this will happen.

In some cases, brownfield FDI is made with an explicit intention of not doing much to improve the productive capabilities of the company bought – a foreign direct investor might buy a company that he thinks is undervalued by the market, especially in times of financial crisis, and run it as it used to be until he finds a suitable buyer.[28] Sometimes the foreign direct investor may even actively *destroy* the existing productive capabilities of the company bought by engaging in 'asset stripping'. For example, when the Spanish airline Iberia bought some Latin American airlines in the 1990s, it swapped its own old planes for the new ones owned by the Latin American airlines, eventually driving some of the latter into bankruptcy due to a poor service record and high maintenance costs.

Of course, the value of foreign direct investment to the host economy is not confined to what it does to the enterprise in which the investment has been made. The enterprise concerned hires local workers (who may learn new skills), buys inputs from local producers (who may pick up new technologies in the process) and has some 'demonstration effects' on domestic firms (by showing them new management techniques or providing knowledge about overseas markets). These effects, known as 'spill-over effects', are real additions to a nation's long-run productive capabilities and not to be scoffed at.

Unfortunately, the spill-over effects may not happen. In the extreme case, a TNC can set up an 'enclave' facility, where all inputs are imported and all that the locals do is to engage in simple assembly, where they do not even pick up new skills. Moreover, even when they occur, spill-over effects tend to be relatively insignificant in magnitude.[29] This is why governments have tried to magnify them by imposing performance requirements – regarding, for example, technology transfer, local contents or exports.[30]

A critical but often ignored impact of FDI is that on the (current and future) domestic competitors. An entry by a TNC through FDI can destroy existing national firms that could have 'grown up' into successful operations without this premature exposure to competition, or it can pre-empt the emergence of domestic competitors. In such cases, short-run productive capabilities are enhanced, as the TNC subsidiary replacing the (current and future) national firms is usually more productive than the latter. But the level of productive capability that the country can attain *in the long run* becomes lower as a result.

This is because TNCs do not, as a rule, transfer the most valuable activities outside their home country, as I will discuss in greater detail later. As a result, there will be a definite ceiling on the level of sophistication that a TNC subsidiary can reach in the long run. To go back to the Toyota example in chapter 1, had Japan liberalized FDI in its automobile industry in the 1960s, Toyota definitely wouldn't be producing the Lexus today – it would have been wiped out or, more likely, have become a valued subsidiary of an American carmaker.

Given this, a developing country may reasonably decide to forego short-term benefits from FDI in order to increase the chance for its domestic firms to engage in higher-level activities in the long run, by banning FDI in certain sectors or regulating it.[31] This is exactly the same logic as that of infant industry protection that I discussed in the earlier chapters – a country gives up the short-run benefits of free trade in order to create higher productive capabilities in the long run. And it is why, historically, most economic success stories have resorted to regulation of FDI, often in a draconian manner, as I shall now show.

'More dangerous than military power'

'It will be a happy day for us when not a single good American security is owned abroad and when the United States shall cease to be an exploiting ground for European bankers and money lenders.' Thus wrote the US *Bankers' Magazine* in 1884.[32]

The reader may find it hard to believe that a *bankers'* magazine published in *America* could be so hostile to foreign investors. But this was in fact true to type at the time. The US had a terrible record in its dealings with foreign investors.[33]

In 1832, Andrew Jackson, today a folk hero to American freemarketeers, refused to renew the licence for the quasi-central bank, the second Bank of the USA – the successor to Hamilton's Bank of the USA (see chapter 2).[34] This was done on the grounds that the foreign ownership share of the bank was too high – 30% (the pre-EU Finns would have heartily approved!). Declaring his decision, Jackson said: 'should the stock of the bank principally pass into the hands of the subjects of a foreign country, and we should unfortunately become involved in a war with that country, what would be our condition? . . . Controlling our currency, receiving our public moneys, and holding thousands of our citizens in dependence, it would be far more formidable and dangerous than the naval and military power of the enemy. If we must have a bank . . . it should be *purely American*.'[35] If the president of a developing country said something like this today, he would be branded a xenophobic dinosaur and blackballed in the international community.

From the earliest days of its economic development right up to the First World War, the US was the world's largest importer of foreign capital.[36] Given this, there was, naturally, considerable concern over 'absentee management' by foreign investors[37]; 'We have no horror of FOREIGN CAPITAL – if subjected to *American management* [italics and capitals original],' declared *Niles' Weekly Register*, a nationalist magazine in the Hamiltonian tradition, in 1835.[38]

Reflecting such sentiment, the US federal government strongly regulated foreign investment. Non-resident shareholders could not vote and only American citizens could become directors in a national (as opposed to state-level) bank. This meant that 'foreign individuals and foreign financial institutions could buy shares in U.S. national banks *if* they were prepared to have American citizens as their representatives on the board of directors', thus discouraging foreign investment in the banking sector.[39] A navigation monopoly for US ships in coastal shipping was imposed in 1817 by Congress and continued until the First World War.[40] There were also strict regulations on foreign investment in natural resource industries. Many state governments barred or restricted investment by non-resident foreigners in land. The 1887 federal Alien Property Act prohibited the ownership of land by aliens – or by companies more than 20% owned by aliens – in the 'territories' (as opposed to the fully fledged states), where land speculation was particularly rampant.[41] Federal mining laws restricted mining rights to US citizens and companies incorporated in the US. In 1878, a timber law was enacted, permitting only US residents to log on public land.

Some state (as opposed to federal) laws were even more hostile to foreign investment. A number of states taxed foreign companies more heavily than the American ones. There was a notorious Indiana law of 1887 that withdrew court protection from foreign firms altogether.[42] In the late 19th century, the New York state government took a particularly hostile attitude towards FDI in the financial sector, an area where it was rapidly developing a world-class position (a clear case of infant industry protection).[43] It instituted a law in the 1880s that banned foreign banks from engaging in 'banking business' (such as taking deposits and discounting notes or bills). The 1914 banking law banned the establishment of foreign bank branches. For example, the London City and Midland Bank (then the world's third largest bank, measured by deposits) could not open a New York branch, even though it had 867 branches worldwide and 45 correspondent banks in the US alone.[44]

Despite its extensive, and often strict, controls on foreign investment, the US was the largest recipient of foreign investment throughout the 19th century and the early 20th century – in the same way strict regulation of TNCs in China has not prevented a large amount of FDI from pouring into that country in recent decades. This flies in the face of the belief by the Bad Samaritans that foreign investment regulation is bound to reduce investment flows, or, conversely, that the liberalization of foreign investment regulation will increase foreign investment flows. Moreover, despite – or, I would argue, partly because of – its strict regulation of foreign investment (as well as having in place manufacturing tariffs that were the highest in the world), the US was the world's fastest-growing economy throughout the 19th century and up until the 1920s. This undermines the standard argument that foreign investment regulation harms the growth prospects of an economy.

Even more draconian than the US in regulating foreign investment was Japan.[45] Especially before 1963, foreign ownership was limited to 49%, while in many 'vital industries' FDI was banned altogether. Foreign investment was steadily liberalized, but only in industries where the domestic firms were ready for it. As a result, of all countries outside the communist bloc, Japan has received the lowest level of FDI as a proportion of its total national investment.[46] Given this history, the Japanese government saying that '[p]lacing constraints on [foreign direct] investment would not seem to be an appropriate decision even from the perspective of development policy' in a recent submission to the WTO is a classic example of selective historical amnesia, double standards and 'kicking away the ladder'[47]

Korea and Taiwan are often seen as pioneers of pro-FDI policy, thanks to their early successes with export-processing zones (EPZs), where the investing foreign firms were little regulated. But, outside these zones, they actually imposed many restrictive policies on foreign investors. These restrictions allowed them to accumulate technological capabilities more rapidly, which, in turn, reduced the need for the 'anything goes' approach found in their EPZs in subsequent periods. They restricted the areas where foreign companies could enter and put ceilings on their ownership shares. They also screened the technologies brought in by TNCs and imposed export requirements. Local content requirements were quite strictly imposed, although they were less stringently applied to exported products (so that lower quality domestic inputs would not hurt export competitiveness too much). As a result, Korea was one of the least FDI-dependent countries in the world until the late 1990s, when the country adopted neo-liberal policies.[48] Taiwan, where the policies were slightly milder than in Korea, was somewhat more dependent on foreign investment, but its dependence was still well below the developing country average.[49]

The bigger European countries – the UK, France and Germany – did not go as far as Japan, the USA or Finland in regulating foreign investment. Before the Second World War, they didn't need to – they were mostly making, rather than receiving, foreign investments. But, after the Second World War, when they started receiving large amounts of American, and then Japanese, investment, they also restricted FDI flows and imposed performance requirements. Until the 1970s, this was done mainly through foreign exchange controls. After these controls were abolished, informal performance requirements were used. Even the ostensibly foreign-investor-friendly UK government used a variety of 'undertakings' and 'voluntary restrictions' regarding local sourcing of components, production volumes and exporting.[50] When Nissan established a UK plant in 1981, it was forced to procure 60% of value added locally, with a time scale over which this would rise to 80%. It is reported that the British government also 'put pressure on [Ford and GM] to achieve a better balance of trade.'[51]

Even cases like Singapore and Ireland, countries that have succeeded by extensively relying on FDI, are *not* proof that host country governments should let TNCs do whatever they want. While welcoming foreign companies, their governments used selective policies to attract foreign investment into areas that they considered strategic for the future development of their economies. Unlike Hong Kong, which *did* have a liberal FDI policy, Singapore has always had a very targeted approach. Ireland started genuinely prospering only when it shifted from an indiscriminate approach to FDI ('the more, the merrier') to a focused strategy that sought to attract foreign investment in sectors like electronics, pharmaceuticals, software and financial services. It also used performance requirements quite widely.[52]

To sum up, history is on the side of the regulators. Most of today's rich countries regulated foreign investment when they were on the receiving end. Sometimes the regulation was draconian – Finland, Japan, Korea and the USA (in certain sectors) are the best examples. There were countries that succeeded by actively courting FDI, such as Singapore and Ireland, but even they did not adopt the *laissez-faire* approach towards TNCs that is recommended to the developing countries today by the Bad Samaritans.

Borderless world?

Economic theory, history and contemporary experiences all tell us that, in order truly to benefit from foreign direct investment, the government needs to regulate it well. Despite all this, the Bad Samaritans have been trying their best to outlaw practically all regulation of foreign direct investment over the last decade or so. Through the World Trade Organisation, they have introduced the TRIMS (Trade-related Investment Measures) Agreement, which bans things like local content requirements, export requirements or foreign exchange balancing requirements. They have been pushing for further liberalization through the current GATS (General Agreement on Trade in Services) negotiations and a proposed investment agreement at the World Trade Organisation. Bilateral and regional free trade agreements (FTAs) and bilateral investment treaties (BITs) between rich and poor countries also restrict the ability of developing countries to regulate FDI.[53]

Forget history, say the Bad Samaritans in defending such actions. Even if it did have some merits in the past, they argue, regulation of foreign investment has become unnecessary *and* futile, thanks to globalization, which has created a new 'borderless world'. They argue that the 'death of distance' due to developments in communications and transportation technologies has made firms more and more mobile and thus stateless – they are not attached to their home countries any more. If firms do not have nationality any more, it is argued, there are no grounds for discriminating against foreign firms. Moreover, any attempt to regulate foreign firms is futile, as, being 'footloose', they would move to another country where there is no such regulation.

There is certainly an element of truth in this argument. But the case is vastly exaggerated. There are, today, firms like Nestlé that produces less than 5% of its output at home (Switzerland), but they are very much the exceptions. Most large internationalized firms produce less than one-third of their output abroad, while the ratio in the case of Japanese companies is well below 10%.[54] There has been some relocation of 'core' activities (such as research & development) overseas, but it is usually to other developed countries, and with a heavy 'regional' bias (the regions here meaning North America, Europe and Japan, which is a region unto itself).[55]

In most companies, the top decision-makers are still mostly home country nationals. Once again, there are cases like Carlos Ghosn, the Lebanese-Brazilian who runs a French (Renault) and Japanese (Nissan) company. But he is also very much an exception. The most telling example is the merger of Daimler-Benz, the German car maker, and Chrysler, the US car maker, in 1998. This was really a takeover of Chrysler by Benz. But, at the time of the merger, it was depicted as a marriage of two equals. The new company, Daimler-Chrysler, even had equal numbers of Germans and Americans on the management board. But that was only for the first few years. Soon, the Germans vastly outnumbered the Americans – usually 10 or 12 to one or two, depending on the year. When they are taken over, even American firms end up run by foreigners (but then that is what take-over means).

Therefore, the nationality of the firm still matters very much. Who owns the firm determines how far its different subsidiaries will be allowed to move into higher-level activities. It would be very naïve, especially on the part of developing countries, to design economic policies on the assumption that capital does not have national roots anymore.

But then how about the argument that, whether necessary or not, it is no longer possible in practice to regulate foreign investment? Now that TNCs have become more or less 'footloose', it is argued, they can punish countries that regulate foreign investment by 'voting with their feet'.

One immediate question one can ask is: if firms have become so mobile as to make national regulation powerless, why are the Bad Samaritan rich countries so keen on making developing countries sign up to all those international agreements that restrict their ability to regulate foreign investment? Following the market logic so loved by the neo-liberal orthodoxy, why not just leave countries to choose whatever approach they want and then let foreign investors punish or reward them by choosing to invest only in those countries friendly towards foreign investors? The very fact that rich countries want to impose all these restrictions on developing countries by means of international agreements reveals that regulation of FDI is not yet futile after all, contrary to what the Bad Samaritans say.

In any case, not all TNCs are equally mobile. True, there are industries – such as garments, shoes and stuffed toys – for which there are numerous potential investment sites because production equipment is easy to move and, the skills required being low, workers can be easily trained. However, in many other industries, firms cannot move that easily for various reasons – the existence of immobile inputs (e.g., mineral resources, a local labour force with particular skills), the attractiveness of the domestic market (China is a good example), or the supplier network that they have built up over the years (e.g., sub-contracting networks for Japanese car makers in Thailand or Malaysia).

Last but not least, it is simply wrong to think that TNCs will necessarily avoid countries that regulate FDI. Contrary to what the orthodoxy suggests, regulation is *not* very important in determining the level of inflow of foreign investment. If that were the case, countries like China would not be getting much foreign investment. But the country is getting around 10% of world FDI because it offers a large and fast-growing market, a good labour force and good infra-structure (roads, ports). The same argument can be applied to the 19th-century US.

Surveys reveal that corporations are most interested in the market potential of the host country (market size and growth), and then in things like the quality of the labour force and infrastructure, with regulation being only a matter of minor interest. Even the World Bank, a well-known supporter of FDI liberalization, once admitted that '[t]he specific incentives and regulations governing direct investment have less effect on how much investment a country receives than has its general economic and political climate, and its financial and exchange rate policies'.[56]

As in the case of their argument about the relationship between international trade and economic development, the Bad Samaritans have got the causality all wrong. They think that, if you liberalize foreign investment regulation, more investment will flow in and help economic growth. But foreign investment follows, rather than causes, economic growth. The brutal truth is that, however liberal the regu-latory regime, foreign firms won't come into a country unless its economy offers an attractive market and high-quality productive resources (labour, infrastructure). This is why so many developing countries have failed to attract significant amounts of FDI, despite giving foreign firms maximum degrees of freedom. Countries have to get growth going *before* TNCs get interested in them. If you are organizing a party, it is not enough to tell people that they can come and do whatever they want. People go to parties where they know there are already interesting things happening. They don't usually come and make things interesting for you, whatever freedom you give them.

'The only thing worse than being exploited by capital . . .'

Like Joan Robinson, a former Cambridge economics professor and arguably the most famous female economist in history, I believe that the only thing that is worse than being exploited by capital is not being exploited by capital. Foreign investment, especially foreign direct investment, can be a very useful tool for economic development. But *how* useful it is depends on the kinds of investment made and how the host country government regulates it.

Foreign financial investment brings more danger than benefits, as even the neo-liberals acknowledge these days. While foreign direct investment is no Mother Teresa, it often does bring benefits to the host country *in the short run*. But it is the long run that counts when it comes to economic development. Accepting FDI unconditionally may actually make economic development in the long run more difficult. Despite the hyperbole about a 'borderless world', TNCs remain national firms with international operations and, therefore, are unlikely to let their subsidiaries engage in higher-level activities; at the same time their presence can prevent the emergence of national firms that might start them in the long run. This situation is likely to damage the long-run development potential of the host country. Moreover, the long-run benefits of FDI depend partly on the magnitude and the quality of the spill-over effects that TNCs create, whose maximization requires appropriate policy intervention. Unfortunately, many key tools of such intervention have already been outlawed by the Bad Samaritans (e.g., local content requirements).

Therefore, foreign direct investment can be a Faustian bargain. In the short run, it may bring benefits, but, in the long run, it may actually be bad for economic development. Once this is understood, Finland's success is unsurprising. The country's strategy was based on the recognition that, if foreign investment is liberalized too early (Finland was one of the poorest European economies in the early-20th century), there will be no space for domestic firms to develop independent technological and managerial capabilities. It took Nokia 17 years to earn any profit from its electronics subsidiary, which is now the biggest mobile phone company in the world.[57] If Finland had liberalized foreign investment from early on, Nokia would not be what it is today. Most probably, foreign financial investors who bought into Nokia would have demanded the parent company stop cross-subsidizing the no-hope electronics subsidiary, thus killing off the business. At best, some TNC would have bought up the electronics division and made it into its own subsidiary doing second-division work.

The flip side of this argument is that regulation of foreign direct investment may paradoxically benefit foreign companies in the long run. If a country keeps foreign companies out or heavily regulates their activities, it would not be good for those companies in the short run. However, if a judicious regulation of foreign direct investment allows a country to accumulate productive capabilities more rapidly and at a higher level than possible without it, it will benefit foreign investors in the long run by offering them an investment location that is more prosperous and possesses better productive inputs (e.g., skilled workers, good infrastructure). Finland and Korea are the best examples of this. Partly thanks to their clever foreign investment regulation, these countries have become richer, better educated and technologically far more dynamic and thus have become more attractive investment sites than would have been possible without those regulations.

Foreign direct investment may help economic development, but only when introduced as part of a long-term-oriented development strategy. Policies should be designed so that foreign direct investment does not kill off domestic producers, which may hold out great potential in the long run, while also ensuring that the advanced technologies and managerial skills foreign corporations possess are transferred to domestic business to the maximum possible extent. Like Singapore and Ireland, some countries can succeed, and have succeeded, through actively courting foreign capital, especially FDI. But more countries will succeed, and have succeeded, when they more actively regulate foreign investment, including FDI. The attempt by the Bad Samaritans to make such regulation by developing countries impossible is likely to hinder, rather than help, their economic development.

CHAPTER 5

Man exploits man

Private enterprise good, public enterprise bad?

John Kenneth Galbraith, one of the most profound economic thinkers of the 20th century, once famously said: 'Under capitalism, man exploits man; under communism, it is just the opposite.' He was *not* suggesting that there is no difference between capitalism and communism, he would have been the last person to do so; Galbraith was one of the leading non-leftist critics of modern capitalism. What he was expressing was the profound disappointment that many people felt about the failure of communism to build the egalitarian society it had promised.

Since its rise in the 19th century, the key goal of the communist movement had been the abolition of private ownership of the 'means of production' (factories and machines). It is easy to understand why the communists saw private ownership as the ultimate source of the distributive injustice of capitalism. But they also saw private owner-ship as a cause of economic inefficiency. They believed that it was the reason for the 'wasteful' anarchy of the market. Too many capitalists routinely invest in producing the same things, they argued, because they do not know the investment plans of their competitors. Eventually, there is over-production and some of the enterprises involved go bank-rupt, condemning some machines to the scrap heap and laying perfectly employable workers idle. The waste caused by this process, it was argued, would disappear if the decisions of different capitalists could be co-ordinated in advance through rational, centralized plan-ning – after all, capitalist firms are islands of planning in the surrounding anarchic sea of the market, as Karl Marx, the leading communist theorist, once put it. Therefore, if private property were abolished, communists believed, the economy could be run as if it were a single firm and thus managed more efficiently.

Unfortunately, the centrally planned economy based on state ownership of enterprises performed very poorly. Communists may have been right in saying that unfettered competition can lead to social waste, but suppressing all competition through total central planning and universal state ownership exacted enormous costs of its own by killing off economic dynamism. Lack of competition and excessive top-down regulation under communism also bred conformism, bureaucratic red tape and corruption.

Few would now dispute that communism failed as an economic system. But it is a huge leap of logic to go from that conclusion to the proposition that state-owned enterprises (SOEs), or public enterprises, do not work. This judgement became popular in the wake of Margaret Thatcher's pioneering privatization programme in Britain in the early 1980s, and acquired the status of a pseudo-religious credo during the 'transformation' of the former communist economies in the 1990s. For a while, it was as if the whole ex-communist world was hypnotised by the mantra, 'private good, public bad', reminiscent of the anti-human slogan, 'four legs good, two legs bad', in George Orwell's *Animal Farm* – that great satire of communism. Privatization of SOEs has also been a centrepiece of the neo-liberal agenda that the Bad Samaritans have imposed on most developing countries in the past quarter of a century.

State ownership in the dock

Why do the Bad Samaritans think state-owned enterprises need to be privatized? At the heart of the argument against SOEs lies a simple but powerful idea. The idea is that people do not fully take care of things that are not theirs. We see the corroboration of this notion on a daily basis. When your plumber takes his third tea break of the morning at 11am, you begin to wonder whether he would do the same if he was fixing his own boiler. You know that most of those people who throw away litter in public parks would never do so in their own gardens. It seems to be human nature for people to do their best to take care of the things they own while maltreating those things that they do not. Therefore, it is argued by the opponents of state ownership, you have to give people ownership, or property rights, over things (including enterprises) if you want them to use them most efficiently.[1]

Ownership gives the owner two important rights in relation to his property. The first is the right to dispose of it. The second is the right to claim the profits from its use. Since profits are, by definition, what are left to the owner of the property after he has paid for all the inputs he has bought in order to use his property productively (e.g., raw materials, labour and other inputs used in his factory), the right to claim the profits is known as the 'residual claim'. The problem is that, if the owner has the residual claim, the amount of the profits does not concern those suppliers of inputs who get fixed payments.

By definition, state-owned enterprises are properties collectively owned by all the citizens, who hire professional managers on fixed salaries to run them. Given that it is the citizenry that has the residual claim as the owner of the enterprise, the hired managers do not care about the profitability of their enterprises. Of course, the citizenry, as the 'principal', can make its 'agents', or the hired managers, interested in the profitability of the SOEs by linking their pay to it. But such incentive systems are notoriously difficult to design. This is because there is a fundamental gap in information between the principals and their agents. For example, when the hired manager says that she has done her best and that the poor performance is due to factors beyond her control, the principal will find it very difficult to prove that she is lying. The difficulty of the principal controlling the agent's behaviour is known as the 'principal-agent problem' and the resulting costs (that is, the reduction in profits due to poor management) the 'agency cost'. The principal-agent problem is at the centre of the neo-liberal argument against SOEs.

But this is not the only cause of inefficiency of state ownership of enterprises. Individual citizens, even if they theoretically own the public enterprises, do not have any incentives to take care of their properties (the enterprises in question) by adequately monitoring the hired managers. The problem is that any increase in profit resulting from the extra monitoring of the SOE managers by some citizens will be shared by every citizen, while only those citizens who do the monitoring pay the costs (e.g., time and energy spent in going through company accounts or alerting the relevant government agencies to any problems). As a result, everyone's preferred course of action will be not to monitor the public enterprise managers at all and simply to 'free-ride' on the efforts of the others. But, if everyone free-rides, no one will monitor the managers and poor performance will be the outcome. The reader will immediately understand the 'free-rider problem' if he tries to recall how often he himself has monitored the performance of any of his country's SOEs (of which he is one of the legal owners) – almost certainly never!

There is yet another argument against state-owned enterprises, known as the 'soft budget constraint' problem. Being a part of the government, the argument goes, SOEs are often able to secure additional finances from the government if they make losses or are threatened with bankruptcy. In this way, it is argued, enterprises can act as if the limits on their budgets are malleable, or 'soft', and get away with lax management. This theory of soft budget constraint was originally advanced by the famous Hungarian economist, Janos Kornai, to explain the behaviour of state-owned enterprises under communist central planning, but it can be applied to similar enterprises in capitalist economies too. Those 'sick enterprises' of India that never go bankrupt are the most frequently cited example of the soft budget constraint problem in relation to state-owned enterprises.[2]

State vs private

So the case against state-owned enterprises, or public ownership, seems very powerful. The citizens, despite being the legal owners of public enterprises, have neither the ability nor the incentive to monitor their agents, who have been hired to run the enterprises. The agents (managers) do not maximize enterprise profits, while it is impossible for the principals (citizens) to make them do so, because of the inherent deficiency in information they possess about the agents' behaviour and the free-rider problem amongst the principals themselves. On top of this, state ownership makes it possible for enterprises to survive through political lobbying rather than through raising productivity.

But all three arguments against state ownership of enterprises actually apply to large private-sector firms as well. The principal-agent problem and the free-rider problem affect many large private-sector firms. Some large companies are still managed by their (majority) owners (e.g., BMW, Peugeot), but most of them are managed by hired managers because they have dispersed share ownership. If a private enterprise is run by hired managers and there are numerous shareholders owning only small fractions of the company, it will suffer from the same problems as state-owned enterprises. The hired managers (like their SOE counterparts) will also have no incentive to put in more than sub-optimal levels of effort (the principal-agent problem), while individual shareholders will not have enough incentive to monitor the hired managers (the free-rider problem).

As for politically generated soft budget constraints, they are not confined to SOEs. If they are politically important (e.g., large employers or enterprises operating in politically sensitive industries, such as armaments or healthcare), private firms can also expect subsidies or even government bail-outs. Right after the Second World War, a lot of large private enterprises were nationalized in many European countries because they were not doing well. In the 1960s and the 1970s, the British industrial decline prompted both Labour and Conservative governments to nationalize key firms (Rolls Royce in 1971 under the Conservatives; British Steel in 1967, British Leyland in 1977, and British Aerospace in the same year under Labour). Or, to take another example, in Greece, 43 virtually bankrupt private-sector firms were nationalized between 1983 and 1987 when the economy was going through a difficult patch.[3] Conversely, state-owned enterprises are *not* totally immune to market forces. Many public enterprises across the world have been shut down and their managers sacked because of bad performance – these are equivalent to corporate bankruptcies and corporate takeovers in the private sector.

Private firms know that they will be able to take advantage of soft budget constraints if they are important enough, and they are not shy about exploiting the opportunity to the full. As one foreign banker reportedly told the *Wall Street Journal* in the middle of the 1980s Third World debt crisis, '[w]e foreign bankers are for the free market when we're out to make a buck and believe in the state when we are about to lose a buck'.[4]

Indeed, many state bail-outs of large private sector firms have been made by avowedly free-market governments. In the late 1970s, the bankrupt Swedish shipbuilding industry was rescued through nation-alization by the country's first right-wing government in 44 years, despite the fact that it had come to power with a pledge to reduce the size of the state. In the early 1980s, the troubled US car maker Chrysler was rescued by the Republican administration under Ronald Reagan, which was in the vanguard of neo-liberal market reforms at the time. Faced with the financial crisis in 1982, following its premature and poorly designed financial liberalization, the Chilean government rescued the entire banking sector with public money. This was General Pinochet's government, which had seized power in a bloody *coup* in the name of defending the free market and private ownership.

The neo-liberal case against state-owned enterprises is further undermined by the fact that there are numerous well-functioning SOEs in real life. Many of them are actually world-class firms. Let me tell you about some of the more important ones.

State-owned success stories

Singapore Airlines is one of the most highly regarded airlines in the world. Often voted the world's favourite airline, it is efficient and friendly. Unlike most other carriers, it has never made a financial loss in its 35-year history.

The airline is a state-owned enterprise, 57% controlled by Temasek, the holding company whose sole shareholder is Singapore's Ministry of Finance. Temasek Holdings owns controlling stakes* (usually the

* There is no agreed definition of what is a controlling stake in an enterprise's shares. A holding of as little as 15% could give the shareholder effective control over an enterprise, depending on the holding structure. But, typically, a holding of around 30% is considered a controlling stake.

majority share) in a host of other highly efficient and profitable enterprises, called GLCs (government-linked companies). The GLCs do not just operate in the usual public 'utility' industries, such as telecommunications, power and transport. They also operate in areas that are owned by the private sector in most other countries, such as semiconductors, shipbuilding, engineering, shipping and banking.[5] The Singapore government also runs the so-called Statutory Boards that provide certain vital goods and services. Virtually all land in the country is publicly owned and around 85% of housing is provided by the Housing and Development Board. The Economic Development Board develops industrial estates, incubates new firms and provides business consulting services.

Singapore's SOE sector is twice as big as that of Korea, when measured in terms of its contribution to national output. When measured in terms of its contribution to total national investment, it is nearly three times bigger.[6] Korea's SOE sector is, in turn, about twice as large as that of Argentina and five times bigger than that of the Philippines, in terms of its share in national income.[7] Yet both Argentina and the Philippines are popularly believed to have failed because of an over-extended state, while Korea and Singapore are often hailed as success stories of private-sector-driven economic development.

Korea also provides another dramatic example of a successful public enterprise in the form of the (now privatized) steel maker, POSCO (Pohang Iron and Steel Company).[8] The Korean government made an application to the World Bank in the late 1960s for a loan to build its first modern steel mill. The bank rejected it on the grounds that the project was not viable. Not an unreasonable decision. The country's biggest export items at the time were fish, cheap apparel, wigs and plywood. Korea didn't possess deposits of either of the two key raw materials – iron ore and coking coal. Furthermore, the Cold War meant it could not even import them from nearby communist China. They had to be brought all the way from Australia. And to cap it all, the Korean government proposed to run the venture as an SOE. What more perfect recipe for disaster? Yet within ten years of starting production in 1973 (the project was financed by Japanese banks), the company became one of the most efficient steel-producers on the planet and is now the world's third largest.

Taiwan's experience with state-owned enterprises has been eve more remarkable.[9] Taiwan's official economic ideology is the so-called 'Three People's Principles' of Dr Sun Yat-Sen, the founder of the Nationalist Party (*Kuomintang*) that engineered the Taiwanese economic miracle.[10] These principles dictate that the key industries should be owned by the state. Accordingly, Taiwan has had a very large SOE sector. Throughout the 1960s and the 1970s, it accounted for over 16% of national output. Little of it was privatized until 1996. Even after the 'privatization' of 18 (of many) state-owned enterprises in 1996, the Taiwanese government still retains a controlling stake in them (averaging 35.5%) and appoints 60% of the directors to their boardrooms. Taiwan's strategy has been to let the private sector grow by creating a good economic environment (including, importantly, the supply of cheap, high-quality inputs by public enterprises) and not bothering about privatization very much.

In the past three decades of its economic ascendancy, China has used a strategy similar to that of Taiwan. All Chinese industrial enterprises had been owned by the state under Maoist communism. Now China's SOE sector only accounts for around 40% of industrial output.[11] Over the past 30 years of economic reform, some smaller state-owned enterprises have been privatized under the slogan of *zhuada fangxiao* (grabbing the big, letting go of the small). But the fall in the share of state ownership has been mainly due to the growth of the private sector. The Chinese have also come up with a unique type of enterprise based on a hybrid form of ownership, called TVEs (township and village enterprises). These enterprises are formally owned by local authorities, but usually operate as if they were privately owned by powerful local political figures.

It is not only in East Asia that we can find good public enterprises. The economic successes of many European economies, such as Austria, Finland, France, Norway and Italy after the Second World War, were achieved with very large SOE sectors at least until the 1980s. In Finland and France especially, the SOE sector was at the forefront of technological modernization. In Finland, public enterprises led technological modernization in forestry, mining, steel, transport equipment, paper machinery and chemical industries.[12] The Finnish government gave up its controlling stake in only a few of these enterprises even after recent privatizations. In the case of France, the reader may be surprised to learn that many French household names, like Renault (automobiles), Alcatel (telecommunications equipment), St Gobain (glass and other building materials), Usinor (steel; merged into Arcelor, which is now part of Arcelor-Mittal, the biggest steel-maker in the world), Thomson (electronics), Thales (defence electronics), Elf Aquitaine (oil and gas), Rhone-Poulenc (pharmaceuticals; merged with the German company Hoechst to form Aventis, which is now part of Sanofi-Aventis), all used to be SOEs.[13] These firms led the country's technological modernization and industrial development under state ownership until their privatization at various points between 1986 and 2000.[14]

Well-performing state-owned enterprises are also found in Latin America. The Brazilian state-owned oil company Petrobras is a world-class firm with leading-edge technologies. EMBRAER (Empresa Brasileira de Aeronáutica), the Brazilian manufacturer of 'regional jets' (short-range jet planes), also became a world-class firm under state ownership. EMBRAER is now the world's biggest producer of regional jets and the world's third largest aircraft manufacturer of any kind, after Airbus and Boeing. It was privatized in 1994, but the Brazilian government still owns the 'golden share' (1% of the capital), which allows it to veto certain deals regarding military aircraft sales and technology transfers to foreign countries.[15]

If there are so many successful public enterprises, why do we rarely hear about them? It is partly because of the nature of reporting, whether journalistic or academic. Newspapers tend to report bad things – wars, natural disasters, epidemics, famines, crime, bankruptcy, etc. While it is natural and necessary for newspapers to focus on these events, the journalistic habit tends to present the public with the bleakest possible view of the world. In the case of SOEs, journalists and academics usually investigate them only when things go wrong – inefficiency, corruption or negligence. Well-performing SOEs attract relatively little attention in the same way that a peaceful and productive day in the life of a 'model citizen' is unlikely to make front-page news.

There is another, perhaps more important, reason for the paucity of positive information on state-owned enterprises. The rise of neo-liberalism during the past couple of decades has made state owner-ship so unpopular in the public mind that successful SOEs themselves want to underplay their connection with the state. Singapore Airlines does not advertise the fact that it is owned by the state. Renault, POSCO and EMBRAER – now all privatized – try to underplay, if not exactly hide, the fact that they became world-class firms under state ownership. Partial state ownership is practically hushed up. For example, few people know that the state (*Land*) government of Lower Saxony (*Niedersachsen*), with an 18.6% stake, is the largest shareholder in the German carmaker Volkswagen.

The unpopularity of state ownership, however, is not entirely, or even mainly, due to the power of neo-liberal ideology. There are many SOEs all over the world that are not performing well. My examples of high-performing SOEs are *not* meant to distract the reader's atten-tion away from the poorly performing ones. They are given to show that there is nothing 'inevitable' about poor performance by public enterprises and that improving their performance does not necessarily require privatization.

The case for state ownership

I have shown that all the reasons cited as causes of poor SOE performance apply also to large private-sector firms with dispersed ownership, if not always to the same degree. My examples also show that there are many public enterprises that do very well. But even that is not the whole story. Economic theory shows that there are circum-stances under which public enterprises are superior to private-sector firms.

One such circumstance is where private-sector investors refuse to finance a venture despite its long-term viability because they think it is too risky. Precisely because money can move around quickly, capital markets have an inherent bias towards short-term gains and do not like risky, large-scale projects with long gestation periods. If the capital

to generate private sector interest in a poorly performing SOE, the government often has to invest heavily in it and/or restructure it. But if its performance can be improved under state ownership, why then privatize it at all?[20] Therefore, unless it is *politically* impossible to restructure a public enterprise without a strong government commitment to privatization, a lot of problems in public enterprises may be solved without privatization.

Moreover, the privatized firm should be sold at *the right price*. Selling at the right price is the duty of the government, as the trustee of the citizens' assets. If it sells them too cheaply, it is transferring public wealth to the buyer. This raises an important distributional question. In addition, if the wealth transferred is taken outside the country, there will be a loss in national wealth. This is more likely to occur when the buyer is based abroad, but national citizens can also stash the money away, if there is an open capital market, as seen in the case of Russian 'oligarchs' following post-communist privatization.

In order to get the right price, the privatization programme must be done at the *right scale* and with the *right timing*. For example, if a government tries to sell too many enterprises within a relatively short period, this would adversely affect their prices. Such a 'fire sale' weakens the government's bargaining power, thus lowering the proceeds it receives: this is what took place in a number of Asian countries after the 1997 financial crisis. What is more, given fluctuations in the stock market, it is important to privatize only when the stock market conditions are good. In this sense, it is a bad idea to set a rigid deadline for privatization, which the IMF often insists on and which some governments have also voluntarily adopted. Such a deadline will force the government to privatize regardless of market conditions.

Even more important is selling the public enterprises to *the right buyers*. If privatization is going to help a country's economic future, the public enterprises need to be sold to people who have the ability to improve their long-term productivity. Obvious as this may sound, it is often not done. Unless the government demands that the buyer has a proven track record in the industry (as some countries have done), the enterprise may be sold to those who are good at financial engineering rather than at managing the enterprise in question.

More importantly, SOEs are often sold off corruptly to people who have no competence to run them well – massive state-owned assets were transferred in a corrupt way to the new 'oligarchy' in Russia after the fall of communism. In many developing countries, the very processes of privatization have also been riddled with corruption, with a large part of the *potential* proceeds ending up in the pockets of a few insiders, rather than in the state coffers. Corrupt transfers can sometimes be effected illegally, through bribery. But they can also be done legally, for example, where government insiders act as consultants and get high fees in the process.

This is ironic, given that one frequent argument against SOEs is that they are rife with corruption. However, the sad fact is that a government that is unable to control or eliminate corruption in its SOEs is not suddenly going to develop the capacity to prevent corruption when it is privatizing them. Indeed, corrupt officials have an incentive to push through privatization at all costs, because it means they do not have to share the bribes with their successors and can 'cash in' all future bribery streams (e.g., bribes that SOE managers can extract from input suppliers). It should also be added that privatization will not necessarily reduce corruption, for private-sector firms can be corrupt too (see chapter 8).

Privatization of natural monopolies or essential services will also fail if they are not subject to the *right regulatory regime* afterwards. When the SOEs concerned are natural monopolies, privatization without the appropriate regulatory capability on the part of the government may replace inefficient but (politically) restrained public monopolies with inefficient and unrestrained private monopolies. For example, the sale of the Cochabamba water system in Bolivia to the American company Bechtel in 1999 resulted in an immediate tripling of water rates, which sparked off riots that resulted in the re-nationalization of the company.[21] When the Argentinian government partially privatized roads in 1990 by awarding contractors the right to collect tolls in return for road maintenance, '[c]ontractors in control of a road leading to a popular beach resort sparked protests by building earthen barriers across alternative routes in order to force motorists to pass through their pay booths. And after travellers complained about the rip-off along another highway, contractors parked a fleet of phony squad cars at tollbooths to give the appearance of police backing'.[22] Commenting on the privatization of the Mexican state-owned telephone company, Telmex, in 1989, even a World Bank study concluded that 'the privatization of Telmex, along with its attendant price-tax regulatory regime, has the result of "taxing" consumers – a rather diffuse, unorganized group – and then distributing the gains among more well-defined groups; [foreign] shareholders, employees and the government'.[23]

The problem of regulatory deficit is particularly severe at the local government level. In the name of political decentralization and 'bringing service providers closer to the people', the World Bank and donor governments have recently pushed for breaking up SOEs into smaller units on a geographical basis, thereby leaving the regulatory function to local authorities. This looks very good on paper, but it has, in effect, often resulted in regulatory vacuums.[24]

Black cat, white cat

The picture regarding the management of state-owned enterprises is complex. There are good state-owned enterprises, and there are bad state-owned enterprises. Even for a similar problem, public ownership may be the right solution in one context and not in another. Many problems that dog SOEs also affect large private-sector firms with dispersed ownership. Privatization sometimes works well, but can be a recipe for disaster, especially in developing countries that lack the necessary regulatory capabilities. Even when privatization is the right solution, it may be difficult to get it right in practice.

Of course, saying that the picture is complex does not mean that 'anything goes'. There are some general lessons that we can draw from economic theories and real life examples.

Enterprises in industries that are natural monopolies, industries that involve large investment and high risk and enterprises that provide essential services should be kept as SOEs, unless the government has very high tax-raising and/or regulatory capabilities. Other things being equal, there is a greater need for SOEs in the developing countries than in the developed countries, as they have underdeveloped capital markets and weak regulatory and taxation capabilities. Privatizing politically important enterprises on the basis of dispersed share sales is unlikely to resolve the underlying problems of poor SOE perform-ance, because the newly privatized firm will have more or less the same problems as when it was under state ownership. When priva-tizing, care must be taken to sell the right enterprise at the right price to the right buyer, and to subject the enterprise to the right regulatory regime thereafter – if this is not done, privatization is not likely to work, even in industries that do not naturally favour state ownership.

SOE performance can often be improved without privatization. One important thing to do is to review critically the goals of the enter-prises and establish clear priorities among them. Very often, public enterprises are charged with serving too many goals – for example, social goals (e.g., affirmative action for women and minorities), employment generation and industrialization. There is nothing wrong with state-owned enterprises serving multiple goals, but what the goals are and the relative priority among them need to be made clear.

The monitoring system can also be improved. In many countries, SOEs are monitored by multiple agencies, which means either that they are not meaningfully supervised by any particular agency or that there is a supervisory over-kill that disrupts daily management – for example, the state-owned Korean Electricity Company was reported to have undergone eight government inspections, lasting 108 days, in 1981 alone. In such cases, it may be helpful if the monitoring respon-sibilities are consolidated into a single agency (as they were in Korea in 1984).

Increase in competition can also be important in improving SOE performance. More competition is *not* always better, but competition is often the best way to improve enterprise performance.[25] Public enter-prises that are not natural monopolies can easily be made to compete with private-sector firms, both domestically or in the export market. This has been the case with many SOEs. For example, in France, Renault (fully state-owned until 1996 and still 30% controlled by the state) faced direct competition from the private firm Peugeot-Citroën, as well as from foreign producers. Even when they were virtual monopolies in their domestic markets, SOEs like EMBRAER and POSCO were required to export and, therefore, had to compete internationally. Moreover, where feasible, competition can be increased by setting up another SOE.[26] For example, in 1991, South Korea set up a new SOE, Dacom, specializing in international calls, whose competition with the existing state-owned monopoly, Korea Telecom, greatly contributed to increasing efficiency and service quality throughout the 1990s. Of course, SOEs are often in industries where there is a natural monopoly, where increasing competition within the industry is either impossible or would be socially unproductive. But, even in these sectors, some degree of competition may be injected by boosting some 'neighbouring' industries (airlines vs railways).[27]

In conclusion, there is no hard and fast rule as to what makes a successful state-owned enterprise. Therefore, when it comes to SOE management, we need a pragmatic attitude in the spirit of the famous remark by China's former leader Deng Xiao-ping: 'it does not matter whether the cat is white or black as long as it catches mice.'

CHAPTER 6

Windows 98 in 1997

Is it wrong to 'borrow' ideas?

In the summer of 1997, I was attending a conference in Hong Kong. The boundless energy and commercial bustle of the city were thrilling even to a Korean, who is no stranger to such things. Walking down the busy street, I noticed dozens of street hawkers selling pirated computer software and music CDs. What caught my eye was the display of the Windows 98 operating system for PCs.

I knew that people in Hong Kong were, like my fellow Koreans, good at pirate-copying, but how could the copy come out before the real thing? Had someone invented a time machine? Unlikely, even in Hong Kong. Someone must have smuggled out the prototype Windows 98 that was being given the final touch in the research labs of Microsoft and knocked off a bootleg version.

Computer software is notoriously easy to duplicate. A new product which is the result of hundreds of man-years of software development effort can be duplicated onto a disk in a few seconds. So, Mr Bill Gates may be exceptionally generous in his charity work, but he is a pretty hard man when it comes to someone copying his software. The entertainment industry and the pharmaceutical industry have the same problem. This is why they are exceptionally aggressive in promoting the strong protection of intellectual property rights (IPRs), such as patents, copyrights and trademarks.

Unfortunately, this handful of industries has been driving the whole international agenda on IPRs over the past two decades. They led the campaign to introduce the so-called TRIPS (Trade-Related Intellectual Property Rights) agreement in the World Trade Organisation. This agreement has widened the scope, extended the duration and heightened the degree of protection for IPRs to an unprecedented extent, making it much more difficult for developing countries to acquire the new knowledge they need for economic development.

'The fuel of interest to the fire of genius'

Many African countries are suffering from an HIV/AIDS epidemic.[1] Unfortunately, HIV/AIDS drugs are very expensive, costing $10–12,000 per patient per year. This is three to four times the annual income per person of even the richest African countries, such as South Africa or Botswana, both of which happen to have the most serious HIV/AIDS epidemic in the world. It is 30–40 times that of the poorest countries, like Tanzania and Uganda, which also have a high incidence of the disease.[2] Given this, it is understandable that some African countries have been importing 'copy' drugs from countries like India and Thailand, which cost only $3–500, or 2–5% of the 'real' thing.

The African governments have not been doing anything revolutionary. All patent laws, including the most pro-patentee US law, have a provision for restricting the rights of IPR-holders when they clash with the public interest. In such circumstances, governments can cancel patents, impose compulsory licensing (forcing the patent holder to license it to third parties – at a reasonable fee) or allow parallel imports (imports of copy products from countries where the product is not patented). Indeed, in the aftermath of the anthrax terror scare in 2001, the US government utilized the public interest provision to maximum effect – it used the threat of compulsory licensing to extract a whopping 80% discount for Cipro, the patent-protected anti-anthrax drug from Bayer, the German pharmaceutical company.[3]

Despite the legitimacy of the actions of African countries concerning the HIV/AIDS drugs, 41 pharmaceutical companies banded together and decided to make an example of the South African government and took it to court in 2001. They argued that the country's drug laws allowing parallel imports and compulsory licensing were contrary to the TRIPS agreement. The ensuing social campaigns and public uproar showed the drug companies in a bad light, and they eventually withdrew the lawsuit. Some of them even offered substantial discounts on their own HIV/AIDS drugs to African countries to make up for the negative publicity generated by the episode.

During the debate surrounding the HIV/AIDS drugs, the pharmaceutical companies argued that, without patents, there will be no more new drugs – if anyone can 'steal' their inventions, they would have no reason to invest in inventing new drugs. Citing Abraham Lincoln – the only US president to be issued a patent* – who said that 'patent adds the fuel of interest to the fire of genius', Harvey Bale, director general of the International Federation of Pharmaceutical Manufacturers Associations, asserted that 'without [intellectual property rights] the private sector will not invest the hundreds of millions of dollars needed to develop new vaccines for AIDS and other infectious and non-infectious diseases.'[4] Therefore, the drug companies went on to say, those who are criticizing the patent system (and other IPRs) are threatening the future supply of new ideas (not just drugs), undermining the very productivity of the capitalist system.

The argument sounds reasonable enough, but it is only a half-truth. It is not as if we always have to 'bribe' clever people into inventing new things. Material incentives, while important, are not the only things that motivate people to invest in producing new ideas. At the height of the HIV/AIDS debate, 13 fellows of the Royal Society, the highest scientific society of the UK, put this point powerfully in an open letter to the *Financial Times*: 'Patents are only one means for promoting discovery and invention. Scientific curiosity, coupled with the desire to benefit humanity, has been of far greater importance throughout history.'[5] Countless researchers all over the world come up with new ideas all the time, even when they do not directly profit from them. Government research institutes or universities often

---

* Lincoln received US Patent #6,469 for 'A Device for Buoying Vessels Over Shoals' on May 22 1849. The invention consists of a set of bellows attached to the hull of a ship just below the waterline. On reaching a shallow place, the bellows are filled with air and the vessel, thus buoyed, is expected to float clear. It was never marketed, probably because the extra weight would have increased the probability of running onto sandbars more frequently.

explicitly refuse to take out patents on their inventions. All these show that a lot of research is not motivated by the profit from patent monopoly.

This is not a fringe phenomenon. A lot of research is conducted by non-profit-seeking organizations – even in the US. For example, in the year 2000, only 43% of US drugs research funding came from the pharmaceutical industry itself. 29% came from the US government and the remaining 28% from private charities and universities.[6] So, even if the US were to abolish pharmaceutical patents tomorrow and, in response, all the country's pharmaceutical companies shut down their research labs (which will not happen), there would still be more than half as much drugs research as there is today in that country. A slight weakening of patentee rights – for example, being forced to charge lower prices to poor people/countries or being made to accept a shorter patent life in developing countries – is even less likely to result in the disappearance of new ideas, despite the patent lobby mantra.

We should also not forget that patents are critical only for some industries, such as pharmaceutical and other chemicals, software, and entertainment, where copying is easy.[7] In other industries, copying new technology is not easy, and innovation automatically gives the inventor a temporary technological monopoly, even in the absence of the patent law. The monopoly is due to the natural advantages accorded to the innovator, such as imitation lag (due to the time it takes for others to absorb new knowledge); reputational advantage (of being the first and so best-known producer); and the head start in 'racing down learning curves' (i.e., the natural increase in productivity through experience).[8] The resulting temporary monopoly profit is reward enough for the innovative activity in most industries. This was indeed a popular argument against patents in the 19th century.[9] This is also why patents do not feature at all in the Austrian-born American economist Joseph Schumpeter's famous theory of innovation – Schumpeter believed that the monopoly rent (or what he calls the entrepreneurial profit) that a technological innovator will enjoy through the above mechanisms is a big enough incentive for investing in generating new knowledge.[10] Most industries actually do not *need* patents and other IPRs to generate new knowledge – although they will be more than happy to take advantage of them, if they are offered to them. The patent lobby talks nonsense when it argues that there will be no new technological progress without patents.

Even in those industries where copying is easy and thus patents (and other IPRs) are necessary, we need to get the balance right between the interests of the patentees (and the holders of copyrights and trademarks) and the rest of society. One obvious problem is that patents, by definition, create monopolies, which impose costs on the rest of society. For example, the patentee could use its technological monopoly to exploit the consumers, as some people believe Microsoft is doing. But it is not just the problem of income distribution between the patentee and the consumers. Monopoly also creates net social loss by allowing the producer to maximize its profit by producing at a less than socially desirable quantity, creating net social loss (this is explained in chapter 5). Also, because it is a 'winner takes all' system, critics point out, the patent system often results in the duplication of research among competitors – this may be wasteful from the social point of view.

The unstated presumption in the pro-patent argument is that such costs will be more than offset by the benefits that flow from increased innovation (that is, higher productivity), but this is not guaranteed. Indeed, in mid-19th-century Europe, the influential anti-patent movement, famously championed by the British free-market magazine, *The Economist*, objected to the patent system on the grounds that its costs would be higher than its benefits.[11]

Of course, the 19th-century anti-patent liberal economists were wrong. They failed to recognize that some forms of monopoly, including the patent, can create more benefits than costs. For example, infant industry protection does produce inefficiency by artificially creating monopoly power for domestic firms, as free-trade economists are only too pleased to point out. But such protection may be justified, if it raises productivity in the long run and more than offsets the damages from the monopoly it creates, as I have repeatedly explained in the earlier chapters. In exactly the same manner, we advocate the protection of patents and other intellectual property rights, despite their potential to create inefficiency and waste, because we believe they will more than compensate for those costs in the long run by generating new ideas that raise productivity. But accepting the potential benefits of the patent system is different from saying that there is no cost involved. If we design it wrong and give too much protection to the patentee, the system can create more costs than benefits, as is the case with excessive infant industry protection.

The inefficiency from monopolies and the waste from 'winner-takes-all' competition are neither the only, nor the most important, problems with the patent system, and other similar forms of intellectual property rights protection. The most detrimental impact lies in its potential to block knowledge flows into technologically backward countries that need better technologies to develop their economies. Economic development is all about absorbing advanced foreign technologies. Anything that makes it more difficult, be it the patent system or a ban on the export of advanced technologies, is not good for economic development. It is as simple as that. In the past, the Bad Samaritan rich countries themselves understood this clearly and did everything to prevent this from happening.

John Law and the first technological arms race

As water flows from high to low, knowledge has always flowed from where there is more to where there is less. Those countries that are better at absorbing the knowledge inflow have been more successful in catching up with the more economically advanced nations. On the other side of the fence, those advanced nations that are good at controlling the outflow of core technologies have retained their technological leadership for longer. The technological 'arms race', between backward countries trying to acquire advanced foreign knowledge and the advanced countries trying to prevent its outflow has always been at the heart of the game of economic development.

The technological arms race started to take on a new dimension in the 18th century, with the emergence of modern industrial technologies that had much greater potential for productivity growth than traditional technologies. The leader in this new technological race was Britain. Not least because of the Tudor and Georgian economic policies that we discussed in chapter 2, it was rapidly becoming Europe's, and the world's, leading industrial power. Naturally, it was reluctant to part with its advanced technologies. It even set up legal barriers to technology outflows. The other industrialising countries in Europe and the US had to violate those laws in order to acquire superior British technologies.

This new technological arms race was started in full spate by John Law (1671–1729), the legendary Scottish financier-economist who even became France's finance minister for just under a year. Law was named the 'moneymaker' by the author of his popular biography, Janet Gleeson.[12] He was a moneymaker in more than one sense. He was an extremely successful financier, making huge killings on currency speculation, setting up and merging large banks and trading companies, getting royal monopolies for them and selling their shares at huge profits. His financial scheme was too successful for its own good. It led to the Mississippi Bubble – a financial bubble three times bigger than the contemporary South Sea Bubble discussed in chapter 2 – which wrecked the French financial system.* Law was also known as

---

*Law was born into a banking family in Scotland. In 1694, he had to flee to the Continent after killing a man in a duel. In 1716, after years of lobbying, Law was given a licence by the French government to set up a note-issuing bank, Banque Générale. His main backer was the Duc d'Orléans, Louis XIV's nephew and the then regent for the child king, Louis XV, the great-grandson of Louis XIV. In 1718, Banque Générale became Banque Royale, with its notes guaranteed by the king. In the meantime, Law bought the Compagnie du Mississippi (the Mississippi Company) in 1717 and floated it as a joint-stock company. The company absorbed other rival trading companies and, in 1719, became Compagnie Perpetuelle des Indes, although it was still commonly called Compagnie du Mississippi. The company had a royal monopoly on all overseas trading. With Law launching high-profile settlement schemes in Louisiana (French North America) and generating rumours vastly exaggerating their prospects, a speculative frenzy on the company's stocks started in the summer of 1719. The share price rose by more than 30 times between early 1719 and early 1720. So many large fortunes were made so quickly – and subsequently lost in many cases – that the term *millionaire* was coined to describe the new mega-rich. In January 1720, Law was even made the finance minister (the Controller General of Finances). But the bubble soon burst, leaving the French financial system in ruins. The Duc d'Orléans dismissed Law in December 1720. Law left France and eventually died penniless in Venice in 1729.

a great gambler with an incredible ability to calculate the odds. As an economist, he advocated the use of paper money backed by a central bank.[13] The idea that we can make worthless paper into money through government fiat was a radical notion then. At the time, most people believed that only things that have a value of their own, like gold and silver, could serve as money.

John Law is today remembered mainly as the financial wheeler-dealer who created the Mississippi Bubble but his understanding of economics went far beyond mere financial engineering. He understood the importance of technology in building a strong economy. While he was expanding his banking operation and building up the Mississippi Company, he also recruited hundreds of skilled workers from Britain in an attempt to upgrade France's technology.[14]

At the time, getting skilled workers was the key to accessing advanced technologies. No one could say, even today, that workers are mindless automata repeating the same task in the manner so hilariously but poignantly depicted by Charlie Chaplin in his classic film, *Modern Times*. What workers know and can do matters greatly in determining a firm's productivity. In earlier times, though, their importance was even more pronounced, since they themselves embodied a lot of technologies. Machines were still rather primitive, so productivity depended very much on how skilled the workers who operated them were. The scientific principles behind industrial operations were poorly understood, so technical instructions could not be written down easily in universal terms. Once again, the skilled worker had to be there to run the operation smoothly.

Galvanized by Law's attempt to poach skilled workers and also by a similar Russian attempt, Britain decided to introduce a ban on the migration of skilled workers. The law, introduced in 1719, made it illegal to recruit skilled workers for jobs abroad – known as 'suborning'. Emigrant workers who did not return home within six months of being warned to do so would lose their right to lands and goods in Britain and have their citizenship taken away. Specifically mentioned in the law were industries such as wool, steel, iron, brass, other metals and watch-making; but in practice the law covered all industries.[15]

With the passage of time, machines became more complex and

began to embody more technologies. This meant that getting hold of key machinery started to become as important as, and increasingly more important than, recruiting skilled workers. Britain introduced a new act in 1750 banning the export of 'tools and utensils' in the wool and silk industries. The ban was subsequently widened and strengthened to include the cotton and linen industries. In 1785, the Tools Act was introduced to ban the export of many different types of machinery.[16]

Other countries intent on catching up with Britain knew that they had to get hold of these advanced technologies, whether the method used to do so was 'legal' or 'illegal' from the British point of view. The 'legal' means included apprenticeships and factory tours.[17] The 'illegal' means involved the governments of continental Europe and the US luring skilled workers contrary to British law. These governments also routinely employed industrial spies. In the 1750s, the French government appointed John Holker, a former Manchester textile finisher and Jacobite officer, as Inspector-General of Foreign Manufactures. While also advising French producers on textile technologies, Holker's main job was running industrial spies and poaching skilled workers from Britain.[18] There was also a lot of machine smuggling. Smuggling was hard to detect. Because machines were still quite simple and had relatively few parts, they could be taken apart and smuggled out bit by bit relatively quickly.

Throughout the 18th century, the technological arms race was fought viciously, using recruitment schemes, machine smuggling and industrial espionage. But by the end of the century, the nature of the game had changed fundamentally with the increasing importance of 'disembodied' knowledge – that is, knowledge that can be separated from the workers and the machines that used to hold them. The development of science meant that a lot of – although not all – knowledge could be written down in a (scientific) language that could be understood by anyone with appropriate training. An engineer who understood the principles of physics and mechanics could reproduce a machine simply by looking at the technical drawings. Similarly, if a chemical formula could be acquired, medicines could be easily reproduced by trained chemists.

Disembodied knowledge is more difficult to protect than knowledge embodied in skilled workers or actual machines. Once an idea is written down in general scientific and engineering language, it becomes much easier to copy it. When you have to recruit a skilled foreign worker, there are all sorts of personal and cultural problems. When you import a machine, you may not get the maximum out of it because you may only poorly understand its operative principles. As the importance of disembodied knowledge grew, it became more important to protect the ideas themselves than the workers or machines that embody them. Consequently, the British ban on skilled worker emigration was abolished in 1825, while that on machinery export was dropped in 1842. In their place, the patent law became the key instrument in managing the flow of ideas.

The first patent system is supposed to have been used by Venice in 1474, when it granted ten years' privileges to inventors of 'new arts and machines'. It was also somewhat haphazardly used by some German states in the 16th century and by Britain from the 17th century.[19] Then, reflecting the growing importance of disembodied knowledge, it spread very quickly from the late 18th century, starting with France in 1791, the US in 1793 and Austria in 1794. Most of today's rich countries established their patent laws within half a century of the French patent law.[20] Other intellectual property laws, such as copyright law (first introduced in Britain in 1709) and trademark law (first introduced in Britain in 1862) were adopted by most of today's rich countries in the second half of the 19th century. Over time, there emerged international agreements on IPRs, such as the Paris Convention on patents and trademarks (1883)[21] and the Berne Convention on copyrights (1886). But even these international agreements did not end the use of 'illegal' means in the technological arms race.

The lawyers get involved

The year 1905 is known as the *annus mirabilis* of modern physics. In that year, Albert Einstein published three papers that changed the course of physics for good.[22] Interestingly, at the time, Einstein was not a professor of physics but a humble patent clerk (an assistant technical examiner) in the Swiss Patent Office, which was his first job.[23]

Had Einstein been a chemist rather than a physicist, his first job could *not* have been in the Swiss Patent Office. For, until 1907, Switzerland did not grant patents to chemical inventions.[24] Switzerland, in fact, had no patent law of any kind until 1888. Its 1888 patent law accorded protection only to 'inventions that can be represented by mechanical models'. The clause automatically (and intentionally) excluded chemical inventions – at the time, the Swiss were 'borrowing' a lot of chemical and pharmaceutical technologies from Germany, the then world leader in those fields. It was thus not in their interest to grant chemical patents.

Only in 1907, under the threat of trade sanctions by Germany, did the Swiss decide to extend patent protection to chemical inventions. However, even the new patent law did not protect chemical technologies to the degree expected in today's TRIPS system. Like many other countries at the time, the Swiss refused to grant patents for chemical substances (as opposed to chemical processes). The reasoning was that those substances, unlike mechanical inventions, already existed in nature and, therefore, the 'inventor' had merely found a way to isolate them, rather than inventing the substance itself. Chemical substances remained unpatentable in Switzerland until 1978.

Switzerland was not the only country at the time without a patent law. The Netherlands actually abolished its 1817 patent law in 1869, not to introduce it again until 1912. When the Dutch abolished the law, they were in no small measure influenced by the anti-patent movement I mentioned above – they were convinced that patent, as artificially created monopoly, went against their free-trade principle.[25] Exploiting the absence of a patent law, the Dutch electronics company, Philips, a household name today, started out in 1891 as a producer of light bulbs based on the patents 'borrowed' from the American inventor, Thomas Edison.[26]

Switzerland and the Netherlands may have been extreme cases. But throughout much of the 19th century, the IPR regimes in today's rich countries were all very bad at protecting *foreigners'* intellectual property rights. This was partly the consequence of the general laxity of early patent laws in checking the originality of an invention. For example, in the US, before the 1836 overhaul of its patent law, patents were granted without any proof of originality; this encouraged rack-eteers to patent devices already in use ('phony patents') and then to demand money from their users under threat of suit for infringe-ment.[27] But the absence of protection for foreigners' intellectual property rights was often deliberate. In most countries, including Britain, the Netherlands, Austria, France and the US, patenting of *imported invention* was explicitly allowed. When Peter Durand took out a patent in 1810 in Britain for canning technology, using the Frenchman Nicolas Appert's invention, the application explicitly stated that it was an 'invention communicated to me by a certain foreigner', then a common proviso used when taking out a patent on a foreigner's invention.[28]

'Borrowing' ideas was not simply done in relation to inventions that could be patented. There was also extensive counterfeiting of trademarks in the 19th century – in a manner similar to what was subsequently done by Japan, Korea, Taiwan and, today, China. In 1862, Britain revised its trademark law, the Merchandise Mark Act, with the specific purpose of preventing foreigners, especially the Germans, from making counterfeit English products. The revised act required the producer to specify the place or country of manufacture as a part of the necessary 'trade description'.[29]

The law underestimated German ingenuity, however – the German firms came up with some brilliant evasive tactics.[30] For example, they placed the stamp indicating the country of origin on the packaging instead of on the individual articles. Once the packaging was removed, customers could not tell the product's country of origin. This tech-nique is said to have been particularly common in the case of imported watches and steel files. Alternatively, German manufacturers would send some articles, like pianos and bicycles, over in pieces and have them assembled in England. Or they would place the stamp indicating the country of origin where it was practically invisible. The 19th-century British journalist Ernest Williams, who wrote a book about German counterfeiting, *Made in Germany*, documents how 'One

German firm, which exports to England large numbers of sewing-machines, conspicuously labeled 'Singer' and 'North-British Sewing Machines', places the Made in Germany stamp in small letters underneath the treadle. Half a dozen seamstresses might combine their strength to turn the machine bottom-upwards, and read the legend: otherwise it would go unread'.[31]

Copyrights were also routinely violated. Despite its currently gung-ho attitude towards copyright, the US in the past refused to protect foreigners' copyrights in its 1790 copyright law. It only signed the international copyright agreement (the Berne Convention of 1886) in 1891. At the time, the US was a net importer of copyright materials and saw the advantage of protecting only American authors. For another century (until 1988), it did not recognize copyrights on materials printed outside the US.

The historical picture is clear. Counterfeiting was not invented in modern Asia. When they were backward themselves in terms of knowledge, all of today's rich countries blithely violated other people's patents, trademarks and copyrights. The Swiss 'borrowed' German chemical inventions, while the Germans 'borrowed' English trademarks and the Americans 'borrowed' British copyrighted materials – all without paying what would today be considered 'just' compensation.

Despite this history, the Bad Samaritan rich countries are now forcing developing countries to strengthen the protection of intellectual property rights to a historically unprecedented degree through the TRIPS agreement and a raft of bilateral free-trade agreements. They argue that stronger protection of intellectual property will encourage the production of new knowledge and benefit everyone, including the developing countries. But is this true?

Making Mickey Mouse live longer

In 1998, the US Copyright Term Extension Act extended the period of copyright protection from 'life of the author plus 50 years, or 75 years for a work of corporate authorship' (as set in 1976) to 'life of the author plus 70 years, or 95 years for a work of corporate authorship'. Historically speaking, this was an incredible extension in the period of copyright protection from the original 14 years (renewable for another 14 years) laid down by the 1790 Copyright Act.

The 1998 act is derogatively known as the Mickey Mouse Protection Act, from the fact that Disney was heading the lobby for it in anticipation of the 75th birthday of Mickey Mouse, first created in 1928 (*Steamboat Willie*). What is particularly remarkable about it is that it was applied *retrospectively*. As should be immediately obvious to anyone, extending the term of protection for existing work can never create new knowledge.[32]

The story does not end with copyrights. The US pharmaceutical industry has already successfully lobbied to extend *de facto* patents by up to eight years, using excuses like the need to compensate for delays in the drugs approval process by the FDA (Food and Drugs Administration) or the need for data protection. Given that US patents, like copyright, used to be for only 14 years, this means that the pharmaceutical industry has effectively doubled the patent life for its inventions.

It is not just in the US that the terms of IPR protection have been lengthening. In the third quarter of the 19th century (1850–75), the average patent life in a sample of 60 countries was around 13 years. Between 1900 and 1975, this was extended to 16 or 17 years. But recently the US has played the leading role in accelerating and consolidating this upward trend. It has now made its 20-year term for patent protection a 'global standard' through enshrining it in the World Trade Organisation's TRIPS agreement – the 60-country average stood at 19 years as of 2004.[33] Anything that goes beyond TRIPS, such as the *de facto* extension of drug patents, the US government has been spreading through bilateral free-trade agreements. I know of no economic theory that says that 20 years is better than 13 years or 16 years as the term of patent protection from social point of view, but it is obvious that the longer it is, the better it is for the patent-holders.

As the protection of intellectual property rights involves monopoly (and its social costs), extending the period of protection clearly increases those costs. Lengthening the term – like any other strengthening of IPR protection – means that society is paying more for new knowledge. Of course, those costs may be justified if the term extension produces more knowledge (by strengthening the incentive for innovation), but there is no evidence that this has been happening – at least not enough to compensate for the increased costs of protection. Given this, we need to carefully examine whether the current terms of IPR protection are appropriate and shorten them if necessary.

Sealed crustless sandwiches and turmeric

One basic assumption behind IPR laws is that the new idea that is awarded protection is worth protecting. This is why all such laws demand the idea to be original (to possess 'novelty' and 'non-obviousness', in the technical jargon). This may sound incontrovertible in abstract terms, but it is more difficult to put into practice, not least because investors have an incentive to lobby for lowering the originality bar.

For example, as I mentioned when discussing the history of Swiss patent law, many people believe that chemical *substances* (as opposed to the process) are *not* worthy of patent protection, because those who have extracted them have not done anything really original. For this reason, chemical and/or pharmaceutical substances could not be patented in most rich countries until the 1960s or the 1970s – Germany, France, Switzerland, Japan and the Nordic countries. Pharmaceutical products remained unpatentable in Spain and Canada right up to the early 1990s.[34] Before the TRIPS agreement, most developing countries did not give pharmaceutical product patents.[35] Most countries had never given them; others, such as India and Brazil, had abolished the pharmaceutical product patents (process patent as well, in the case of Brazil) that they once had.[36]

Even for things whose patentability is not disputed, there is no obvious way to judge what is a worthy invention. For example, when Thomas Jefferson was the US patent commissioner – quite ironic given that he opposed patents (more on this later), but this was *ex officio* as secretary of state – he did a very good job of rejecting patent applications at the slightest excuse. It is reported that the number of patents granted each year trebled after Jefferson resigned from his secretarial post and thus ceased to be the patent commissioner. This was, of course, not because the Americans suddenly became three times more inventive.

Since the 1980s, the originality hurdle for patents has been significantly lowered in the US. In their important book on the current state of the US patent system, Professors Adam Jaffe and Josh Lerner point out that patents have been granted to some very obvious things, like Amazon.com's 'one click' internet shopping, the Smuckers food company's 'sealed crustless sandwiches', and even things like a 'bread refreshing method' (essentially toasting the stale bread) or a 'method of swinging on a swing' (apparently 'invented' by a five-year-old).[37] In the first two cases, the patent holders even used their new rights to take their competitors to court – barnesandnoble.com in the former case and a small Michigan catering company called Albie's Foods, Inc. in the latter.[38] While these cases are at the wackier end of the spectrum, they reflect the general trend that 'the tests for novelty and non-obviousness, which are supposed to ensure that the patent monopoly is granted only to truly original ideas, have become largely non-operative'.[39] The result of this has been what Jaffe and Lerner call a 'patent explosion'. They document how the number of patents granted in the US grew by 1% a year between 1930 and 1982, the year when the American patent system was loosened, but grew by 5.7% a year during 1983–2002, when patents were more liberally granted.[40] This increase is definitely not due to some sudden explosion in American creativity![41]

But why should the rest of the world care if the Americans are issuing silly patents? They should care because the new American system has encouraged the 'theft' of ideas that are well-known in other countries, especially developing countries, but are not legally protected precisely because they have been so well known for such a long time. This is known as the theft of 'traditional knowledge'. The best example in this regard is the patent granted in 1995 to two Indian researchers at the University of Mississippi for the medicinal use of turmeric, whose wound-healing properties have been known in India for thousands of years. The patent was only cancelled thanks to the challenge mounted in the American courts by the New Delhi-based Council for

Agriculture Research. This patent might be still there if the wronged country had been some small and very poor developing country that lacked India's human and financial resources to fight such battles.

Shocking though these examples may be, the consequences of the lowering of originality bar is not the biggest problem with the recent unbalancing of the intellectual property rights system. The most serious problem is that the IPR system has begun to be an obstacle, rather than a spur, to technological innovation.

The tyranny of interlocking patents

Sir Isaac Newton once famously said, 'if I have seen a little further, it is by standing on the shoulders of giants'.[42] He was referring to the fact that ideas develop in a cumulative manner. In the early controversy around patents, some people used this as an argument against them – when new ideas emerge from a ferment of intellectual endeavour, how can we say that the person who put the 'finishing touches' to an invention should take all the glory – and the profit? Thomas Jefferson opposed patents on this very basis. He argued that ideas were 'like air' and cannot, therefore, be owned (although he saw no problem in owning people – he himself owned many slaves).[43]

The problem is inherent in the patent system. Ideas are the most important inputs in producing new ideas. But if other people own the ideas you need in order to develop your own new ideas, you cannot use them without paying for them. This can make producing new ideas expensive. Worse, you run the danger of being sued for patent infringement by your competitors, who may own patents closely related to yours. Such a lawsuit would not only waste your money but also keep you from further developing the technology in dispute. In this sense, patents can become an obstacle, rather than a spur, to technological development.

Indeed, patent infringement suits have been major obstacles to technological progress in US industries like sewing machines (mid-19th century), aeroplanes (early 20th century) and semiconductors (mid-20th century). The sewing machine industry (Singer and a few other companies) came up with a brilliant solution to this particular problem – a 'patent pool', where all the companies involved cross-licensed all the relevant patents to one another. In the cases of the aeroplanes (the Wright brothers vs Glenn Curtiss) and the semi-conductors (Texas Instrument vs Fairchild), the firms concerned could not reach a compromise, so the US government stepped in to impose patent pools. Without these government-imposed patent pools, these industries could not have progressed as they have done.

Unfortunately, the problem of interlocking patents has recently become worse. More and more minute pieces of knowledge have become patentable, down to the level of individual genes, thereby increasing the risk of patents becoming an obstacle to technological progress. The recent debate surrounding so-called golden rice illustrates this point very well.

In 2000, a group of scientists led by Ingo Potrykus (Swiss) and Peter Beyer (German) announced a new technology to genetically engineer rice with extra beta carotene (which turns into Vitamin A when digested). Because of the natural colour of beta carotene, the rice has a golden hue, which gives it its name. The rice is also considered 'golden' by some because it can potentially bring important nutritional benefits to millions of poor people in countries where rice is the basic staple.[44] Rice is nutritionally very effective, able to sustain more people than wheat, given the same area of land. But it lacks one critical nutrient – Vitamin A. Poor people in rice-eating countries tend to eat little else other than rice and therefore suffer from Vitamin A deficiency (VAD). At the beginning of the 21st century, it is estimated that 124 million people in 118 countries in Africa and Asia are affected by VAD. VAD is thought to be responsible for one or two million deaths, half a million cases of irreversible blindness and millions of cases of the debilitating eye-disease, xerophthalmia, every year.[45]

In 2001, Potrykus and Beyer caused controversy by selling the technology to the multinational pharmaceutical/biotechnology firm, Syngenta (AstraZeneca at the time).[46] Syngenta already had a legitimate partial claim on the technology, thanks to its indirect funding of the research through the European Union. And the two scientists, to their credit, negotiated hard with Syngenta to allow farmers making less than $10,000 a year out of golden rice to use the technology for free. Even so, some people found the sale of such a valuable 'public good' technology to a profit-making firm unacceptable.

In response to the criticisms, Potrykus and Beyer said they had had to sell their technology to Syngenta because of the difficulties involved in negotiating licences for the other patented technologies they needed in order to operationalize their technology. They argued that, as scientists, they simply did not have the necessary resources or the skills to negotiate for the 70 relevant patents belonging to 32 different companies and universities. Critics countered that they were exaggerating the difficulties. They pointed out that there are only a dozen or so patents that are truly relevant for countries where the golden rice would bring about the largest benefits.

But the point remains. The days are over when technology can be advanced in laboratories by individual scientists alone. Now you need an army of lawyers to negotiate the hazardous terrain of interlocking patents. Unless we find a solution to the problem of interlocking patents, the patent system may actually become a major obstacle, rather than a spur, to technological progress.

Harsh rules and developing countries

The recent changes in the system of intellectual property rights have magnified its costs, while reducing the benefits. Lowering the originality bar and the extension of patent (and other IPR) life have meant that we are, in effect, paying more for each patent, whose average quality, however, is lower than before. Changes in the attitudes of rich country governments and corporations have also made it more difficult to override the commercial interests of patent holders for the sake of the public interest, as we saw in the HIV/AIDS case. And making increasingly minute pieces of knowledge patentable has worsened the problem of interlocking patents, slowing down technological progress.

These negative impacts have been much greater for developing countries. The lower originality bar set in the rich countries, especially the US, has made the theft of already existing traditional knowledge from developing countries easier. Much needed medicines have become far more expensive, as developing countries are not allowed to make (or import) copy drugs any more, while their political weakness *vis-à-vis* rich country pharmaceutical companies constrains their ability to use the public interest provision.

But the biggest problem is, to put it bluntly, that the new IPR system has made economic development more difficult. When 97% of all patents and the vast majority of copyrights and trademarks are held by rich countries, the strengthening of the rights of IPR-holders means that acquiring knowledge has become more expensive for developing countries. The World Bank estimates that, following the TRIPS agreement, the increase in technology licence payments alone will cost developing countries an extra $45 billion a year, which is nearly half of total foreign aid given by rich countries ($93 billion a year in 2004–5).[47] Although it is hard to quantify the impact, strengthening of copyright has made education, especially higher education that uses specialized and advanced foreign books, more costly.

This is not all. If they are to comply with the TRIPS agreement, each developing country needs to spend a lot of money building up and implementing a new IPR system. The system does not run itself. Enforcement of copyright and trademarks requires an army of inspectors. The patent office needs scientists and engineers to process the patent applications and the courts need patent lawyers to help sort out disputes. Training and hiring all these people costs money. In a world with finite resources, training more patent lawyers or hiring more inspectors to hunt down DVD pirates means training fewer medical doctors and teachers while hiring fewer nurses or police officers. It is obvious which of these professions developing countries need more.

The wretched thing is that developing countries are going to get hardly anything in return for paying increased licensing fees and incurring additional expenditures to implement the new IPR system. When rich countries strengthen their IPR protection, they can at least expect some increase in innovation, even if its benefits are not enough to cover the increased costs arising from strengthened protection. In contrast, most developing countries do not have the capabilities to conduct research. The incentive to conduct research may have been increased, but there is no one to take advantage of it. It is like the story of my son, Jin-Gyu, that I discussed in chapter 3. If the capability is not there, it does not matter what the incentives are. This is why even the renowned British financial journalist Martin Wolf, a self-proclaimed defender of globalization (despite his full awareness of its problems and limitations), describes IPR as 'a rent-extraction device' for most developing countries, 'with potentially devastating consequences for their ability to educate their people (because of copyright), adapting designs for their own use (ditto) and deal with severe challenges of public health'.[48]

As I keep emphasizing, the foundation of economic development is the acquisition of more productive knowledge. The stronger the international protection for IPRs is, the more difficult it is for the follower countries to acquire new knowledge. This is why, historically, countries did not protect foreigners' intellectual property very well (or at all) when they needed to import knowledge. If knowledge is like water that flows downhill, then today's IPR system is like a dam that turns potentially fertile fields into a technological dustbowl. This situation clearly needs fixing.

Getting the balance right

One common question that I am asked when I criticize the current IPR system in my lectures is: 'seeing that you are against intellectual property, would you let other people steal your research papers and publish them under their own names?' This is symptomatic of the simplistic mentality that pervades our debate on intellectual property rights. Criticizing the IPR regime as it exists today is not the same as arguing for the wholesale abolition of intellectual property itself.

I am *not* arguing that we should abolish patents, copyrights or trademarks. They do serve useful purposes. But the fact that some protection of intellectual property rights is beneficial, or even necessary, does not mean that more of it is always better. An analogy with salt may be useful in explaining this point more clearly. Some salt is essential to our survival. Some more of it makes our eating more pleasurable, even though it may do some harm to our health. But, above a certain level, the harm that salt does to our health outweighs the benefits we get from tastier food. Protection of intellectual property rights is like this. Some minimum amount of it may be essential in creating incentives for knowledge creation. Some more of it may bring more benefits than costs. But too much of it may create more costs than benefits so that it ends up harming the economy.

So the real question is not whether IPR protection is good or bad in abstract. It is how we get the balance right between the need to encourage people to produce new knowledge and the need to ensure that the costs from the resulting monopoly do not exceed the benefits that the new knowledge brings about. In order to do that, we need to weaken the degree of IPR protection prevailing today – by shortening the period of protection, by raising the originality bar, and by making compulsory licensing and parallel imports easier.

If a weaker protection leads to insufficient incentives for potential inventors, which may or may not be the case, the public sector can step in. This may involve the direct conduct of research by public bodies – national (e.g., the US National Institutes of Health) or international (e.g., the International Rice Research Institute that developed the Green Revolution varieties of rice). It may be done by means of targeted R&D subsidies to private-sector companies, with a condition attached regarding public access to the end product.[49] The public sector, at the national and international level, is already doing these things anyway, so it would not be a radical departure from existing practice. It would simply be a matter of stepping up and redirecting existing efforts.

Above all, the international IPR system should be reformed in a way that helps developing countries become more productive by allowing them to acquire new technical knowledge at reasonable costs. Developing countries should be allowed to grant weaker IPRs – shorter patent life, lower licensing royalty rates (probably graduated according to their abilities to pay) or easier compulsory licensing and parallel imports.[50]

Last but not least, we should not only make technology acquisition easier for developing countries but also help them develop *the* *capabilities to use and develop* more productive technologies. For this purpose, we could institute an international tax on patent royalties and use it to provide technological support to developing countries. The cause may also be promoted by a modification to the international copyright system, which makes access to academic books easier.*

Like all other institutions, intellectual property rights (patents, copyrights and trademarks) may or may not be beneficial, depending on how they are designed and where they are used. The challenge is not to decide whether to scrap them altogether or strengthen them to the hilt, but to get the balance right between the interests of the IPR-holders and the rest of the society (or the rest of the world, if you like). Only when we get the balance right will the IPR system serve the useful purpose it was originally set up to serve – that is, encouraging the generation of new ideas at the lowest possible costs to society.

---

* Access to academic books is crucial in enhancing the productive capabilities of developing countries, as my own experience with pirate-copied books, described in the Prologue, suggests. Rich country publishers should be encouraged to allow cheap reproduction of academic books in developing countries – they are not going to lose much by this, because their books are too expensive for developing country consumers anyway. We could also set up a special international fund to subsidize the purchase of academic books by developing country libraries, academics and students. A similar argument can put the current hysteria in the rich countries about counterfeit products from developing countries into perspective. As I pointed out in the Prologue, it is not as if those people who buy counterfeit products in developing countries (including many tourists who buy them there) can afford the genuine articles. So, as long as they are not smuggled into the rich countries and sold as the genuine articles (which rarely happens), the original manufacturers lose little actual revenue from the counterfeit goods. One could even argue that the developing country consumers are, in effect, doing free advertising for the original manufacturers. Especially in high-growth economies, today's counterfeit consumers are going to be tomorrow's consumers of the genuine articles. Many Koreans who used to buy fake luxury goods in the 1970s are now buying the real things.

CHAPTER 7

Mission impossible?

Can financial prudence go too far?

Most people who have watched the blockbuster movie *Mission Impossible III* must have been mightily impressed by the urban splendour that is Shanghai, the centre of the Chinese economic miracle. They would also remember the frantic final chase set in the quaint but shabby neighbourhood by the canal, which seems to be stuck in the 1920s. The contrast between that district and the skyscrapers in the city centre symbolizes the challenge that China faces with soaring inequality and the discontent it is producing.

Some who have watched previous episodes of *Mission Impossible* may also have had a small source of curiosity satisfied. For the first time in the series, we were told the meaning of the acronym IMF, the formidable intelligence agency for which the movie's leading character, Ethan Hunt (Tom Cruise), works. It is called the Impossible Mission Force.

The real IMF, the International Monetary Fund, may not send secret agents to blow up buildings or assassinate undesirables, but it is much feared by developing countries all the same, for it plays the role of gatekeeper *vis-à-vis* the these countries, controlling their access to international finance.

When developing countries get into a balance of payments crisis, as they often do, signing an agreement with the IMF is crucial. The money that the IMF itself lends is only a minor part of the story, for the IMF does not have much money of its own. More important is the agreement itself. It is seen as a guarantee that the country will mend its 'profligate' ways and adopt a set of 'good' policies that will ensure its future ability to repay its debts. Only when such agreement is made do other potential lenders – the World Bank, rich country governments and private-sector lenders – agree to continue their supplies of finance to the country concerned. The agreement with the IMF involves accepting conditions on a wide (and, indeed, ever-widening, as I discussed in chapter 1) range of economic policies, from trade liberalization to the adoption of new company law. But the most important and feared of IMF conditions concern macroeconomic policies.

Macroeconomic policies – monetary policy and fiscal policy – are intended to change the behaviour of the whole economy (as distinct from the sum total of the behaviours of the individual economic actors that make it up).[1] The counter-intuitive idea that the whole economy may behave differently from the sum total of its parts comes from the famous Cambridge economist John Maynard Keynes. Keynes argued that what is rational for individual actors may not be rational for the entire economy. For example, during an economic downturn, firms see the demand for their products fall, while workers face increased chances of redundancy and wage cuts. In this situation, it is prudent for individual firms and workers to reduce their spending. But if all economic actors reduced their expenditure, they will all be worse off, for the combined effect of such actions is a lower aggregate demand, which, in turn, further increases everyone's chances of bankruptcy and redundancy. Therefore, Keynes argued, the government, whose job it is to manage the whole economy, cannot simply use scaled-up versions of action plans that are rational for individual economic agents. It should always deliberately do the opposite of what other economic actors do. In an economic downturn, therefore, it should increase its spending to counter the tendency of the private sector firms and workers to reduce their spending. In an economic upturn, it should reduce its expenditure and increase taxes, so that it can prevent demand from outstripping supply.

Reflecting this intellectual origin, until the 1970s, the main aim of macroeconomic policies was reducing the magnitude of the swings in the level of economic activity – known as the business cycle. But since the rise of neo-liberalism, and its 'monetarist' approach to macroeconomics, in the 1980s, the focus of macroeconomic policies has radically changed. The 'monetarists' are called as such because they believe that prices rise when too much money is chasing after a given quantity of goods and services. They also argue that price stability (i.e., keeping inflation low) is the foundation of prosperity and, therefore, that monetary discipline (that is required for price stability) should be the paramount goal of macroeconomic policy.

When it comes to developing countries, the need for monetary discipline is even more emphasized by the Bad Samaritans. They believe that most developing countries do not have the self-discipline to 'live within their means'; it is alleged that they print money and borrow as if there were no tomorrow. Domingo Cavallo, a famous (or infamous, after the financial collapse in 2002) former finance minister of Argentina, once described his own country as a 'rebel teenager' who could not control his behaviour and needed to 'grow up'.[2] Therefore, the firm guiding hand of the IMF is seen as crucial by the Bad Samaritans in securing macroeconomic stability and hence growth in these countries. Unfortunately, the macro-economic policies promoted by the IMF have produced almost the exact opposite effect.

'Mugger, armed robber and hit man'

Neo-liberals see inflation as public enemy number one. Ronald Reagan once put it most graphically: 'inflation is as violent as a mugger, as frightening as an armed robber and as deadly as a hit man'.[3] They believe that the lower the rate of inflation is, the better it is. Ideally, they want zero inflation. At most, they would accept a very low single-digit rate of inflation. Stanley Fischer, the Northern-Rhodesia-born American economist, who was the chief economist of the IMF between 1994 and 2001, explicitly recommended 1–3% as the target inflation rate.[4] But why is inflation considered so harmful?

To begin with, it is argued that inflation is a form of stealth tax that unjustly robs people of their hard-earned income. The late Milton Friedman, the guru of monetarism, argued that 'inflation is the one form of taxation that can be imposed without legislation'.[5] But the illegitimacy of 'inflation tax', and the 'distributive injustice' arising out of it, is only the beginning of the problem.

Neo-liberals argue that inflation is bad for economic growth as well.[6] Most of them would hold that the lower a country's rate of inflation, the higher its economic growth is likely to be. The thinking behind this is as follows: investment is essential for growth; investors do not like uncertainty; so we must keep the economy stable, which means keeping prices flat; thus low inflation is a prerequisite of investment and growth. This argument has had a particularly strong appeal in those Latin American countries, where memories of disastrous hyperinflation in the 1980s combined with collapse in economic growth were strong (especially Argentina, Bolivia, Brazil, Nicaragua and Peru).

Neo-liberal economists argue that two things are essential in achieving low inflation. First, there should be monetary discipline – the central bank should not increase the money supply over and above what is absolutely necessary to support real growth in the economy. Second, there should be financial prudence – no government should live beyond its means (more on this later).

In order to achieve monetary discipline, the central bank, which controls the money supply, should be made to pursue price stability single-mindedly. Fully embracing this argument, for example, New Zealand in the 1980s indexed the central bank governor's salary to the rate of inflation in inverse proportion, so that he/she would have a very personal interest in controlling inflation. Once we ask the central bank to consider other things, like growth and employment, the argument goes, the political pressure on it would be unbearable. Stanley Fischer argues: 'A central bank given multiple and general goals may choose among them and will certainly be subject to political pressures to shift among its goals depending on the state of the electoral cycle'.[7] The best way to prevent this from happening is to 'protect' the central bank from politicians (who do not understand economics very well and, more importantly, have short time-horizons) by making it 'politically independent'. This orthodox belief in the virtues of central bank independence is so strong that the IMF often makes it a condition for its loans, as, for example, it did in the agreement with Korea following the country's currency crisis in 1997.

In addition to monetary discipline, neo-liberals have traditionally emphasized the importance of government prudence – unless
the government lives within its means, the resulting budget deficits
would cause inflation by creating more demands than the economy
can meet.[8] More recently, following the wave of developing country
financial crises in the late 1990s and the early 2000s, it was recognized that governments do not have a monopoly in 'living beyond
one's means'. In those crises, much of the over-borrowing was by
private-sector firms and consumers, rather than by governments. As
a result, an increasing emphasis has been put on the 'prudential
regulations' of the banks and other financial-sector firms. The most
important among these is the so-called capital adequacy ratio for
banks, recommended by the BIS (Bank for International Settlements),
the club of central banks based in the Swiss city of Basel (more on
this later).*

There is inflation and there is inflation

Inflation is bad for growth – this has become one of the most widely
accepted economic nostrums of our age. But see how you feel about
it after digesting the following piece of information.

During the 1960s and the 1970s, Brazil's average inflation rate was
42% a year.[9] Despite this, Brazil was one of the fastest growing
economies in the world for those two decades – its *per capita* income
grew at 4.5% a year during this period. In contrast, between 1996 and
2005, during which time Brazil embraced the neo-liberal orthodoxy,
especially in relation to macroeconomic policy, its inflation rate averaged a much lower 7.1% a year. But during this period, *per capita*
income in Brazil grew at only 1.3% a year.

If you are not entirely persuaded by the Brazilian case – understandable, given that hyperinflation went side by side with low growth
in the 1980s and the early 1990s – how about this? During its 'miracle'
years, when its economy was growing at 7% a year in *per capita* terms,

---

* This ratio recommends that the total lending of a bank should not be more than
a certain multiple of its capital base (12.5 is the recommended ratio).

Korea had inflation rates close to 20%–17.4% in the 1960s and 19.8% in the 1970s. These were rates higher than those found in several Latin American countries, and totally contrary to the cultural stereotypes of the hyper-saving, prudent East Asian versus fun-loving, profligate Latinos (more on cultural stereotypes in chapter 9). In the 1960s, Korea's inflation rate was *much higher* than that of five Latin American countries (Venezuela, Bolivia, Mexico, Peru and Colombia) and not much lower than that infamous 'rebel teenager', Argentina.[10] In the 1970s, the Korean inflation rate was higher than that found in Venezuela, Ecuador and Mexico, and not much lower than that of Colombia and Bolivia.[11] Are you still convinced that inflation is incompatible with economic success?

With these examples, I am not arguing that all inflation is good. When prices rise very fast, they undermine the very basis of rational economic calculation. The experience of Argentina in the 1980s and the early 1990s is quite illustrative in this regard.[12] In January 1977, a carton of milk cost 1 peso. Fourteen years later, the same container cost over 1 billion pesos. Between 1977 and 1991, inflation ran at an annual rate of 333%. There was a twelve-month period, ending in 1990, during which actual inflation was 20,266%. The story has it that, during this period, prices rose so fast that some supermarkets resorted to using blackboards rather than price tags. There is no question that this kind of price inflation makes long-range planning impossible. Without a reasonably long time-horizon, rational investment decisions become impossible. And without robust investment, economic growth becomes very difficult.

But there is a big logical jump between acknowledging the destructive nature of hyperinflation and arguing that the lower the rate of inflation, the better.[13] As the examples of Brazil and Korea show, the inflation rate does not have to be in the 1–3% range, as Stanley Fischer and most neo-liberals want, for an economy to do well. Indeed, even many neo-liberal economists admit that, below 10%, inflation does not seem to have any adverse effect on economic growth.[14] Two World Bank economists, Michael Bruno, once the chief economist, and William Easterly, have shown that, below 40%, there is no systematic correlation between a country's inflation rate and its growth rate.[15]

They even argue that, below 20%, higher inflation seemed to be associated with higher growth during some time periods.

In other words, there is inflation and there is inflation. High inflation is harmful, but moderate inflation (up to 40%) is not only not necessarily harmful, but may even be compatible with rapid growth and employment creation. We may even say that some degree of inflation is inevitable in a dynamic economy. Prices change because the economy changes, so it is natural that prices go up in an economy where there are lots of new activities creating new demand.

But, if moderate inflation is not harmful, why are neo-liberals so obsessed with it? Neo-liberals would argue that all inflation – moderate or not – is still objectionable, because it disproportionately hurts people on fixed incomes – notably wage earners and pensioners, who are the most vulnerable sections of the population. Paul Volcker, the chairman of the US Federal Reserve Board (the US central bank) under Ronald Reagan (1979–87), argued: 'Inflation is thought of as a cruel, and maybe the cruellest, tax because it hits in a many-sectored way, in an unplanned way, and it hits the people on a fixed income hardest'.[16]

But this is only half the story. Lower inflation may mean that what the workers have already earned is better protected, but the policies that are needed to generate this outcome may reduce what they can earn in the future. Why is this? The tight monetary and fiscal policies that are needed to lower inflation, especially to a very low level, are likely also to reduce the level of economic activity, which, in turn, will lower the demand for labour and thus increase unemployment and reduce wages. So a tough control on inflation is a two-edged sword for workers – it protects their existing incomes better, but it reduces their future incomes. It is only the pensioners and others (including, significantly, the financial industry) whose incomes derive from financial assets with fixed returns for whom lower inflation is a pure blessing. Since they are outside the labour market, tough macroeconomic policies that lower inflation cannot adversely affect their future employment opportunities and wages, while the incomes they already have are better protected.

Neo-liberals have made a big deal out of the fact that inflation hurts the general public, as we can see from the earlier quote from Volcker. But this populist rhetoric obscures the fact that the policies needed to generate low inflation are likely to reduce the future earnings of most working people by reducing their employment prospects and wage rates.

The price of price stability

Upon taking power from the apartheid regime in 1994, the new ANC (African National Congress) government of South Africa declared that it would pursue an IMF-style macroeconomic policy. Such a cautious approach was considered necessary if it was not to scare away investors, given its leftwing, revolutionary history.

In order to maintain price stability, interest rates were kept high; at their peak in the late 1990s and the early 2000s, the real interest rates were 10–12%. Thanks to such tight monetary policy, the country has been able to keep its inflation rate during this period at 6.3% a year.[17] But this was achieved at a huge cost to growth and jobs. Given that the average non-financial firm in South Africa has a profit rate of less than 6%, real interest rates of 10–12% meant that few firms could borrow to invest.[18] No wonder the investment rate (as a proportion of GDP) fell from the historical 20-25% (it was once over 30% in the early 1980s) down to about 15%.[19] Considering such low levels of investment, the South African economy has not done too badly – between 1994 and 2005, its *per capita* income grew at 1.8% a year. But that is only 'considering . . .'

Unless South Africa is going to engage in a major programme of redistribution (which is neither politically feasible nor economically wise), the only way to reduce the huge gap in living standards between the racial groups in the country is to generate rapid growth and create more jobs, so that more people can join the economic mainstream and improve their living standards. Currently, the country has an *official* unemployment rate of 26–8%, one of the highest in the world*; a 1.8% annual growth rate is way too

* Unemployment rates in developing countries underestimate the true extent of unemployment, as many poor people cannot afford to remain unemployed (as there is no welfare state) and, therefore, end up working in extremely low-productivity jobs (e.g., selling trinkets on the street, catching doors for people for small changes). This is known as 'disguised unemployment' among economists.

inadequate to bring about a serious reduction in unemployment and poverty. In the last few years, the South African government has thankfully seen the folly of this approach and has brought the interest rates down, but real interest rates, at around 8%, are still too high for vigorous investment.

In most countries, firms outside the financial sector make a 3–7% profit.[20] Therefore, if real interest is above that level, it makes more sense for potential investors to put their money in the bank, or buy bonds, rather than invest it in a productive firm. Also taking into account all the trouble involved in managing productive enterprises – labour problems, problems with delivery of parts, trouble with payments by customers, etc. – the threshold rate may even be lower. Given that firms in developing countries have little capital accumulated internally, making borrowing more difficult means that firms cannot invest much. This results in low investment, which, in turn, means low growth and scarce jobs. This is what has happened in Brazil, South Africa and numerous other developing countries when they followed the Bad Samaritans' advice and pursued a very low rate of inflation.

However, the reader would be surprised to learn that the rich Bad Samaritan countries, which are so keen to preach to developing countries the importance of high real interest rates as a key to monetary discipline, themselves have resorted to lax monetary policies when they have needed to generate income and jobs. At the height of their post-Second-World-War growth boom, real interest rates in the rich countries were all very low – or even negative. Between 1960 and '73, the latter half of the 'Golden Age of Capitalism' (1950–1973), when all of today's rich nations achieved high investment and rapid growth, the average real interest rates were 2.6% in Germany, 1.8% in France, 1.5% in the USA, 1.4% in Sweden and -1.0% in Switzerland.[21]

Monetary policy that is too tight lowers investment. Lower investment slows down growth and job creation. This may not be a huge problem for rich countries with already high standards of living, generous welfare state provision and low poverty, but it is a disaster for developing countries that desperately need more income and jobs and often are trying to deal with a high degree of income inequality without resorting to a large-scale redistribution programme that, anyway, may create more problems than it solves.

Given the costs of pursuing a restrictive monetary policy, giving independence to the central bank with the sole aim of controlling inflation is the last thing a developing country should do, because it will institutionally entrench monetarist macroeconomic policy that is particularly unsuitable for developing countries. This is all the more so when there is actually *no* clear evidence that greater central bank independence even lowers the rate of inflation in developing countries, let alone helps to achieve other desirable aims, like higher growth and lower unemployment.[22]

It is a myth that central bankers are non-partisan technocrats. It is well known that they tend to listen very closely to the view of the financial sector and implement policies that help it, if necessary at the cost of the manufacturing industry or wage-earners. So, giving them independence allows them to pursue policies that benefit their own natural constituencies without appearing to do so. The policy bias would be even worse if we explicitly tell them that they should not worry about any policy objectives other than inflation.

Moreover, central bank independence raises an important issue for democratic accountability (more on this in chapter 8). The flip side of the argument that central bankers can take good decisions only because their jobs do not depend on making the electorate happy is that they can pursue policies that hurt the majority of people with impunity – especially if they are told not to worry about anything other than the rate of inflation. Central bankers need to be supervised by elected politicians, so that they can be, even if at one remove, responsive to the popular will. This is exactly why the charter of the US Federal Reserve Board defines its first responsibility as 'conducting the nation's monetary policy by influencing the monetary and credit conditions in the economy in pursuit of *maximum employment, stable prices, and moderate long-term interest rates* [italics added]'[23] and why the Fed chairman is subject to regular grilling by Congress. Ironic, then, that the US government acts internationally as a Bad Samaritan and encourages developing countries to create an independent central banks solely focused on inflation.

When prudence isn't prudent

Gordon Brown prided himself on having earned the nickname 'the iron chancellor' during the ten years he spent in that post before becoming prime minister. This sobriquet used to be associated with the former German chancellor (prime minister), Otto von Bismarck, but, unlike Bismarck's 'ironmongery', which was in foreign policy, Brown's 'ironmongery' was in the area of public finance. He has been praised for his resolve in not giving in to the demand for deficit spending, coming from his supporters in the public sector, who were understandably clamouring for more money after years of Conservative budget cuts. Mr Brown constantly emphasized the importance of prudence in fiscal management, so much so that William Keegan, a leading British financial journalist, called his book on Brown's economic policy *The Prudence of Mr. Gordon Brown*. Prudence, it seems, has become the supreme virtue in a finance minister.

Emphasis on fiscal prudence has been a central theme in the neoliberal macroeconomics promoted by the Bad Samaritans. They argue that government should not live beyond its means and must always balance its budget. Deficit spending, they argue, only leads to inflation and undermines economic stability, which, in turn, reduces growth and diminishes the living standards of people on fixed income.

Once again, who can argue against prudence? But, as in the case of inflation, the real question is what exactly it means to be prudent. For one thing, being prudent does not mean that the government has to balance its books every year, as is preached to developing countries by the Bad Samaritans. The government budget may have to be balanced, but this needs to be achieved over a business cycle, rather than every year. The year is an extremely artificial unit of time in economic terms, and there is nothing sacred about it. Indeed, if we followed this logic, why not tell governments to balance its books every month or even every week? As Keynes's central message had it, what is important is that, over the business cycle, the government acts as a counterweight to the behaviour of the private sector, engages in deficit spending during economic downturns and generates a budget surplus during economic upturns.

For a developing country, it may even make sense to run a budget deficit on a permanent basis in the medium term, as long as the resulting debt is sustainable. Even at the level of individuals, it is perfectly prudent to borrow money when you are studying or raising a young family and to re-pay the debt when your earning power is higher. Similarly, it makes sense for a developing country to 'borrow from future generations' by running budget deficits in order to invest beyond its current means and thereby accelerate economic growth. If the country succeeds in accelerating its growth, future generations will be rewarded with higher standards of living than would have been possible without such government deficit spending.

Despite all this, the IMF is obsessed with developing country governments balancing the books every year, regardless of business cycles or longer-term development strategy. So it imposes budget balancing conditions, or even the requirement to run a surplus on countries in macroeconomic crisis that could actually benefit from deficit spending by the government.

For example, when Korea signed an agreement with the IMF in December 1997 in the wake of a currency crisis, it was required to generate budget surplus equivalent to 1% of GDP. Given that a huge exodus of foreign capital was already pushing the country into a deep recession, it should have been allowed to increase government budget deficits. If any country could afford to do this, it was Korea – at the time, it had one of the smallest stocks of government debt as a proportion of GDP in the world, including all the rich nations. Despite this, the IMF barred the country from using deficit spending. Little wonder that the economy nose-dived. In the early months of 1998, over 100 firms *a day* were going bankrupt and the unemployment rate nearly trebled – no surprise, then, that some Koreans dubbed the IMF 'I'M Fired'. Only when this uncontrollable downward economic spiral looked set to continue did the IMF relent and allow the Korean government to run a budget deficit – but only a very small one (up to 0.8% of GDP).[24] In a more extreme example, following its financial crisis in the same year, Indonesia was also instructed by the IMF to cut government spending, especially food subsidies. When combined with a rise in interest rates to 80%, the result was widespread corporate bankruptcy, mass unemployment and urban riots. As a result, Indonesia saw a massive 16% fall in output in 1998.[25]

If they were in similar circumstances, the rich Bad Samaritan countries would never do what they tell the poor countries to do. Instead they would cut interest rates and increase government deficit spending in order to boost demand. No rich country finance minister would be stupid enough to raise interest rates and run a budget surplus during economic downturns. When the US economy was reeling from the aftermath of the burst of the so-called dot.com bubble and the September 11 bombing of the World Trade Center at the beginning of the 21st century, the solution taken by the supposedly 'fiscally responsible', anti-Keynesian republican government of George W. Bush was – you've guessed it – government deficit spending (combined with a monetary policy of unprecedented laxity). In 2003 and 2004, the US budget deficit reached nearly 4% of its GDP. Other rich country governments have done the same. During 1991–1995, a period of economic downturn, the ratio of government deficit to GDP was 8% in Sweden, 5.6% in the UK, 3.3% in the Netherlands and 3% in Germany.[26]

The 'prudent' financial sector policies recommended by the Bad Samaritans have also created other problems for macroeconomic management in developing countries. The BIS capital adequacy ratio, which I explained above, has been particularly important in this regard.

The BIS ratio requires that a bank's lending changes in line with changes in its capital base. Given that the prices of the assets that make up a bank's capital base go up when the economy is doing well and fall when it is not, this means that the capital base grows and shrinks along with the economic cycle. As a result, banks are able to increase their loans in good times even without any inherent improvement in the quality of the assets that they hold, simply because their capital base expands due to asset price inflation. This feeds into the boom, overheating the economy. During a downturn, the capital base of the banks shrinks, as asset prices fall, forcing them to call in loans, which, in turn, pushes the economy down further. While it may be prudent for individual banks to observe the BIS capital adequacy ratio, if all the banks follow it, the business cycle will be greatly magnified, ultimately hurting the banks themselves.*

When the economic fluctuations become bigger, the swings in fiscal policy have to become bigger too, if they are to play an adequate counter-cyclical role. But big adjustments in government spending generate problems. On the one hand, a big increase in government spending during an economic downturn makes it more likely that the spending goes into ill-prepared projects. On the other hand, making large cuts in govern-ment spending during an economic upturn is difficult due to political resistance. Given this, the greater volatility created by strictly enforcing the BIS ratio (and the opening-up of capital markets, as discussed in chapter 4) has actually made good fiscal policy more difficult to conduct.[27]

Keynesianism for the rich, monetarism for the poor

Gore Vidal, the American writer, once famously described the American economic system as 'free enterprise for the poor and socialism for the rich'.[28] Macroeconomic policy on the global scale is a bit like that. It is Keynesianism for the rich countries and monetarism for the poor.

When the rich countries get into recession, they usually relax mone-tary policy and increase budget deficits. When the same thing happens in developing countries, the Bad Samaritans, through the IMF, force them to raise interest rates to absurd levels and balance their budgets, or even generate budget surplus – even if these actions treble unemploy-ment and spark riots in the streets. When Korea was in its biggest-ever financial crisis in 1997, the IMF allowed the country to run budget deficits equivalent to only 0.8% of GDP (and, at that, after trying the opposite for several months, with disastrous consequences); when Sweden had a similar problem (due to the ill-managed opening-up of its capital market,

---

* More recently, the BIS has suggested an even more 'prudent' system called BIS II, where the loans are weighted by their risk rating. For example, riskier loans (e.g., corporate lending) need to be supported by a larger capital base than safer loans (e.g., mortgaged loans for house purchase) of the same nominal value. This will be particularly bad for developing countries, whose firms have low credit rating, as this means that banks would have a particular incentive to reduce their lending to developing country corporations.

as was the case with Korea in 1997) in the early 1990s, its budget deficits were, in proportional terms, ten times that (8% of its GDP).

Ironically, when the citizens of developing countries voluntarily tighten their belts, they are derided for not understanding basic Keynesian economics. For example, when some Korean housewives campaigned for voluntary austerity measures, including serving smaller meals at home in the wake of the 1997 financial crisis, the *Financial Times* correspondent in Korea sneered at their stupidity, saying that such actions 'could deepen the country's plunge into recession since it would further reduce the demand needed to bolster growth'.[29] But what is the difference between what these Korean housewives were doing and the spending cuts imposed by the IMF, which the *FT* correspondent thought were eminently sensible?

The Bad Samaritans have imposed macroeconomic policies on developing countries that seriously hamper their ability to invest, grow and create jobs in the long run. The categorical – and simplistic – denunciation of 'living beyond one's means' has made it impossible for them to 'borrow to invest' in order to accelerate economic growth. If we categorically denounce people for living beyond their means, we should, amongst other things, condemn young people for borrowing to invest in their career development or in their children's education. That cannot be right. Living beyond one's means may or may not be right; it all depends on the stage of development that the country is in and the use to which the borrowed money is put.

Mr Cavallo, the Argentine finance minister, may have been right in saying that developing countries are like 'rebel teenagers' who need to 'grow up'. But acting like a grown-up is not really growing up. The teenager needs to get an education and find a proper job; it is not enough just to pretend that he is grown up and quit his school so that he can increase his savings. Similarly, in order really to 'grow up', it is not enough for developing countries to use policies that suit 'grown-up' countries. What they need to do is to invest in their future. In order to do that, they should be allowed to pursue macroeconomic policies that are *more* pro-investment and pro-growth than the ones used by the rich countries, and that are *a lot more* aggressive than those they are allowed to pursue today by the Bad Samaritans.

CHAPTER 8

Zaire vs Indonesia

Should we turn our backs on corrupt and undemocratic countries?

Zaire: In 1961, Zaire (now the Democratic Republic of the Congo) was a desperately poor country with a *per capita* annual income of $67. Mobutu Sese Seko came to power in a military coup in 1965 and ruled until 1997. He is estimated to have stolen $5 billion during his 32-year rule, or about 4.5 times the country's national income in 1961 ($1.1 billion).

Indonesia: In that same year, with a *per capita* annual income of only $49, Indonesia was even poorer than Zaire. Mohamed Suharto came to power in a military coup in 1966 and ruled until 1998. He is estimated to have stolen at least $15 billion during his 32-year rule. Some suggest the figure may even have been as high as $35 billion. His children became some of the country's richest business people. If we take the mid-point of these two estimates ($25 billion), Suharto has stolen the equivalent of 5.2 times his country's national income in 1961 ($4.8 billion).

Zaire's income *per capita* in purchasing power terms in 1997, when Mobutu was deposed, was *one third* of its level in 1965, when he came to power. In 1997, the country stood 141st among the 174 countries for which the UN calculated a 'human development index' (HDI). The HDI takes into account not only income but also 'quality of life' measured by life expectancy and literacy.

Considering the corruption statistics, Indonesia should have performed even worse than Zaire. Yet where Zaire's living standards *fell* by three times during Mobutu's rule, Indonesia's *rose* by more than three times during Suharto's rule. Its HDI ranking in 1997 was 105th – not the score of a 'miracle' economy, but creditable nonetheless, especially considering where it had started.

The Zaire-Indonesia contrast shows the limitations of the increasingly popular view propagated by the Bad Samaritans that corruption is one of the biggest, if not necessarily *the* biggest, obstacle to economic development. The argument goes that there is no point in helping poor countries with corrupt leaders, because they will 'do a Mobutu' and waste the money. This view is reflected in the World Bank's recent anti-corruption drive, under the leadership of former US deputy defence secretary Paul Wolfowitz, who declared: 'The fight against corruption is a part of the fight against poverty, not just because corruption is wrong and bad but because it really retards economic development'.[1] During Wolfowitz's leadership, from July 2005 to June 2007, the World Bank suspended loan disbursements to several developing countries on grounds of corruption.[2]

Corruption is a big problem in many developing countries. But the Bad Samaritans are using it as a convenient justification for the reduction in their aid commitments, despite the fact that cutting aid will hurt the poor more than it will a country's dishonest leaders, especially in the poorst countries (which tend to be more corrupt, for reasons I shall explain).[3] Moreover, they are increasingly using corruption as an 'explanation' for the failures of the neo-liberal policies that they have promoted over the past two and a half decades. Those policies have failed because they were wrong, not because they have been overwhelmed by local anti-developmental factors, like corruption or 'wrong' culture (as I will discuss in the next chapter), contrary to what is becoming increasingly popular to argue among the Bad Samaritans.

Does corruption hurt economic development?

Corruption is a violation of the trust vested by its 'stakeholders' in the holders of offices in any organization, be it a government, a corporation, a trade union or even an NGO (non-governmental organization).

True, there can be instances of 'noble cause corruption'; one such example being Oscar Schindler's bribing of Nazi officials that saved the lives of hundreds of Jews, as immortalized in the Steven Spielberg movie, *Schindler's List*.[4] But they are the exceptions, and corruption is, in general, morally objectionable.

Life would be simpler if morally objectionable things like corruption also had unambiguously negative economic consequences. But the reality is a lot messier. Looking at just the last half a century, there are certainly countries, like Zaire under Mobutu or Haiti under Duvalier, whose economy was ruined by rampant corruption. At the other extreme, we have countries like Finland, Sweden and Singapore, which are known for their cleanliness and have also done very well economically. Then we have countries like Indonesia that were very corrupt but performed well economically. Some other countries – Italy, Japan, Korea, Taiwan and China come to mind – have done even better than Indonesia during this period, despite ingrained corruption on a widespread and often massive scale (though not as serious as in Indonesia).

And corruption is not just a 20th-century phenomenon. Most of today's rich countries successfully industrialised despite the fact that their public life was spectacularly corrupt.* In Britain and France, the open sale of public offices (not to speak of honours) was a common practice at least until the 18th century.[5] In Britain, until the early 19th century, it was considered perfectly normal for ministers to 'borrow' their departmental funds for personal profit.[6] Until 1870, appointments of high-ranking civil servants in Britain were made on the basis of patronage, rather than merit. The government chief whip (equivalent to the majority leader in the US Congress) was then actually called the patronage secretary of the Treasury, because (distributing)

---

* Their corruption was such that the very definition of corruption was different from what prevails today. When he was accused of corruption in Parliament in 1730, Robert Walpole freely admitted that he had great estates and asked: 'having held some of the most lucrative offices for nearly 20 years, what could anyone expect, unless it was a crime to get estates by great office'. He turned the tables on his accusers by asking them, 'how much greater a crime it must be to get an estate out of lesser offices.' See Nield (2002), *Public Corruption – The Dark Side of Social Evolution* (Anthem Press, London), p. 62.

patronage *was* his main job.[7] In the USA, the 'spoils' system, where public offices were allocated to the loyalists of the ruling party regardless of their professional qualifications, became entrenched in the early 19th century and was particularly rampant for a few decades after the Civil War. Not a single US federal bureaucrat was appointed through an open, competitive process until the 1883 Pendleton Act.[8] But this was a period when the US was one of the fastest growing economies in the world.

The electoral process was also spectacularly venal. In Britain, bribery, 'treating' (typically done by giving free drinks in party-affiliated public houses), promises of jobs and threats to voters were widespread in elections until the Corrupt and Illegal Practices Act of 1883. Even after the Act, electoral corruption persisted well into the 20th century in local elections. In the US, public officials were often used for party political campaigns (including being forced to donate to electoral campaign funds). Electoral fraud and vote-buying were widespread. Elections in the US, where there were a lot of immigrants, involved turning ineligible aliens into instant citizens who could vote, which was done 'with no more solemnity than, and quite as much celerity as, is displayed in converting swine into pork in a Cincinnati packing house', according to the *New York Tribune* in 1868.[9] With expensive election campaigns, it was no big surprise that many elected officials actively sought bribes. In the late 19th century, legislative corruption in the US, especially in state assemblies, got so bad that the future US president Theodore Roosevelt lamented that the New York assemblymen, who engaged in the open selling of votes to lobbying groups, 'had the same idea about Public Life and Civil Service that a vulture has of a dead sheep'.[10]

How is it possible that corruption has such different economic consequences in different economies? Many corrupt countries do disastrously (e.g., Zaire, Haiti), some others have done decently (e.g., Indonesia), while still others do very well (e.g., the US in the late 19th century and post-Second-World-War East Asian countries). In order to answer the question, we need to open the 'black box' called corruption and understand its inner workings.

A bribe is a transfer of wealth from one person to another. It does not *necessarily* have negative effects on economic efficiency and growth. If the minister (or some other public official) taking a bribe from a capitalist is investing that money in another project that is at least as productive as that which the capitalist would have otherwise invested in (had he not had to pay the bribe), the venality involved may have no effect on the economy in terms of efficiency or growth. The only difference is that the capitalist is poorer and the minister richer – i.e., it is a question of income distribution.

Of course, it is always possible that the money is not used by the minister as productively as by the capitalist. The minister may blow his ill-gotten gains in conspicuous consumption, while the capitalist might have invested the same money wisely. This is often the case. But it cannot be assumed to be so *a priori*. Historically, many bureaucrats and politicians have proved to be wily investors, while many capitalists squandered their fortunes. If the minister uses the money more effectively than the capitalist, corruption may even help economic growth.

A critical issue in this regard is whether the dirty money stays in the country. If the bribe is deposited in a Swiss bank, it cannot contribute to creating further income and jobs through investment – which is one way in which such odious money can partially 'redeem' itself. And, indeed, this is one of the main reasons for the difference between Zaire and Indonesia. In Indonesia, the money from corruption mostly stayed inside the country, creating jobs and incomes. In Zaire, much of the corrupt money was shipped out of the country. If you must have corrupt leaders, you at least want them to keep their loot at home.

Whether or not the income transfer due to corruption results in a more (or less) productive use of the money paid out as bribes, corruption can create a variety of economic problems by 'distorting' government decisions.

For example, if a bribe allows a less efficient producer to get the licence to build, say, a new steel mill, it will lower the economy's efficiency. But, once again, such an outcome is not a foregone conclusion. It has been argued that the producer who is willing to pay the highest bribe is likely to be the most efficient producer – as the producer who expects to make more money out of the licence would be, by definition, willing to offer the bigger bribe to secure the licence. If that is the case, giving the licence to the producer paying the highest bribe is essentially the same as a government auctioning the licence off and is thus the best way to choose the most efficient producer – except that the potential auction income goes to the unscrupulous official, rather than to the state exchequer, as it would have done in a transparent auction. Of course, this 'bribing as an unofficial (and efficient) auction' argument falls apart if the more efficient producers are morally upright and refuse to pay bribes, in which case corruption will allow a less efficient producer to get the licence.

Corruption may also 'distort' government decisions by hampering regulation. If a water company supplying sub-standard water can continue the practice by bribing the relevant officials, there will be negative economic consequences – a higher incidence of water-borne diseases that will increase health care costs and, in turn, reduce labour productivity, for example.

But if the regulation was an 'unnecessary' one, corruption may increase economic efficiency. For example, before the legal reform in 2000, opening a factory in Vietnam required the submission of dozens of documents (including the applicant's character references and medical certificates), including 20 or so issued by the government; it is said to have taken between six and twelve months to prepare all the paperwork and get all the necessary approvals.[11] In such a situation, it may be better if the potential investor bribes the relevant government officials and gets the licence quickly. The investor wins by earning more money, it may be argued, the consumer gains by having his demand satisfied more quickly, and the government official gains by getting richer (though there is a breach of confidence and the government loses legitimate revenue). For this reason, it has often been argued that bribery may enhance the economic efficiency of an over-regulated economy by re-introducing market forces, if through illegal means. This is what the American veteran political scientist Samuel Huntington meant in his classic passage: 'In terms of economic growth, the only thing worse than a society with a rigid, over-centralized dishonest bureaucracy is one with a rigid, over-centralized honest bureaucracy.'[12] Once again, bribery that lets enterprises subvert regulations may or may not be economically beneficial (if still illegal and at best morally ambiguous), depending on the nature of the regulation.

So the economic consequences of corruption depend on which decisions the corrupt act affects, how the bribes are used by the recipients and what would have been done with the money had there been no corruption. I could have also talked about things like the predictability of corruption (e.g., is there a 'fixed price' for a certain kind of 'service' by the corrupt official?) or the degree of 'monopoly' in the bribery market (e.g., how many people do you have to bribe to get a licence?). But the point is that the combined result of all these factors is difficult to predict. This is why we observe such vast differences across countries in terms of the relationship between corruption and economic performance.

Prosperity and honesty

If the impact of corruption on economic development is ambiguous, how about the latter's impact on the former? My answer is that economic development makes it easier to reduce corruption, but that there is no automatic relationship. Quite a lot depends on the conscious efforts made to reduce corruption.

As I discussed earlier, history shows that, at earlier stages of economic development, corruption is difficult to control. The fact that today no country that is very poor is very clean suggests that a country has to rise above absolute poverty before it can significantly reduce venality in the system. When people are poor, it is easy to buy their dignity – starving people find it difficult not to sell their votes for a bag of flour, while under-paid civil servants will often fail to resist the temptation to take a bribe. But it is not just a matter of personal dignity. There are also more structural causes.

Economic activities in developing countries are mostly dispersed across a large number of small units (e.g., small peasant farms, corner shops, hawkers' stalls and backyard workshops). This provides a fertile ground for petty corruption, which may be too numerous to detect for under-resourced developing country governments. These small economic units also have very poor, if at all, accounts, making them 'invisible' for tax purposes. This invisibility combines with the lack of administrative resources within revenue services to produce low tax collection capacity. This inability to collect taxes limits the government budget, which, in turn, encourages corruption in a number of ways.

First of all, low government revenue makes it difficult to pay decent salaries to public officials, which makes them vulnerable to bribery. It is actually quite remarkable how so many developing country government officials live honestly despite being paid a pittance. But, the poorer the salaries are, the higher the chance that officials will succumb to the temptation. Also, a limited government budget leads to a weak (or even absent) welfare state. So the poor have to rely on patronage from politicians who give out loyalty-based welfare benefits in return for votes. In order to do this, the politicians need money, so they take bribes from corporations, national and international, that need their favour. Finally, a limited government budget makes it difficult for the government to spend resources on fighting corruption. In detecting and prosecuting dishonest officials, the government needs to hire (in-house or from outside) expensive accountants and lawyers. Fighting corruption is not cheap.

With better living conditions, people can achieve higher behavioural standards. Economic development also increases the capacity of the government to collect taxes – as economic activities become more 'visible' and as government administrative capacity rises. This, in turn, allows it to increase public salaries, expand the welfare state and spend more resources on detecting and punishing malfeasance among officials – all of which help reduce corruption.

Having said all this, it is important to point out that economic development does not automatically create a more honest society. For example, the US was more corrupt in the late 19th century than earlier in that century, as I mentioned earlier. Moreover, some rich countries are far more corrupt than poor ones. To illustrate this point, let's look at the Corruption Perception Index published in 2005 by Transparency International, the influential anti-corruption watchdog.* According to the index, Japan (*per capita* income $37,180 in 2004) was jointly ranked 21st with Chile ($4,910), a country with barely 13% of its income. Italy ($26,120) ranked joint 40th with Korea ($13,980), with half its income level, and Hungary ($8,270), with one-third its income level. Botswana ($4,340) and Uruguay ($3,950), despite having *per capita* incomes only about 15% that of Italy or 30% that of Korea, ranked well *ahead* of them, at joint 32nd. These examples suggest that economic development does not automatically reduce corruption. Deliberate actions need to be taken to achieve that goal.[13]

Too many market forces

Not only are the Bad Samaritans using corruption as an unwarranted 'explanation' for the failures of neo-liberal policies (for they believe that those policies cannot be wrong) but the solution to the corruption problem that they have been promoting has often worsened, rather than alleviated, it.

The Bad Samaritans, basing their argument on neo-liberal

---

* The index should be taken with a grain of salt. As the name makes it clear, it is only measuring the 'perception' revealed in surveys of technical experts and businessmen, who have their own limited knowledge and biases. The problem with such a subjective measure is well illustrated by the fact that the perceptions of corruption in the Asian countries affected by the 1997 financial crisis suddenly rose significantly after the crisis, despite having almost constantly fallen in the preceding decade (see H-J. Chang [2000], 'The Hazard of Moral Hazard – Untangling the Asian Crisis', *World Development*, vol. 28, no. 4). Also, what is perceived as corruption depends on the country, thus affecting the expert perception too. For example, in a lot of countries, US-style spoils disbursement of government jobs will be considered corrupt, but it is not considered so in the US. Applying, say, the Finnish definition will make the US more corrupt than is captured by the index (the US was ranked the 17th). Also, a lot of corruption in developing countries involves firms (or sometimes even governments) from rich countries paying bribes, which is *not* captured in the perception of corruption in the rich countries themselves. So the rich countries may be more corrupt than they appear, once we include their overseas activities. The index can be downloaded from http://www.transparency.org/content/download/1516/7919.

economics, say that the best way to tackle corruption is to introduce more market forces into both the private and the public sectors – a solution that neatly dovetails into their market-fundamentalist economic programme. They argue that freeing the market forces in the private sector – that is, deregulation – will not only increase economic efficiency but also reduce corruption by depriving politicians and bureaucrats of the very powers to allocate resources that give them the ability to extract bribes in the first place. In addition, the Bad Samaritans have implemented measures based on the so-called New Public Management (NPM), which tries to increase administrative efficiency and reduce corruption by introducing more market forces into the government itself – more frequent contracting out, a more active use of performance-related pay and short-term contracts and a more active exchange of personnel between the public and private sectors.

Unfortunately, NPM-inspired reforms have often increased, rather than reduced, corruption. Increased contracting out has meant more contracts with the private sector, creating new opportunities for bribes. The increased flow of people between the public and private sectors has had an even more insidious effect. Once lucrative private-sector employment becomes a possibility, public officials may be tempted to befriend future employers by bending, or even breaking, the rules for them. They may do this even without being paid for it right away. With no money changing hands, no law has been broken (and, therefore, no corruption has occurred) and, at most, the official can be accused of bad judgment. But the payoff is in the future. It may not even be made by the same corporations that benefited from the original decision. Having built up his reputation as a 'pro-business' person or, even more euphemistically, a 'reformer', he can later move to a plum job with a private law firm, a lobbying organization or even an international agency. He may even use his pro-business credentials to set up a private equity fund. The incentive to do favours for the private sector becomes all the greater if the careers of the civil servants are made insecure through short-term contracting in the name of increasing market discipline. If they know that they are not going to stay in the civil service very long, they will have all the more incentive to cultivate their future employment prospects.*

In addition to the impact of the introduction of New Public Management, neo-liberal policies have also indirectly, and unintentionally, increased corruption by promoting trade liberalization, which weakens government finances, which, in turn, makes corruption more likely and difficult to fight.[14]

Also, deregulation, another key component of the neo-liberal policy package, has increased corruption in the private sector. Private sector crookedness is often ignored in the economic literature because corruption is usually *defined* as the abuse of *public* office for personal gain.[15] But dishonesty exists in the private sector too. Financial deregulation and relaxation of accounting standards have led to insider trading and false accounting even in rich nations – recall cases like the energy company Enron, and the telecommunications company WorldCom and their accountancy firm Arthur Andersen in the 'Roaring Nineties' in the US.[16] Deregulation can also increase the power of private-sector monopolies, which expands the opportunities for their unscrupulous purchasing managers to take bribes from sub-contractors.

Corruption often exists because there are too many market forces, not too few. Corrupt countries have shadow markets in the wrong things, such as government contracts, jobs and licences. Indeed, it is only after they made the sale of things like government offices illegal that today's rich countries could significantly reduce profiteering through the abuse of public office. Unleashing more market forces through deregulation, as the neo-liberal orthodoxy constantly pushes for, may worsen the situation. This is why corruption has often *increased*, rather than decreased, in many developing countries following liberalization pushed by the Bad Samaritans. The extreme racketeering seen in the process of liberalization and privatization in

---

* The marked increase in corruption in post-Thatcher Britain, the pioneer of NPM, is a salutary lesson regarding market-based anti-corruption campaigns. Commenting on the experience, Robert Nield, a retired Cambridge economics professor and a member of the famous 1968 Fulton civil service reform committee, laments that 'I cannot think of another instance where a modern democracy has systematically undone the system by which incorrupt public services were brought into being'. See Nield (2002), *Public Corruption* (Anthem Press, London), p. 198.

post-communist Russia has become notorious, but similar phenomena have been observed in many developing countries.[17]

Democracy and the free market

In addition to corruption, there is another political issue that occupies an important place in the neo-liberal policy agenda. It is democracy. But democracy, especially its relationship with economic development, is a complex and highly charged issue. So, unlike on issues like free trade, inflation or privatization, there is no united position on it among the Bad Samaritans.

Some suggest that democracy is essential for economic development, as it protects citizens from arbitrary expropriation by the rulers; without such protection, there will be no incentive to accumulate wealth; thus the USAID argues that '[e]xpanding democracy improves individual opportunity for prosperity and improved well-being'.[18] Others think that democracy may be sacrificed if it becomes necessary in defence of a free market, as evidenced by the strong support offered by some neo-liberal economists to the Pinochet dictatorship in Chile. Still others think that democracy will naturally develop once the economy develops (which, of course, can be best achieved by free-trade, free-market policies), because it will produce an educated middle class that naturally wants democracy. Yet others sing the praises of democracy all the time but keep quiet when the undemocratic country in question is a 'friend' – in keeping with the *realpolitik* tradition represented by Franklin Roosevelt's famous comment on the Nicaraguan dictator, Anastasio Somoza, that 'he may be a son of a bitch, but he is our son of a bitch'.[19]

Despite this diversity of views, there is a strong consensus among neo-liberals that democracy and economic development reinforce each other. Of course, neo-liberals are not unique in holding such a view. But what distinguishes them is their belief that this relationship is mainly, if not exclusively, mediated by the (free) market. They argue that democracy promotes free markets, which, in turn, promote economic development, which then promotes democracy: 'The market underpins democracy, just as democracy should normally strengthen the market', writes Martin Wolf, the British financial journalist, in his renowned book, *Why Globalisation Works*.[20]

According to the neo-liberal view, democracy promotes free markets because a government that can be unseated without resorting to violent measures has to be restrained in its predatory behaviour. If they don't have to worry about losing power, rulers can impose excessive taxes with impunity and even confiscate private property, as numerous autocrats have done throughout history. When this happens, incentives to invest and generate wealth are destroyed and market forces distorted, impeding economic development. By contrast, under democracy, the predatory behaviour of the government is restrained and thus free markets can flourish, promoting economic development. In turn, free markets promote democracy because they lead to economic development, which produces wealth-holders independent of the government, who will demand a mechanism through which they can counter the arbitrary actions of the politicians – democracy. This is what the former US president Bill Clinton had in mind when he said in support of China's accession to the WTO: 'as China's people become more mobile, prosperous, and aware of alternative ways of life, they will seek greater say in the decisions that affect their lives'.[21]

Leaving aside for the moment the question as to whether the free market is the best vehicle for economic development (to which I have repeatedly said no throughout this book), can we at least say that democracy and (free) markets are, indeed, natural partners and reinforce each other?

The answer is no. Unlike what neo-liberals say, market and democracy clash at a fundamental level. Democracy runs on the principle of 'one man (one person), one vote'. The market runs on the principle of 'one dollar, one vote'. Naturally, the former gives equal weight to each person, regardless of the money she/he has. The latter gives greater weight to richer people. Therefore, democratic decisions usually subvert the logic of market. Indeed, most 19th-century liberals opposed democracy because they thought it was *not* compatible with a free market.[22] They argued that democracy would allow the poor majority to introduce policies that would exploit the rich minority (e.g., a progressive income tax, nationalization of private property), thus destroying the incentive for wealth creation.

Influenced by such thinking, all of today's rich countries initially gave voting rights only to those who owned more than a certain amount of property or earned enough income to pay more than a certain amount of tax. Some of them had qualifications related to literacy or even educational achievement (so, for example, in some German states, a university degree gave you one extra vote) – which were, of course, closely related to people's economic status anyway and were usually used in conjunction with property/tax conditions. So, in England, the supposed birthplace of modern democracy, only 18% of men could vote, even after the famous 1832 Reform Act.[23] In France, before the introduction of universal male suffrage in 1848 (the first in the world), only around 2% of the male population could vote due to restrictions regarding age (you had to be over 30) and, more importantly, payment of tax.[24] In Italy, even after the lowering of the voting age to 21 in 1882, only around two million men (equivalent to about 15% of the male population) could vote, due to tax payment and literacy requirements.[25] The economic qualification for suffrage was, then, the flip side of the famous colonial American slogan against the British, 'no taxation without representation' – there was also to be 'no representation without taxation'.

By pointing out the contradiction between democracy and market, I am not saying that market logic should be rejected. Under communism, total rejection of the 'one dollar, one vote' principle not only created economic inefficiency but also propagated inequities based on other criteria – political power, personal connections or ideological credentials. It should also be noted that money can be a greater leveller. It can work as a powerful solvent of undesirable prejudices against people of particular races, social castes or occupational groups. It is much easier to make people treat members of discriminated groups better if the latter have money (that is, when they are potential customers or investors). The fact that even the openly racist apartheid regime in South Africa gave the Japanese 'honorary white' status is a powerful testimony to the 'liberating' power of the market.

But, however positive market logic may be in some respects, we should not, and cannot, run society solely on the principle of 'one dollar, one vote'. Leaving everything to the market means that the rich may be able to realize even the most frivolous element of their desires, while the poor may not be able even to survive – thus the world spends twenty times more research money on slimming drugs than on malaria, which claims more than a million lives and debilitates millions more in developing countries every year. Moreover, there are certain things that should simply not be bought and sold – even for the sake of having healthy markets. Judicial decisions, public offices, academic degrees and qualifications for certain professions (lawyers, medical doctors, teachers, driving instructors) are such examples. If these things can be bought, there would be serious problems not just with the legitimacy of the society in question but also with economic efficiency: sub-standard medical doctors or unqualified teachers can lower the quality of the labour forces; venal judicial decisions will undermine the efficacy of the contract law.

Democracy and markets are both fundamental building blocks for a decent society. But they clash at a fundamental level. We need to balance them. When we add the fact that free markets are not good at promoting economic development (as I have shown throughout the book), it is difficult to say that there is a virtuous circle between democracy, the free market and economic development, contrary to what the Bad Samaritans argue.

When democracies undermine democracy

Free market policies promoted by the Bad Samaritans have brought more areas of our life under the 'one dollar, one vote' rule of market. In so far as there is a natural tension between free markets and democracy, this means that democracy is constrained by such policies, even if that was not the intention. But there is more. The Bad Samaritans have recommended policies that actively seek to undermine democracy in developing countries (although they would never put them in those terms).

The argument starts reasonably enough. Neo-liberal economists

worry that politics opens the door for perversion of market ration-
ality: inefficient firms or farmers may lobby the parliamentarians to
get tariffs and subsidies, imposing costs on the rest of society that has
to buy expensive domestic products; populist politicians may put pressure on the central bank to 'print money' in time for election campaign,
which causes inflation and hurts people in the longer run. So far, so
good.

The neo-liberal solution to this problem is to 'depoliticize' the
economy. They argue that the very scope of government activity
should be reduced – through privatization and liberalization – to a
minimal state. In those few areas where it is still allowed to operate,
the room for policy discretion should be minimized. It is argued that
such restraints are particularly needed in developing nations where
the leaders are less competent and more corrupt. Such restraints can
be provided by rigid rules that constrain government choices – for
example, a law requiring a balanced budget – or by the establishment of politically independent policy agencies – an independent
central bank, independent regulatory agencies and even an independent tax office (known as ARA, or autonomous revenue authority,
and tried in Uganda and Peru[26]). For developing countries, it is seen
as particularly important to sign up to international agreements –
for example, the WTO agreements, bilateral/regional free trade agreements or investment agreements – because their leaders are less
responsible and thus more likely to stray from the righteous path of
neo-liberal policy.

The first problem with this argument for de-politicization is the
assumption that we can clearly know where economics should end
and politics should begin. But that is not possible because markets
– the domain of economics – are political constructs themselves.
Markets are political constructs in so far as all property rights and
other rights that underpin them have political origins. The political origins of economic rights can be seen in the fact that many
of them that are seen as natural today were hotly contested politically in the past – examples include the right to own ideas (not
accepted by many before the introduction of intellectual property
rights in the 19th century) and the right not to have to work when

young (denied to many poor children).[27] When these rights were still politically contested, there were plenty of 'economic' arguments as to why honouring them was incompatible with the free market.[28] Given this, when neo-liberals propose de-politicizing the economy, they are presuming that the particular demarcation between economics and politics that they want to draw is the correct one. This is unwarranted.

More importantly for our concern in this chapter, in pushing for the depoliticization of the economy, the Bad Samaritans are undermining democracy. Depoliticization of policy decisions in a democratic polity means – let's not mince our words – weakening democracy. If all the really important decisions are taken away from democratically elected governments and put in the hands of un-elected technocrats in the 'politically independent' agencies, what is the point of having democracy? In other words, democracy is acceptable to neo-liberals only in so far as it does not contradict the free market; this is why some of them saw no contradiction between supporting the Pinochet dictatorship and praising democracy. To put it bluntly, they want democracy only if it is largely powerless – like the title of the book published is 1987 by Ken Livingstone, the current left-wing mayor of London, *If Voting Changed Anything They'd Abolish It*.[29]

Thus seen, like the old liberals, neo-liberals believe deep down that giving political power to those who 'do not have a stake' in the existing economic system will inevitably result in an 'irrational' modification of the *status quo* in terms of distribution of property (and other economic) rights. However, unlike their intellectual predecessors, neo-liberals live in an era when they cannot openly oppose democracy, so they try to do it by discrediting *politics in general*.[30] By discrediting politics in general, they gain legitimacy for their actions that take away decision powers from the democratically elected representatives. In doing so, neo-liberals have succeeded in diminishing the scope of democratic control without ever openly criticizing democracy itself. The consequence has been particularly damaging in developing countries, where the Bad Samaritans have been able to push through 'anti-democratic' actions well beyond what would be acceptable in rich countries (such as political independence for the tax office).*

Democracy and economic development

Democracy and economic development obviously influence each other, but the relationship is much more complex than what is envisaged in the neo-liberal argument, where democracy would promote economic development by making private property more secure and markets freer.

To begin with, given the fundamental tension between democracy and market, it is unlikely that democracy will promote economic development through promoting the free market. Indeed, the old liberals feared that democracy may discourage investment and thus growth (e.g., excessive taxation, nationalization of enterprises).[31] On the other hand, democracy may promote economic development through other channels. For example, democracy may re-direct government spending into more productive areas – e.g., away from military spending to education or infrastructure investment. This will help economic development. As another example, democracy may promote economic growth by creating the welfare state. Contrary to the popular perception, a well-designed welfare state, especially if combined with a good retraining programme, can reduce the cost of unemployment to the workers and thus make them less resistant to automation that raises productivity (it is not a coincidence that Sweden has the world's highest number of industrial robots per worker). I could mention

---

* All this is, of course, not to deny that a certain degree of de-politicization of the resource allocation process may be necessary. For one thing, unless the resource allocation process is at least, to a degree, accepted as 'objective' by the members of the society, the political legitimacy of the economic system itself may be threatened. Moreover, high costs would be incurred in search and bargaining activities if every allocative decision is regarded as potentially contestable, as was the case in the ex-communist countries. However, this is not the same as arguing, as the neo-liberals do, that no market under any circumstance should be subject to political modifications, because, in the final analysis, there is no market that can be really free from politics.

some more possible channels through which democracy may influence economic development, positively or negatively, but the point is that the relationship is very complex.

It is no wonder, then, that there is no systematic evidence either for or against the proposition that democracy helps economic development. Studies that have tried to identify statistical regularities across countries in terms of the relationship between democracy and economic growth have failed to come up with a systematic result either way.[32] Even at the individual country level, we see a huge diversity of outcomes. Some developing countries did terribly in economic terms under dictatorships – the Philippines under Marcos, Zaire under Mobutu or Haiti under Duvalier are the best-known examples. But there are cases like Indonesia under Suharto or Uganda under Museveni, where dictatorship resulted in decent, if not spectacular, economic performance. Then there are cases like South Korea, Taiwan, Singapore and Brazil in the 1960s and the 1970s or today's China that have done very well economically under dictatorship. By contrast, today's rich countries notched up their best-ever economic record when they significantly extended democracy between the end of the Second World War and the 1970s – during this period, many of them adopted universal suffrage (Australia, Belgium, Canada, Finland, France, Germany, Italy, Japan, Switzerland and the US), strengthened minority rights and intensified the dreaded 'exploitation' of the rich by the poor (such as nationalization of enterprises or a rise in progressive income tax to finance, among other things, a welfare state).

Of course, we don't need to show that democracy positively affects economic growth in order to be able to support it. As Amartya Sen, the Nobel Laureate economist, argues, democracy has an intrinsic value and should be a criterion in any reasonable definition of development.[33] Democracy contributes to building a decent society by making certain things immune to the 'one dollar, one vote' rule of the market – public offices, judicial decisions, educational qualifications, as I discussed earlier. Participation in democratic political processes has intrinsic values that may not be easily translated into monetary value. And so on. Therefore, even if democracy negatively affected economic growth, we may still support it for its intrinsic values. Especially when there is no evidence that it does, we may support it even more strongly.

If the impact of democracy on development is ambiguous, the impact of economic development on democracy seems more straightforward. It seems fairly safe to say that, in the long run, economic development brings democracy. But this broad picture should not obscure the fact that some countries have sustained democracy from when they are fairly poor, while many others have not become democracies until they are very rich. Without people actually fighting for it, democracy does not automatically grow out of economic prosperity.[34]

Norway was the second democracy in the world (it introduced universal suffrage in 1913, after New Zealand in 1907), despite the fact that it was one of the poorest economies in Europe at the time. By contrast, the US, Canada, Australia and Switzerland became democracies, even in the purely formal sense of giving everyone a vote, only in the 1960s and the 1970s, when they were already very rich. Canada gave native Americans voting rights only in 1960. Australia abandoned its 'White Australia' policy and allowed non-whites to vote as late as 1962. Only in 1965 did the Southern states in the US allow the African Americans to vote, thanks to the civil rights movement led by people like Martin Luther King, Jr.[35] Switzerland allowed women to vote as late as 1971 (even later if you count the two renegade cantons, Appenzell Ausser Rhoden and Appenzell Inner Rhoden, which refused to give women votes until 1989 and 1991 respectively). Similar observations may be made in relation to developing countries today. Despite being one of the world's poorest countries until recently, India has maintained democracy well for the last six decades, while Korea and Taiwan were not democracies until the late-1980s, when they had become fairly prosperous.

Politics and economic development

Corruption and lack of democracy are big problems in many developing countries. But the relationships between them and economic development are far more complex than the Bad Samaritans suggest.

The failure to think through the complexity of the corruption issue is, for example, why so many developing country politicians who come to power on an anti-corruption platform not only fail to clean up the system but often end up being ousted or even jailed for corruption themselves. Latin American presidents, like Brazil's Fernando Collor de Mello and Peru's Alberto Fujimori, come to mind. When it comes to democracy, the neo-liberal view that democracy promotes a free market, which, in turn, promotes economic development, is highly problematic. There is a strong tension between democracy and a free market, while a free market is unlikely to promote economic development. If democracy promotes economic development, it is usually through some other channel than the promotion of a free market, contrary to what the Bad Samaritans argue.

Moreover, what the Bad Samaritans have recommended in these areas have not solved the problems of corruption and lack of democracy. In fact, they have often made them worse. Deregulation of the economy in general, and the introduction of greater market forces in the management of the government more specifically, has often increased, rather than reduced, corruption. By forcing trade liberalization, the Bad Samaritans have also inadvertently encouraged corruption; the resulting fall in government revenue has depressed public salaries and thus encouraged petty corruption. While all the time paying lip service to democracy, the Bad Samaritans have promoted measures that have weakened democracy. Some of this happened through deregulation itself, which expanded the domain of the market and thus reduced the domain of democracy. But the rest of it happened through deliberate measures: binding governments to rigid domestic laws or international treaties, and giving political independence to the central bank and other government agencies.

Having once dismissed political factors as minor details that should not get in the way of good economics, neo-liberals have recently become very interested in them. The reason is obvious – their economic programme for developing countries as implemented by the Unholy Trinity of the IMF, World Bank and WTO has had spectacular failures (just think of Argentina in the 1990s) and very few successes.

Because it is unthinkable to the Bad Samaritans that free trade, privatization and the rest of their policies could be wrong, the 'explanation' for policy failure is increasingly found in non-policy factors, such as politics and culture.

In this chapter, I have shown how the neo-liberal attempt to explain the failures of their policies with political problems such as corruption and lack of democracy is not convincing. I have also pointed out that their alleged solutions to these problems have often made things worse. In the next chapter, I will turn to another non-policy factor, culture, which is rapidly becoming a fashionable explanation for development failure, thanks to the recent popularity of the idea of a 'clash of civilizations'.

CHAPTER 9

Lazy Japanese and thieving Germans

Are some cultures incapable of economic development?

Having toured lots of factories in a developing country, an Australian management consultant told the government officials who had invited him: 'My impression as to your cheap labour was soon disillusioned when I saw your people at work. No doubt they are lowly paid, but the return is equally so; to see your men at work made me feel that you are a very satisfied easy-going race who reckon time is no object. When I spoke to some managers they informed me that it was impossible to change the habits of national heritage.'

This Australian consultant was understandably worried that the workers of the country he was visiting did not have the right work ethic. In fact, he was being quite polite. He could have been blunt and just called them lazy. No wonder the country was poor – not dirt poor, but with an income level that was less than a quarter of Australia's.

For their part, the country's managers agreed with the Australian, but were smart enough to understand that the 'habits of national heritage', or culture, cannot be changed easily, if at all. As the 19th-century German economist-cum-sociologist Max Weber opined in his seminal work, *The Protestant Work Ethic and the Spirit of Capitalism*, there are some cultures, like Protestantism, that are simply better suited to economic development than others.

The country in question, however, was Japan in 1915.[1] It doesn't feel quite right that someone from Australia (a nation known today for its ability to have a good time) could call the Japanese lazy. But this is how most westerners saw Japan a century ago.

In his 1903 book, *Evolution of the Japanese*, the American missionary

Sidney Gulick observed that many Japanese 'give an impression . . . of being lazy and utterly indifferent to the passage of time'.[2] Gulick was no casual observer. He lived in Japan for 25 years (1888–1913), fully mastered the Japanese language and taught in Japanese universities. After his return to the US, he was known for his campaign for racial equality on behalf of Asian Americans. Nevertheless, he saw ample confirmation of the cultural stereotype of the Japanese as an 'easy-going' and 'emotional' people who possessed qualities like 'lightness of heart, freedom from all anxiety for the future, living chiefly for the present'.[3] The similarity between this observation and that of today's Africa, in this case by an African himself – Daniel Etounga-Manguelle, a Cameroonian engineer and writer – is striking: 'The African, anchored in his ancestral culture, is so convinced that the past can only repeat itself that he worries only superficially about the future. However, without a dynamic perception of the future, there is no planning, no foresight, no scenario building; in other words, no policy to affect the course of events'.[4]

After her tour of Asia in 1911–1912, Beatrice Webb, the famous leader of British Fabian socialism, described the Japanese as having 'objectionable notions of leisure and a quite intolerable personal independence'.[5] She said that, in Japan, 'there is evidently no desire to teach people to think'.[6] She was even more scathing about my ancestors. She described the Koreans as '12 millions of dirty, degraded, sullen, lazy and religionless savages who slouch about in dirty white garments of the most inept kind and who live in filthy mudhuts'.[7] No wonder she thought that '[i]f anyone can raise the Koreans out of their present state of barbarism I think the Japanese will', despite her rather low opinion of the Japanese.[8]

This was not just a western prejudice against eastern peoples. The British used to say similar things about the Germans. Before their economic take-off in the mid-19th century, the Germans were typically described by the British as 'a dull and heavy people'.[9] 'Indolence' was a word that was frequently associated with the Germanic nature.[10] Mary Shelley, the author of *Frankenstein*, wrote in exasperation after a particularly frustrating altercation with her German coach-driver: 'the Germans never hurry'.[11] It wasn't just the British. A French manufacturer who employed German workers complained that they 'work as and when they please'.[12]

The British also considered the Germans to be slow-witted. According to John Russell, a travel writer of the 1820s, the Germans were a 'plodding, easily contented people ... endowed neither with great acuteness of perception nor quickness of feeling'. In particular, according to Russell, they were not open to new ideas; 'it is long before [a German] can be brought to comprehend the bearings of what is new to him, and it is difficult to rouse him to ardour in its pursuit.'[13] No wonder that they were 'not distinguished by enterprise or activity', as another mid-19th century British traveller remarked.[14]

Germans were also deemed to be too individualistic and unable to co-operate with each other. The Germans' inability to co-operate was, in the view of the British, most strongly manifested in the poor quality and maintenance of their public infrastructure, which was so bad that John McPherson, a viceroy of India (and, therefore, well used to treacherous road conditions), wrote, 'I found the roads so bad in Germany that I directed my course to Italy'.[15] Once again, compare this with a comment by the African observer that I quoted above: 'African societies are like a football team in which, as a result of personal rivalries and a lack of team spirit, one player will not pass the ball to another out of fear that the latter might score a goal'.[16]

British travellers in the early 19th century also found the Germans dishonest – 'the tradesman and the shopkeeper take advantage of you wherever they can, and to the smallest imaginable amount rather than not take advantage of you at all ... This knavery is universal', observed Sir Arthur Brooke Faulkner, a physician serving in the British army.[17]

Finally, the British thought the Germans to be overly emotional. Today many British seem to think that Germans have an almost genetic emotional deficiency. Yet talking about excessive German emotion, Sir Arthur observed that 'some will laugh all sorrows away and others will always indulge in melancholy'.[18] Sir Arthur was an Irishman, so his calling the Germans emotional would be akin to a Finn calling the Jamaicans a gloomy lot, according to the cultural stereotypes prevailing now.

So there you are. A century ago, the Japanese were lazy rather than hardworking; excessively independent-minded (even for a British socialist!) rather than loyal 'worker ants'; emotional rather than inscrutable; light-hearted rather than serious; living for today instead of considering the future (as manifested in their sky-high savings rates). A century and half ago, the Germans were indolent rather than efficient; individualistic rather than co-operative; emotional rather than rational; stupid rather than clever; dishonest and thieving rather than law-abiding; easy-going rather than disciplined.

These characterizations are puzzling for two reasons. First, if the Japanese and the Germans had such 'bad' cultures, how have they become so rich? Second, why were the Japanese and the Germans then so different from their descendants today? How could they have so completely changed their 'habits of national heritage'?

I will answer these questions in due course. But before I do, I need first to clear up some widespread misunderstandings about the relationship between culture and economic development.

Does culture influence economic development?

The view that cultural differences explain the variations in economic development across societies has been around for a long time. The underlying insight is obvious. Different cultures produce people with different values, which manifest themselves in different forms of behaviour. As some of these forms of behaviour are more helpful for economic development than others, those countries with a culture that produces more pro-developmental forms of behaviour will do better than others economically.

Samuel Huntington, the veteran American political scientist and author of the controversial book, *The Clash of Civilizations*, put this idea succinctly. In explaining the economic divergence between South Korea and Ghana, two countries that were at similar levels of economic development in the 1960s, he argued: 'Undoubtedly, many factors played a role, but ... culture had to be a large part of the explanation. South Koreans valued thrift, investment, hard work, education, organization, and discipline. Ghanaians had different values. In short, cultures count'.[19]

Few of us would dispute that people who display forms of behaviour like 'thrift, investment, hard work, education, organization, and discipline' will be economically successful. Cultural theorists, however, say more than that. They argue that these forms of behaviour are largely, or even entirely, fixed because they are determined by culture. If economic success is really determined by 'habits of national heritage', some people are destined to be more successful than others, and there is not much that can be done about it. Some poor countries will just have to stay that way.

Culture-based explanations for economic development were popular right up to the 1960s. But in the era of civil rights and de-colonization, people began to feel that these explanations had cultural-supremacist (if not necessarily racist) overtones. They fell into disrepute as a result. Such explanations have, however, made a comeback in the past decade or so. They have come back into fashion just as the more dominant cultures (narrowly Anglo-American, more broadly European) have started to feel 'threatened' by other cultures – Confucianism in the economic sphere; Islam in the realm of politics and international relations.[20] They also offered a very convenient excuse to the Bad Samaritans – neo-liberal policies have not worked very well, not because of some inherent problems but because the people practising them had 'wrong' values that diminished their effectiveness.

In the current renaissance of such views, some cultural theorists do *not* actually talk about culture *per se*. Recognising that culture is too broad and amorphous a concept, they try to isolate only those components that they think are most closely related to economic development. For example, in his 1995 book, *Trust*, Francis Fukuyama, the neo-con American political commentator, argues that the existence or otherwise of trust extending beyond family members critically affects economic development. He argues that the absence of such trust in the cultures of countries like China, France, Italy and (to some extent) Korea makes it difficult for them to run large firms effectively, which are key to modern economic development. This is, according to Fukuyama, why high-trust societies, such as Japan, Germany and the US, are economically more developed.

But whether or not the word 'culture' is used, the essence of the argument is the same – different cultures make people behave differently, with resulting differences in economic development across different societies. David Landes, the distinguished American economic historian and a leader in the renaissance of culturalist theories, claims that 'culture makes all the difference.'[21]

Different cultures produce peoples with different attitudes towards work, saving, education, cooperation, trust, authority and countless other things that affect a society's economic progress. But this proposition does not get us very far. As we shall see in a moment, it is very difficult to define cultures precisely. Even if we can, it is not possible to establish clearly whether a particular culture is inherently good or bad for economic development. Let me explain.

What is a culture?

Many westerners mistake me for a Chinese or Japanese. It is understandable. With 'slanted' eyes, straight black hair and prominent cheekbones, East Asians all 'look the same' – at least to a westerner who does not understand all the subtle differences in facial features, mannerisms and dress sense among people from different East Asian countries. To westerners who apologise for mistaking me for a Chinese or Japanese, I tell them it's OK, because most Koreans call all westerners 'Americans' – a notion that some Europeans might find disagreeable. To the uninitiated Korean, I tell them, all westerners look the same, with their big noses, round eyes and excessive facial hair.

This experience warns against excessively broad categorization of people. Of course, what is 'excessively broad' depends on the purpose of the categorisation. If we are comparing the human brain with that of, say, the dolphin, even the over-arching category of *Homo sapiens* may be good enough. But if we are studying how culture makes a difference to economic development, even the relatively narrow category 'Korean' may be problematic. Broader categories, like 'Christian' or 'Muslim', obscure much more than they reveal.

In most culturalist arguments, however, cultures are defined very loosely. We are often offered incredibly coarse categories, such as East-West, which I am not even going to bother to criticize. Very often, we are offered broad 'religious' categories, like Christian (which from time to time is lumped together with Judaism into Judaeo-Christian, and which is regularly divided into Catholic and Protestant), Muslim, Jewish, Buddhist, Hindu and Confucian (this latter category is particularly controversial, because it is not a religion).*

Yet think for a minute about these categories. Within the ostensibly homogeneous group 'Catholic', we have both the ultra-conservative Opus Dei movement, which has become well-known through Dan Brown's bestselling novel, *The Da Vinci Code*, and left-wing liberation theology, epitomized in the famous saying by the Brazilian archbishop of Olinda and Recife, Dom Hélder Câmara: 'When I give food to the poor, they call me a saint. When I ask why the poor have no food, they call me a communist.' These two 'Catholic' sub-cultures produce people with very different attitudes towards wealth accumulation, income redistribution and social obligations.

Or, to take another example, there are ultra-conservative Muslim societies that seriously limit women's public participation. Yet more than half the professional staff at the Malaysian central bank are women – a much higher proportion than at any central bank in the supposedly more 'feminist' Christian countries. And here is another example: some people believe that Japan succeeded economically because of its unique variety of Confucianism, which emphasizes loyalty rather than the personal edification stressed in the Chinese and Korean varieties.[22] Whether or not one agrees with

---

* Confucianism is named after Confucius, the Latinized name of the great Chinese political philosopher, Kong Zi, who lived in the 6th century BC. Confucianism is *not* a religion, as it does not have gods or heaven and hell. It is mainly about politics and ethics, but it also has a bearing on the organization of family life, social ceremonies and etiquette. Although it has had its ups and downs, Confucianism has remained the basis of Chinese culture since it became the official state ideology during the Han Dynasty (206 BC to AD 220). It spread to other East Asian countries, like Korea, Japan and Vietnam, over the next several hundred years.

this particular generalization (more on this later), it shows that there isn't just one kind of Confucianism.

If categories like Confucian or Muslim are too broad, how about taking countries as cultural units? Unfortunately, this does not solve the problem. As the culturalists themselves would be prepared to acknowledge, a country often contains different cultural groups, especially in large and culturally diverse ones, like India and China. But even in a country like Korea, one of the most culturally homogeneous societies in the world, there are significant cultural differences between regions. In particular, people from the south-east (*Kyungsang*) think of those from the south-west (*Cholla*) as clever but totally untrustworthy double-dealers. South-westerners return the compliment by regarding the south-easterners as a crude and aggressive, albeit determined and well-organized, bunch of people. It wouldn't be too far-fetched to say that the stereotypes of these two Korean regions are similar to the stereotypes the French and the Germans have of each other. The cultural animosity between the two regions of Korea is so intense that some families won't even allow their children to marry into families from the other region. So is there a single 'Korean' culture or not? And, if things are as complicated as that for Korea, do we even need to talk about other countries?

I could go on, but I think I have made the point that broad categories, like 'Catholic' or 'Chinese', are simply too crude to be analytically meaningful, and that even a country is too big a cultural unit to generalize about. The culturalists may well retort that all we have to do is work with finer categories like Mormon or Japanese Confucian, rather than broader ones like Christian or Confucian. If only matters were that simple. There are more fundamental problems with culturalist theories, to which I turn now.

Dr Jekyll vs Mr Hyde

Ever since the East Asian economic 'miracle', it has become very popular to argue that it was Confucian culture that was responsible, at least partly, for the region's economic successes. Confucian culture, it was pointed out, emphasizes hard work, education, frugality, co-operation and obedience to authority. It seemed obvious that a culture that encourages the accumulation of human capital (with its emphasis on education) and physical capital (with its emphasis on thrift), while encouraging co-operation and discipline, must be good for economic development.

But, before the East Asian economic 'miracle', people used to blame Confucianism for the region's underdevelopment. And they were right. For Confucianism does have a lot of aspects that are inimical to economic development. Let me mention the most important ones.

Confucianism discourages people from taking up professions like business and engineering that are necessary for economic development. At the pinnacle of the traditional Confucian social system were scholar-bureaucrats. They formed the ruling class, together with the professional soldiers, who were second-class rulers. This ruling class presides over a hierarchy of commoners made up of peasants, artisans and merchants, in that order (below them were slaves). But there was a fundamental divide between the peasantry and the other subordinate classes. At least in theory, individual peasants could gain entry into the ruling class if they passed the competitive civil service examination (and they occasionally did). Artisans and merchants, however, were not even allowed to sit for the examination.

To make matters worse, the civil service examination only tested people for their scholastic knowledge of the Confucian classics, which made the ruling class scornful of practical knowledge. In the 18th century, Korean Confucian politicians slaughtered rival factions in a row over how long the king should wear mourning following his mother's death (one year or three years?). Scholar-bureaucrats were supposed to live in 'clean poverty' (although the practice was often different) and thus they actively looked down upon money-making. In the modern setting, Confucian culture encourages talented people to study law or economics in order to become bureaucrats, rather than engineers (artisans) or businessmen (merchants) – occupations that contribute much more directly to economic development.

Confucianism also discourages creativity and entrepreneurship. It has a rigid social hierarchy and, as I have noted, prevents certain segments of society (artisans, merchants) from moving upwards. This rigid hierarchy is sustained by an emphasis on loyalty to superiors and deference to authority, which breeds conformism and stifles creativity. The cultural stereotype of East Asians being good at mechanical things that do not need much creativity has a basis in this aspect of Confucianism.

Confucianism, it can also be argued, hampers the rule of law. Many people, particularly neo-liberals, believe that the rule of law is crucial for economic development, because it is the ultimate guarantor against arbitrary expropriation of property by rulers. Without the rule of law, it is said, there can be no security of property rights, which, in turn, will make people reluctant to invest and create wealth. Confucianism may *not* encourage arbitrary rule, but it is true that it does not like the rule of law, which it regards as ineffectual, as seen in the following famous passage from Confucius: 'If the people be led by laws, and uniformity sought to be given them by punishments, they will try to avoid the punishment, but have no sense of shame. If they be led by virtue, and uniformity sought to be given them by the rules of propriety, they will have the sense of shame, and moreover will become good.' I agree. With strict legal sanctions, people will abide by the law out of fear of punishment, but too much emphasis on law can make them feel that they are not trusted as moral actors. Without that trust, people will not go that extra mile that makes their behaviour moral and not just law-abiding. Having said all this, however, it cannot be denied that Confucian denigration of the rule of law makes the system vulnerable to arbitrary rule – for what do you do when your ruler is not virtuous?

So which is an accurate portrait of Confucianism? A culture that values 'thrift, investment, hard work, education, organization, and discipline', as Huntington put it in relation to South Korea, or a culture that disparages practical pursuits, discourages entrepreneurship and retards the rule of law?

Both are right, except that the first singles out only those elements that are good for economic development and the second only the bad. In fact, creating a one-sided view of Confucianism does not even have to involve selecting different elements. The same cultural element can be interpreted as having positive or negative implications, depending on the result you seek. The best example is loyalty. As I mentioned above, some people think that the emphasis on loyalty is what makes the Japanese variety of Confucianism more suited to economic development than other varieties. Other people judge the emphasis on loyalty to be exactly what is wrong with Confucianism, since it stifles independent thinking and thus innovation.

It is not just Confucianism, however, that has a split personality like the protagonist in Robert Louis Stevenson's *Dr Jekyll and Mr Hyde*. We can perform the same exercise with any culture's belief system. Take the case of Islam.

Muslim culture is today considered by many to hold back economic development. Its intolerance of diversity discourages entrepreneurship and creativity. Its fixation on the afterlife makes believers less interested in worldly things, like wealth accumulation and productivity growth.[23] The limits on what women are allowed to do not only wastes the talents of half the population but also lowers the likely quality of the future labour force; poorly educated mothers provide poor nutrition and little educational help to their children, thereby diminishing their achievements at school. The 'militaristic' tendency (exemplified by the concept of *jihad*, or holy war, against the infidels) glorifies making war, not money. In short, a perfect Mr Hyde.

Alternatively, we could say that, unlike many other cultures, Muslim culture does *not* have a fixed social hierarchy (which is why many low caste Hindus have converted to Islam in South Asia). Therefore, people who work hard and creatively are rewarded. Moreover, unlike in the Confucian hierarchy, there is no disdain for industrial or business activities. Muhammad, the Prophet, was a merchant himself. And being a merchant's religion, Islam has a highly developed sense of contracts – even at wedding ceremonies, marriage contracts are signed. This orientation encourages the rule of law and justice[24] – Muslim countries had trained judges hundreds of years before Christian countries. There is also an emphasis on rational thinking and learning – the Prophet famously said that 'the ink of the scholar is more sacred than the blood of the martyr'. This is one of the reasons why the Arab world once led the world in mathematics, science and medicine.

What is more, although there are conflicting interpretations of the Koran, there is no question that, in practice, most pre-modern Muslim societies were far more tolerant than Christian societies – after all, this is why many Iberian Jews escaped to the Ottoman Empire after the Christian *reconquista* of Spain in 1492.

Such are the roots of the Dr Jekyll picture of Muslim culture: it encourages social mobility and entrepreneurship, respects commerce, has a contractual frame of mind, emphasizes rational thinking, and is tolerant of diversity and thus creativity.

This Jekyll-and-Hyde exercise of ours shows that there is no culture that is either unequivocally good or bad for economic development. Everything depends on what people do with the 'raw material' of their culture. Positive elements may predominate, or negative ones. Two societies at different points in time or located in different geographical locations, and working with the same raw material (Islam, Confucianism or Christianity), can produce, and have produced, markedly different behavioural patterns.

Not being able to see this, culture-based explanations for economic development have usually been little more than *ex post facto* justifications based on a 20/20 hindsight vision. So, in the early days of capitalism, when most economically successful countries happened to be Protestant Christian, many people argued that Protestantism was uniquely suited to economic development. When Catholic France, Italy, Austria and southern Germany developed rapidly, particularly after the Second World War, Christianity, rather than Protestantism, became the magic culture. Until Japan became rich, many people thought East Asia had not developed because of Confucianism. But when Japan succeeded, this thesis was revised to say that Japan was developing so fast because its unique form of Confucianism emphasized co-operation over individual edification, which the Chinese and Korean versions allegedly valued more highly. And then Hong Kong, Singapore, Taiwan and Korea also started doing well, so this judgement about the different varieties of Confucianism was forgotten. Indeed, Confucianism as a whole suddenly became the best culture for development because it emphasized hard work, saving, education and submission to authority. Today, when we see Muslim Malaysia and Indonesia, Buddhist Thailand and even Hindu India doing well economically, we can soon expect to encounter new theories that will trumpet how uniquely all these cultures are suited for economic development (and how their authors have known about it all along).

Lazy Japanese and thieving Germans

So far, I have shown how difficult it is to define cultures and to understand their complexities, let alone finding some kind of ideal culture for economic development. But, if defining culture is difficult, trying to explain something else (say, economic development) in terms of it seems to be an exercise fraught with even greater problems.

All this is not to deny that how people behave makes a difference to economic development. But the point is that people's behaviour is not determined by culture. Moreover, cultures change; so it is wrong to treat culture as destiny, as many culturalists are wont to do. To understand this, let's go back for a moment to those puzzles of the lazy Japanese and the thieving Germans.

One reason why Japanese or German culture in the past looked so bad for economic development is that observers from richer countries tended to be prejudiced against foreigners (especially poor foreigners). But there was also an element of genuine 'misinterpretation' due to the fact that rich countries are very differently organized to poor countries.

Take laziness – the most frequently cited 'cultural' trait of people in poor countries. People from rich countries routinely believe that poor countries are poor because their people are lazy. But many people in poor countries actually work long hours in backbreaking conditions. What makes them *appear* lazy is often their lack of an 'industrial' sense of time. When you work with basic tools or simple machinery, you don't have to keep time strictly. If you are working in an automated factory, it's essential. People from rich countries often interpret this difference in sense of time as laziness.

Of course, it was not *all* prejudice or misinterpretation. Early-19th-century Germans and early-20th-century Japanese *were*, on average, not as organized, rational, disciplined, etc. as the citizens of the successful countries of the time or, for that matter, as people are in today's Germany or Japan. But the question is whether we can really describe the origins of those 'negative' forms of behaviour as 'cultural' in the sense that they are rooted in beliefs, values and outlooks that have been passed on through generations and are, therefore, very difficult, if not necessarily impossible, to change.

My short answer is no. Let us consider 'laziness' again. It *is* true that there are a lot more people 'lazing around' in poor countries. But is it because those people culturally prefer lounging about to working hard? Usually not. It is mainly because poor countries have a lot of people who are unemployed or underemployed (i.e., people may have jobs but do not have enough work to occupy them fully). This is the result of economic conditions rather than culture. The fact that immigrants from poor countries with 'lazy' cultures work much harder than the locals when they move to rich countries proves the point.

As for the once much-vaunted 'dishonesty' of the Germans in the past, when a country is poor, people often resort to unethical, or even illegal, means to make a living. Poverty also means weak law enforcement, which lets people get away with illegal behaviour, and makes breaking the law more 'culturally' acceptable.

How about the 'excessive emotions' of the Japanese and the Germans? Rational thinking, whose absence is often manifested as excessive emotion, develops largely as a result of economic development. Modern economies require a rational organization of activity, which then changes people's understanding of the world.

'Living for today' or being 'easy-going' – words that many people associate with Africa and Latin America nowadays – are also the consequences of economic conditions. In a slowly changing economy, there is not much need to plan for the future; people plan for the future only when they anticipate new opportunities (e.g., new careers) or unexpected shocks (e.g., a sudden inflow of new imports). Moreover, poor economies offer few devices with which people can plan for the future (e.g., credit, insurance, contracts).

In other words, many of the 'negative' forms of behaviour of the Japanese and Germans in the past were largely the outcomes of economic conditions common to all economically underdeveloped countries, rather than of their specific cultures. This is why the Germans and the Japanese in the past were 'culturally' far more similar to people in today's developing countries than to the Germans and the Japanese of today.

Many of these apparently unchangeable 'habits of national heritage' can be, and have been, transformed quite quickly by changes in economic conditions. This is what some observers actually witnessed in late-19th-century Germany and early-20th-century Japan. Sidney Gulick, the American missionary whom I cited previously, observed that 'the Japanese give the double impression of being industrious and diligent on the one hand and, on the other, of being lazy and utterly indifferent to the passage of time'.[25] If you looked at the workers in the new factories, they looked very industrious. But if you looked at under-employed farmers and carpenters, they looked 'lazy'. With economic development, people would also develop an 'industrial' sense of time very quickly. My country Korea offers an interesting example in this regard. Twenty, maybe even 15, years ago, we used to have the expression, 'Korean time'. It described the widespread practice whereby people could be an hour or two late for an appointment and not even feel sorry about it. Nowadays, with the pace of life far more organized and faster, such behaviour has almost disappeared, and with it the expression itself.

In other words, culture changes with economic development.* That is why the Japanese and the German cultures of today are so different from those of their ancestors. Culture is the *result*, as well as the cause, of economic development. It would be far more accurate to say that

---

* Of course, culture, with economic stagnation, can also change for the worse (at least from the point of view of economic development). The Muslim world used to be rational and tolerant, but, following centuries of economic stagnation, many Muslim countries have turned ultra-religious and intolerant. These 'negative' elements have become stronger because of economic stagnation and lack of future prospects. The fact that such forms of behaviour are not an inevitable manifestation of Muslim culture is proven by the rational thinking and tolerance prevalent in many prosperous Muslim empires in the past. It is also corroborated by contemporary examples, like Malaysia, whose economic prosperity has made its Islam tolerant and rational, as all those female central bankers I wrote about earlier will tell you.

countries become 'hardworking' and 'disciplined' (and acquire other 'good' cultural traits) because of economic development, rather than the other way around.

Many culturalists accept, in theory, that cultures change. But in practice most of them treat culture as pretty immutable. This is why, despite endless contemporary accounts to the contrary, culturalists today describe the Japanese on the cusp of economic development in the most flattering light. David Landes, a leading proponent of the cultural theory of economic development, says: 'The Japanese went about modernization with characteristic intensity and system. They were ready for it by virtue of a tradition (recollection) of effective government, by their high levels of literacy, by their tight family structure, by their work ethic and self-discipline, by their sense of national intensity and inherent superiority'.[26] Despite the frequent contemporary observation that the Japanese were lazy, Fukuyama claims in his book, *Trust*, that there was 'the Japanese counterpart to the Protestant work ethic, formulated at around the same time'.[27] When he classifies Germany as an inherently 'high-trust' society, he is also oblivious to the fact that, before they became rich, many foreigners thought the Germans were cheating others all the time and unable to co-operate with one another.

A good cultural argument should be able to admit that the Germans and the Japanese *were* a pretty hopeless bunch in the past and *still* be able to explain how they developed their economies. But most culturalists, blinded by their conviction that only countries with the 'right' value systems can develop, re-interpret German or Japanese histories so as to 'explain' their subsequent economic success.

The fact that culture changes far more quickly than the culturalists assume should give us hope. Negative behavioural traits, like laziness or lack of creativity, do hamper economic development. If these traits are fully, or even predominantly, culturally determined, we would need a 'cultural revolution' in order to get rid of them and start economic development.[28] If we need a cultural revolution before we can develop the economy, economic development would be next to impossible, since cultural revolutions rarely, if ever, succeed. The failure of the Chinese Cultural Revolution, albeit launched for other reasons than economic development, should serve as a salutary warning.

Fortunately, we do *not* need a cultural revolution before economic development can happen. A lot of behavioural traits that are meant to be good for economic development will follow from, rather than be prerequisites for, economic development. Countries can get development going through means other than a cultural revolution, as I explained in the preceding chapters. Once economic development gets going, it will change people's behaviour and even the beliefs underlying it (namely, culture) in ways that help economic development. A 'virtuous circle' between economic development and cultural values can be created.

This is, essentially, what happened in Japan and Germany. And it is what will happen in all future economic success stories. Given India's recent economic success, I am sure we will soon see books that say how Hindu culture – once considered the source of sluggish growth in India (recall the once-popular expression, 'Hindu rate of growth'[29]) – is helping India grow. If my Mozambique fantasy in the Prologue comes true in the 2060s, we will then be reading books discussing how Mozambique has had a culture uniquely suited to economic development all along.

Changing culture

So far, I have argued that culture is not immutable and changes as a result of economic development. However, this is not to say that we can change culture only through changing the underlying economic conditions. Culture can be changed deliberately through persuasion. This is a point rightly emphasized by those culturalists who are not fatalists (for the fatalists, culture is almost impossible to change, so it is destiny).

The problem is that those culturalists tend to believe that cultural changes require only 'activities that promote progressive values and attitudes', in the words of Lawrence Harrison, the author of *Underdevelopment is a State of Mind*.[30] But there is a limit to changes that can be made through ideological exhortation alone. In a society without enough jobs, preaching hard work will not be very effective in changing people's work habits. In a society with little industry, telling people that disparaging the engineering profession is wrong will not make many young people choose to pursue it as a career. In societies where workers are treated badly, appealing for co-operation will fall upon deaf, if not cynical, ears. Changes in attitudes need to be supported by real changes – in economic activities, institutions and policies.

Take the fabled Japanese culture of company loyalty. Many observers believe it is the manifestation of an ingrained cultural trait rooted in the Japanese variety of Confucianism emphasizing loyalty. Now, if true, such an attitude should have been more pronounced as we go back further in time. Yet, a century ago, Beatrice Webb remarked that the Japanese have a 'quite intolerable personal independence'.[31] Indeed, the Japanese workers used to be a pretty militant bunch until fairly recently. Between 1955 and 1964, Japan lost more days per worker in strikes than Britain or France, countries which were not exactly famous for co-operative industrial relations at the time.[32] Co-operation and loyalty came about only because Japanese workers were given institutions such as lifetime employment and company welfare schemes. Ideological campaigns (and government bashing of militant communist trade unions) did play a role, but they would not have been enough on their own.

Similarly, despite its current reputation for peaceful industrial relations, Sweden used to have a terrible labour problem. In the 1920s, it lost more man-hours per worker due to strikes than any other country. But after the 'corporatist' compromise of the 1930s (the 1938 Saltjöbaden Agreement), it all changed. In return for workers restraining their wage demands and strike activities, the country's capitalists delivered a generous welfare state combined with good retraining programmes. Ideological exhortation alone would not have been convincing.

When Korea started its industrialization drive in the 1960s, the government tried to persuade people to abandon the traditional Confucian disdain for industrial professions. The country needed more engineers and scientists. But with few decent engineering jobs, not many bright young people wanted to become engineers. So the government increased funding and the number of places in university for engineering and science departments, while doing the reverse (in relative terms) in humanities departments. In the 1960s there were only 0.6 engineering and science graduates for every humanities graduate, but the ratio became one-to-one by the early 1980s.[33] Of course, the policy worked ultimately because the economy was industrializing fast and, as a result, there were more and more well-paid jobs for engineers and scientists. It was thanks to the combination of ideological exhortation, educational policy and industrialization – and not just promotion of 'progressive values and attitudes' – that Korea has come to boast one of the best-trained armies of engineers in the world.

The above examples show that ideological persuasion is important but not, by itself, enough in changing culture. It has to be accompanied by changes in policies and institutions that can sustain the desired forms of behaviour over an extended period of time so that that they turn into 'cultural' traits.

Reinventing culture

Culture influences a country's economic performance. At a given point in time, a particular culture may produce people with particular behavioural traits that are more conducive to achieving certain social goals, including economic development, than other cultures. At this abstract level, the proposition seems uncontroversial.

But when we try to apply this general principle to actual cases, it proves elusive. It is very difficult to define what the culture of a nation is. Things are complicated further by the fact that very different cultural traditions may co-exist in a single country, even in allegedly 'homogeneous' ones like Korea. All cultures have multiple characteristics, some positive and others negative for economic development. Given all this, it is not possible, nor useful, to 'explain' a country's economic success or failure in terms of its culture, as some Bad Samaritans have tried to do.

More importantly, even though having people with certain behavioural traits may be better for economic development, a country does not need a 'cultural revolution' before it can develop. Though culture and economic development influence each other, the causality is far stronger from the latter to the former; economic development to a large extent creates a culture that it needs. Changes in economic structure change the way people live and interact with one another, which, in turn, changes the way they understand the world and behave. As I have shown with the cases of Japan, Germany and Korea, many of the behavioural traits that are supposed to 'explain' economic development (e.g., hard work, time-keeping, frugality) are actually its consequences, rather than its causes.

Saying that culture changes largely as a result of economic development is not to say that culture cannot be changed by ideological persuasion. Actually, this is what some optimistic culturalists believe. 'Underdevelopment is a state of mind', they declare. For them, therefore, the obvious solution to underdevelopment is to change the way people think through ideological exhortation. I don't deny that such an exercise may be helpful, or even important in certain cases, for changing culture. But a 'cultural revolution' will not take root unless there are complementary changes in the underlying economic structures and institutions.

So, in order to promote behavioural traits that are helpful for economic development, we need a combination of ideological exhortation, policy measures to promote economic development and the institutional changes that foster the desired cultural changes. It is not an easy job to get this mix right, but once you do, culture can be changed much more quickly than is normally assumed. Very often what seemed like an eternal national character can change within a couple of decades, if there are sufficient supporting changes in the underlying economic structure and institutions. The rather rapid disappearance of the Japanese 'national heritage' of laziness since the 1920s, the quick development of co-operative industrial relations in Sweden since the 1930s, and the end of 'Korean time' in the 1990s are some prominent examples.

The fact that culture can be deliberately changed – through economic policies, institution building and ideological campaigns – gives us hope. No country is condemned to underdevelopment because of its culture. But at the same time we must not forget that culture cannot be reinvented at will – the failure to create the 'new man' under communism is a good proof of that. The cultural 'reformer' still has to work with existing cultural attitudes and symbols.

We need to understand the role of culture in economic development in its true complexity and importance. Culture is complex and difficult to define. It does affect economic development, but economic development affects it more than the other way around. Culture is not immutable. It can be changed through: a mutually reinforcing interaction with economic development; ideological persuasion; and complementary policies and institutions that encourage certain forms of behaviour, which over time turn into cultural traits. Only then can we free our imagination both from the unwarranted pessimism of those who believe culture is destiny and from the naïve optimism of those who believe they can persuade people to think differently and bring about economic development that way.

São Paulo, October 2037

Can things get better?

Luiz Soares is a worried man. His family engineering firm – Soares Tecnologia, *S.A.*, which his grandfather, Jose Antonio, founded in 1997 – is on the brink of collapse.

The first years of Soares Tecnologia were difficult. The high interest rate policy, which lasted between 1994 and 2009, severely constrained its ability to borrow and expand. But, by 2013, it had grown into a solid middle-sized firm producing watch parts and other precision equipment, thanks to Jose Antonio's skills and determination.

In 2015, Luiz's father, Paulo, came back with a Ph.D. in nano-physics from Cambridge and persuaded his father to set up a nano-technology division, which he headed. That proved a lucky escape. The Tallinn Round of the WTO concluded in 2017 abolished all industrial tariffs except for a handful of 'reserved' sectors for each country. As a result, most manufacturing industries, other than low-technology, low-wage ones, got wiped out in most developing countries, including Brazil. The Brazilian nano-technology industry survived the so-called Tallinn *tsunami* only because it was one of the 'reserved' industries.

Paulo's foresight paid off. Soon after he took over the firm in 2023, after Jose Antonio's yacht sank in a freak hurricane in the Caribbean (a result of global warming, they said), Soares Tecnologia launched a molecular machine which converted sea water into fresh water with greater efficiency than its American or Finnish rivals. It was a big hit in a country that was suffering from increasingly frequent droughts due to global warming – by that time, the Amazon forest was barely 40% of its 1970 size due to lack of rain (with a helping hand from pasture-hungry cattle ranchers). In 2028, Paulo was even selected as one of the world's 500 leading technology entrepreneurs by the Shanghai-based *Qiye* (Enterprise), the world's most influential business magazine.

Then disaster struck. In 2029, China was hit by a massive financial crisis. Back in 2021, commemorating the 100th anniversary of the foundation of its ruling Communist Party, China had decided to join the OECD (Organisation for Economic Co-operation and Development), the club of rich countries. Opening up its capital market was to be the price of its membership. China had already been resisting for some years the pressure from the rich countries to behave 'responsibly' as the world's second biggest economy and to open up its financial market, but once it started negotiating the terms of OECD accession, there was no escape. Some urged caution, saying that China was still a relatively poor country, with an income level that was only 20% of that of the US, but most others were confident that China would do as well in finance as in manufacturing, where its ascendancy seemed unstoppable. Wang Xing-Guo, the pro-liberalization governor of the People's Bank of China, the central bank (granted full independence in 2017), summed up this optimism perfectly: 'What are we afraid of? The money game is in our genes – after all, paper money is a Chinese invention!' When it joined the organization in 2024, China revalued its currency, the renminbi, by four times and fully opened its capital market. For a while, the Chinese economy boomed as though the sky was the limit. But the resulting real estate and stock market bubbles burst in 2029, requiring the largest IMF rescue package in history.

Soaring unemployment and IMF-imposed cuts to government food subsidies led to riots and eventually to the rise of the Yuan-Gongchandang (Real Communist) movement, fuelled by the seething resentment of the 'losers' in a society that had moved from the near-absolute equality of Maoist communism to Brazilian-style inequality in the space of less than two generations. The Real Communists have been contained, at least for the moment, following the arrest of all their leaders in 2035, but the resulting political turmoil and social unrest marked the end of the Chinese economic miracle.

The Chinese economy being so big by then, it brought the whole world down with it. What came to be known as the Second Great Depression has been going on for several years now and there seems to be no end in sight. With its largest export market collapsing, Brazil has suffered greatly, although not as heavily as some other countries.

The other leading Asian economies – such as India, Japan and Vietnam – went belly up. Many African countries could not survive the collapse of what, by then, was the biggest buyer of their raw materials. The US economy suffered withdrawal symptoms from the massive flight of Chinese capital from its Treasury bill market. The ensuing deep recession in the US economy triggered an even deeper one in Mexico, leading to an armed uprising by the Nuevos Zapatistas, the left-wing guerrillas claiming to be the legitimate heirs of the legendary early-20th century revolutionary Emiliano Zapata. The Nuevos Zapatistas swore to take Mexico out of the IAIA (Inter-American Integration Agreement) – the high-octane version of NAFTA that was formed by the US, Canada, Mexico, Guatemala, Chile and Colombia in 2020. The guerrillas were narrowly defeated after a brutal military operation, aided by the US air force and the Colombian army.

The Second Great Depression was bad enough for Soares Tecnologia, but then came the *coup de grace*. In 2033, driven by his free trade convictions and using the dire economic situation as a means to bully the opposition, the maverick Korean-Brazilian president, Alfredo Kim, a former chief economist of the World Bank, took the country into the IAIA.

For the Brazilian nano-technology industry, it was a catastrophe. As a part of the terms of entry into the IAIA, all federal R&D subsidies and government procurement programmes – lifelines for the industry – were phased out within three years. Tariffs in nano-technology and a few other 'reserved' sectors that had survived the Tallinn Round were immediately scrapped *vis-à-vis* the IAIA member countries. With the overall level of technology still 20, perhaps even 30, years behind US firms, most Brazilian nano-technology companies collapsed. Even Soares Tecnologia, considered to be Brazil's best, survived only by selling a 45% stake to a firm from – of all countries! – Ecuador. Ecuador had done surprisingly well after forming the Bolivarian Economic Union with

Venezuela, Bolivia, Cuba, Nicaragua and Argentina in 2010 – the BEU members left the WTO in 2012 in protest at the Tallinn Round agenda.

But even survivors like Soares Tecnologia were devastated by the new patent law that had now come into force. The US had already extended its patent life from 28 years (instituted in 2018) to 40 years in 2030. By contrast, Brazil was one of the few countries still clinging on to the 20-year patent life allowed under the increasingly obsolete WTO TRIPS agreement of 1995 (most others having moved to 28 years or even 40 years, in the case of the IAIA countries). When Brazil joined the IAIA, the main concession it had to make – in return for the abolition of beef and cotton subsidies in the US (to be phased in over the next 25 years) – was the patent law, which the Americans insisted should be applied *retrospectively*. At one stroke, the Brazilian nano-technology firms became liable to patent suits, and American nano-technology corporations parachuted in their army of patent lawyers.

With no tariffs against American imports, disappearing subsidies and shrivelling government procurement programmes, compounded by a flood of lawsuits, Soares Tecnologia was in a dire state when Paulo – may his soul rest in peace – had a massive stroke and died in 2035. As a result, Luiz was forced to quit his MBA course at the Singapore campus of INSEAD, the French business school (which, by that time, was considered to be better than the original campus in Fontainebleau), break up with Miriam, his half-Xhosa/half-Uzbek girl-friend (a distant cousin of Nelson Mandela on her Xhosa side), and return to Brazil to take over the family firm at the age of 27.

Things have not improved much since Luiz took over. True, he has successfully fought off several patent suits. But if he loses even one of the three that are still pending (none of them is looking hopeful), he will face ruin. His Ecuadorian partner, Nanotecnologia Andina, is already threatening to sell off its share in the company. When his firm disappears with the rest of the Brazilian nano-technology industry, most of Brazil's manufacturing industries – except for aerospace and alcohol fuel, in which Brazil had established a world class position in the late 20th century before the rise of neo-liberalism – will have disappeared. Brazil will be back to square one.

Unlikely? Yes – and I hope it stays that way. Brazil is far too smart and independent-minded to sign something like my IAIA, even if it had a former World Bank chief economist as its president. Mexico has enough wise people and vibrant popular movements to be able to mend its ways before it is thrown into a full-scale civil war. The Chinese leadership is fully aware of the threats posed by the country's widening inequality. They also know the dangers of any premature opening of its capital market, thanks to the 1997 Asian crisis. Even the mighty US patent lobby would find it difficult to secure a retrospective application of 40-year patents in any international agreement. There is a growing consensus that something has to be done about global warming soon. The next round of the WTO talks is not likely to lead to a near-total abolition of industrial tariffs.

But what I have just sketched out is not an impossible scenario. Many of the things I have made up have been deliberately exaggerated, but they all have a strong basis in reality.

For example, the near-total abolition of industrial tariffs following my imaginary Tallinn Round may sound fanciful, but it is actually a little milder than what was proposed by the US at the WTO in 2002 – it called for a total abolition of industrial tariffs by 2015 – and is not far off from what other rich countries are proposing.[1] My Inter-American Integration Agreement is really a (geographically) broader and stronger (content-wise) version of NAFTA (North American Free Trade Agreement). The countries mentioned as possible members of the Bolivarian Economic Union are already working together closely (I have deliberately omitted Brazil, a member of this group, in my story). Of these, Venezuela, Cuba and Bolivia have already formed ALBA (Alternativa Bolivariana para las Américas: Bolivarian Alternatives for the Americas).

Given the growing importance of the Chinese economy, it is not totally fanciful that a major economic crisis in China in the late 2020s could turn into a Second Great Depression, especially if there was political turmoil in the country. The chances of upheaval in such circumstances would be strongly influenced by the gravity of its inequality problem which, while not yet at the Brazilian level, as in my story, could reach that in another generation, if no counteraction is taken. As for a civil war in Mexico, this may sound like a fantasy, but, in today's Mexico, we already have one state, Chiapas, which has been, in effect, ruled by an armed guerrilla group, the Zapatistas under Subcomandante Marcos, since 1994. It would not be impossible for the conflict to escalate if the country were thrown into a major economic crisis, especially if it had continued for another two decades with the neo-liberal policies that have so ill-served it in the past two decades.

My US patent scenario is certainly exaggerated, but US pharmaceutical patents can already be *de facto* extended up to 28 years through data protection and in consideration of the time needed for FDA (Food and Drugs Administration) approval. The US has made sure that these provisions are written into all its free trade agreements. And, as I discussed in the story of Mickey Mouse in chapter 6, in 1998, US copyright *was* retrospectively extended.

The reader may find it particularly implausible that China would prematurely open its capital market. But when your economy becomes the second biggest in the world, it is hard to resist the pressure to act 'responsibly'. This is exactly what happened to Japan when it was made to revalue its currency by three times almost overnight in the 1985 Plaza Accord. That currency revaluation was an important cause of Japan's huge asset bubble, whose bursting in the early 1990s (and the incompetent management of its aftermath) resulted in economic stagnation for a decade. As for my saying that China would join the OECD to celebrate the 100th birthday of its Communist Party, that was certainly said tongue-in-cheek. But countries can become over-confident when they are very successful, as the case of Korea shows. Until the late 1980s, Korea had skilfully used capital controls to great economic benefit. But, in the mid-1990s, it opened its capital market wide, and without careful planning. This was partly due to American pressure, but also because, after three decades of its economic 'miracle', the country had become too full of itself. It decided to join the OECD in 1996 and act like a rich country when it really wasn't one. At the time, its *per capita* income was still only one-third that of most OECD member countries and one quarter that of the richest ones (or slightly above the level China is likely to reach by the mid-2020s). The outcome was the 1997 financial crisis. So my imaginary China story is really a combination of what actually happened in Japan in the 1980s and Korea in the 1990s.

Is it really plausible that Brazil would sign up to something like the IAIA? Absolutely not in today's world, but I am talking about a world in the middle of the Second Great Depression and an economy ravaged by another quarter of a century of neo-liberalism. Also, we should not underestimate how political leaders driven by ideological convictions can do things which are so 'out of character' with their countries' history, if they are there in the right place at the right time. For example, despite the famous British tradition of gradualism and pragmatism, Margaret Thatcher was radical and ideologically driven. Her government changed the character of British politics for the foreseeable future. Likewise, Brazil may have a history of independent-minded and pragmatic foreign policy, but that is not an absolute guarantee against someone like my Alfredo Kim driving it into the IAIA, especially when Brazil does not lack its own supply of free-market ideologues.

So, my 'alternative history of the future' is not a total fantasy. It is grounded in reality a lot more strongly than may appear at first. If I have been deliberately pessimistic in painting this scenario, it is to remind the reader how big the stakes are. I really hope that, 30 years from now, I will be proved completely wrong. But if the world continues with neo-liberal policies currently propagated by the Bad Samaritans, many of the events that I 'document' in the story, or something very like them, could happen.

Throughout this book, I have made many detailed proposals as to how policies, both nationally and globally, need to be changed in all sorts of areas in order to help poor countries develop and to avert the kind of disaster scenario that I have just described in my 'history of the future'. In this concluding chapter, I will not repeat or summarize these suggestions, but rather discuss the key principles that lie behind them. In the process, I hope to show how national economic policies and the rules of international economic interactions need to be changed if we are to promote economic development in poor countries and make the world a better place.

Defying the market

As I have constantly stressed, markets have a strong tendency to rein-force the status quo. The free market dictates that countries stick to what they are already good at. Stated bluntly, this means that poor countries are supposed to continue with their current engagement in low-productivity activities. But their engagement in those activities is exactly what makes them poor. If they want to leave poverty behind, they *have to* defy the market and do the more difficult things that bring them higher incomes – there are no two ways about it.

'Defying the market' may sound radical – after all, have many coun-tries not failed miserably because they have tried to go against the market? But it is something that is done by business managers all the time. Business managers, of course, get judged ultimately by the market, but they – especially the successful ones – do not accept market forces blindly. They have their long-term plans for their companies, and these sometimes demand that they buck market trends for considerable periods of time. They foster the growth of their subsidiaries in the new sectors they choose to move into and make up for the losses with profits from their subsidiaries in the existing sectors. Nokia subsidized its fledg-ling electronics business for 17 years with money from its businesses in logging, rubber boots and electric cable. Samsung subsidized its infant electronics subsidiaries for over a decade with money made in textiles and sugar refining. If they had faithfully followed market signals in the way developing countries are told to by the Bad Samaritans, Nokia would still be felling trees and Samsung refining imported sugar cane. Likewise, countries should defy the market and enter difficult and more advanced industries if they want to escape poverty.

The trouble is that there are good reasons why low-earning coun-tries (or, for that matter, low-earning firms or individuals) are engaged in less productive activities – they lack the capabilities to do more productive ones. A backyard motor repair shop in Maputo simply cannot produce a Beetle, even if Volkswagen were to give it all the necessary drawings and instruction manuals, because it lacks the tech-nological and organizational capacities that Volkswagen enjoys. This is why, free market economists would argue, Mozambicans should be realistic and not mess around with things like cars (let alone hydrogen fuel cells!); instead they should just concentrate on what they are already (at least 'comparatively') good at – growing cashew nuts.

The free market recommendation is correct – in the short run, when capabilities cannot be changed very much. But this does not mean that Mozambicans should not produce something like a Beetle – one day. In fact, they need to – if they are going to make progress. And they can – given enough determination and the right investment, both at the firm level and at the national level, in accumulating the necessary abilities. After all, a backyard auto repair shop is exactly how the famous Korean car maker, Hyundai, started in the 1940s.

Needless to say, investment in capability-building requires short-term sacrifices. But that is not a reason not to do it, contrary to what free-trade economists say. In fact, we often see individuals making short-term sacrifices for a long-term increase in their capacities, and heartily approve of them. Suppose a low-skilled worker quits his low-paying job and attends a training course to acquire new skills. If someone were to say the worker is making a big mistake because he is now not able to earn even the low wage he used to earn, most of us would criticize that person for being short-sighted; an increase in a person's future earning power justifies such short-term sacrifice. Likewise, countries need to make short-term sacrifices if they are to build up their long-term productive capabilities. If tariff barriers or subsidies allow domestic firms to accumulate new abilities – by buying better machinery, improving their organization and training their workers – and become internationally competitive in the process, the temporary reduction in the country's level of consumption (because it is refusing to buy higher-quality, lower-price foreign goods) may be totally justified.

This simple but powerful principle – sacrificing the present to improve the future – is why the Americans refused to practise free trade in the 19th century. It is why Finland did not want foreign investment until recently. It is why the Korean government set up steel mills in the late 1960s, despite the objections of the World Bank. It is why the Swiss did not issue patents and the Americans did not protect foreigners' copyrights until the late 19th century. And it is, to cap it all, why I send my six-year-old son, Jin-Gyu, to school rather than making him work and earn his living.

Investment in capacity-building can take quite a long time to bear fruit. I may not go as far as Zhou Enlai, the long-time prime minister of China under Mao Zedong – when asked to comment on the impact of the French Revolution, he famously replied that 'it is too early to tell'. But when I say long, I mean long. I have just mentioned that it took the electronics division of Nokia 17 years to make any profit, but that is just the beginning. It took Toyota more than 30 years of protection and subsidies to become competitive in the international car market, even at the lower end of it. It was a good 60 years before it became one of the world's top car makers. It took nearly 100 years from the days of Henry VII for Britain to catch up with the Low Countries in woollen manufacturing. It took the US 130 years to develop its economy enough to feel confident about doing away with tariffs. Without such long time horizons, Japan might still be mainly exporting silk, Britain wool and the US cotton.

Unfortunately, these are time frames that are not compatible with the neo-liberal policies recommended by the Bad Samaritans. Free trade demands that poor countries compete immediately with more advanced foreign producers, leading to the demise of firms before they can acquire new capabilities. A liberal foreign investment policy, which allows superior foreign firms into a developing country, will, in the long run, restrict the range of capabilities accumulated in local firms, whether independent or owned by foreign companies. Free capital markets, with their pro-cyclical herd behaviour, make long-term projects vulnerable. A high interest rate policy raises the 'price of future', so to speak, making long-term investment unviable. No wonder neo-liberalism makes economic development difficult – it makes the acquisition of new productive capabilities difficult.

Like any other investment, of course, investment in capability-building does not guarantee success. Some countries (as well as firms or individuals) make it; some don't. Some countries will be more successful than others. And even the most successful countries will bungle things in certain areas (but then, when we talk about 'success', we are talking about batting averages, rather than infallibility). But economic development without investment in enhancing productive capabilities is a near impossibility. History – recent and more distant – tells us that, as I have shown throughout this book.

Why manufacturing matters

Having accepted that increasing capabilities is important, where exactly should a country invest in order to increase them? Industry – or, more precisely, manufacturing industry* – is my answer. It is also the answer that would have been given by generations of successful engineers of economic development from Robert Walpole onwards, had they been asked the same question.

Of course, this is not to say that it is impossible to become rich by relying on natural resources: Argentina was rich in the early 20th century through the trans-Atlantic export of wheat and beef (it was once the fifth richest country in the world); today, a number of countries are rich mainly due to oil. But one has to have a huge stock of natural resources in order to be able to base high living standards solely on them. Few countries are so fortunate. Moreover, natural resources can run out – mineral deposits are finite, while over-exploitation of renewable resources whose supplies are, in principle, infinite (e.g., fish, forests) can make them disappear. Worse, wealth based on natural resources can be rapidly eroded, if technologically more advanced nations come up with synthetic alternatives – in the mid-19th century, Guatemala's wealth, based on the highly prized crimson dye extracted from the insect, *cochinilla* (cochineal), was almost instantly wiped out when the Europeans invented artificial dye.

History has repeatedly shown that the single most important thing that distinguishes rich countries from poor ones is basically their higher capabilities in manufacturing, where productivity is generally higher, and, more importantly, where productivity tends to (although does not always) grow faster than in agriculture or services. Walpole knew

---

* In some definitions, industry includes activities like mining or the generation and distribution of electricity or gas.

this nearly 300 years ago, when he asked George I to say in the British Parliament: 'nothing so much contributes to promote the public well-being as the exportation of manufactured goods and the importation of foreign raw material', as I mentioned in chapter 2. In the US, Alexander Hamilton knew it when he defied the world's then most famous economist, Adam Smith, and argued that his country should promote 'infant industries'. Many developing countries pursued import substitution 'industrialization' in the mid-20th century precisely for this reason. Contrary to the advice of the Bad Samaritans, poor countries should *deliberately* promote manufacturing industries.

Of course, today there are those who challenge this view on the grounds that we are now living in a post-industrial era and that selling services is therefore the way to go. Some of them even argue that developing countries can, and really should, skip industrialization and move directly to the service economy. In particular, many people in India, encouraged by that country's recent success in service outsourcing, seem to be quite taken by this idea.

There are certainly some services that have high productivity and considerable scope for further productivity growth – banking and other financial services, management consulting, technical consulting and IT support come to mind. But most other services have low productivity and, more importantly, have little scope for productivity growth due to their very nature (how much more 'efficient' can a hairdresser, a nurse or a call centre telephonist become *without diluting the quality of their services*?). Moreover, the most important sources of demand for those high-productivity services are manufacturing firms. So, without a strong manufacturing sector, it is impossible to develop high-productivity services. This is why no country has become rich solely on the basis of its service sector.

If I say this, some of you may wonder: what about a country like Switzerland, which has become rich thanks to service industries like banking and tourism? It is tempting to take the rather condescending but popular view of Switzerland that the legendary American actor-film director Orson Welles summed up brilliantly in the movie, *The Third Man*. 'In Italy for thirty years under the Borgias,' he said, 'they had warfare, terror, murder, bloodshed, but they produced

Michelangelo, Leonardo da Vinci and the Renaissance. In Switzerland, they had brotherly love – they had five hundred years of democracy and peace, and what did that produce? The cuckoo clock[2] This view of the Swiss economy, however, is a total misconception.

Switzerland is *not* a country living off black money deposited in its secretive banks and gullible tourists buying tacky souvenirs like cow bells and cuckoo clocks. It is, in fact, literally the most industrialized country in the world. As of 2002, it had the highest *per capita* manufacturing output in the world by far – 24% more than that of Japan, the second highest; 2.2 times that of the US; 34 times that of China, today's 'workshop of the world'; and 156 times that of India.[3] Similarly, Singapore, commonly considered to be a city state that has succeeded as a financial centre and trading port, is a highly industrialized country, producing 35% more manufacturing output per head of population than the 'industrial powerhouse' Korea and 18% more than the US.[4]

Despite what the free trade economists recommend (concentrating on agriculture) or the prophets of post-industrial economy tout (developing services), manufacturing is the most important, though not the only, route to prosperity. There are good theoretical reasons for this, and an abundance of historical examples to prove the point. We must not look at spectacular contemporary examples of manufacturing-based success, like Switzerland and Singapore, and mistakenly think that they prove the opposite. It may be that the Swiss and the Singaporeans are playing us along because they don't want other people to find out the real secret of their success!

Don't try this at home

So far, I have shown that it is important for developing countries to defy the market and deliberately promote economic activities that will raise their productivity in the long run – mainly, though not exclusively, manufacturing industries. I have argued that this involves capability-building, which, in turn, requires sacrificing certain short-term gains for the sake of raising long-term productivity (and thus standards of living) – possibly for decades.

215

But neo-liberal economists may respond by asking: what about the low capacities of developing country governments that are supposed to orchestrate all this? If these countries are to defy the logic of the market, someone has to choose which industries to promote and what capabilities to invest in. But capable government officials are the last thing that developing countries have. If those making these important choices are incompetent, their intervention can only make things worse.

This was the argument used by the World Bank in its famous *East Asian Miracle* report, published in 1993. Advising other developing countries against emulating interventionist Japanese and Korean trade and industrial policies, it argued that such policies cannot work in countries without 'the competence, insulation, and relative lack of corruptibility of the public administrations in Japan and Korea'[5] – that is, practically all developing countries. Alan Winters, a professor of economics at the University of Sussex and the director of the Development Research Group at the World Bank, was even more blunt. He argued that 'the application of second-best economics [economics that allows for imperfect markets and therefore potentially beneficial government intervention – my note] needs first-best economists, not its usual complement of third- and fourth-raters'.[6] The message is clear – 'Do not try this at home', as TV captions say when showing people doing dangerous stunts.

There can be no dispute that, in many developing countries, government officials are not highly trained. But it is also not true that countries like Japan, Korea and Taiwan succeeded with interventionist policies because their bureaucracies were manned by exceptionally well-trained government officials. They were not – at least in the beginning.

Korea used to send its bureaucrats for extra training to – of all places – Pakistan and the Philippines until the late 1960s. Pakistan was then a 'star pupil' of the World Bank, while the Philippines was the second-richest country in Asia after Japan. Years ago, as a graduate student, I had a chance to compare the early economic planning documents of Korea and India. The early Indian plans were cutting-edge stuff for their time. They were based on a sophisticated economic model developed by the world-famous statistician Prasanta Chandra Mahalanobis. The Korean ones, I am embarrassed to say, were definitely written by Professor Winters's 'usual complement of third- and fourth-raters'. But the Korean economy did far better than the Indian one. Perhaps we don't need 'first-best economists' to run good economic policy.

Indeed, Professor Winters's first-best *economists* are one thing that the East Asian economies did *not* have. Japanese economic officials may have been 'first-best', but they were certainly not economists – they were mostly lawyers by training. Until the 1980s, what little economics they knew were mostly of the 'wrong' kind – the economies of Karl Marx and Friedrich List, rather than of Adam Smith and Milton Friedman. In Taiwan, most key economic bureaucrats were engineers and scientists, rather than economists, as is the case in China today.[7] Korea also had a high proportion of lawyers in its economic bureaucracy until the 1970s.[8] The brains behind President Park's Heavy and Chemical Industrialisation (HCI) programme in the 1970s, Oh Won-Chul, was an engineer by training.

It is entirely reasonable to say that we need smart people to run good economic policy. But those 'smart people' do not have to be Professor Winters's 'first-best economists'. Actually, the 'first best economists' may not be very good for economic development, if they are trained in neo-liberal economics. Moreover, the quality of the bureaucracy can be improved as we go along. Such improvement, of course, requires investment in bureaucratic capabilities. But it also needs some experiments with 'difficult' policies. If the bureaucrats stick to (allegedly) 'easy' policies, like free trade, they will never develop the abilities to run 'difficult' policies. You need some 'trying at home', if you aspire to become good enough to appear on TV with your own stunt act.

Tilting the playing field

Knowing what policies are right for your particular circumstances is not enough. A country must be able to implement them. Over the past quarter of a century, the Bad Samaritans have made it increasingly difficult for developing countries to pursue the 'right' policies for their development. They have used the Unholy Trinity of the IMF, the World Bank and the WTO, the regional multilateral financial institutions, their aid budgets and bilateral and regional free-trade or investment agreements in order to block them from doing so. They argue that nationalist policies (like trade protection and discrimination against foreign investors) should be banned, or severely curtailed, not only because they are supposed to be bad for the practising countries themselves but also because they lead to 'unfair' competition. In arguing this, the Bad Samaritans constantly invoke the notion of the 'level playing field'.

The Bad Samaritans demand that developing countries should not be allowed to use extra policy tools for protection, subsidies and regulation, as these constitute unfair competition. If they were allowed to do so, developing countries would be like a football team, the Bad Samaritans argue, attacking from uphill, while the other team (the rich countries) are struggling to climb the un-level playing field. Get rid of all protective barriers and make everyone compete on an equal footing; after all, the benefits of the market can only be reaped when the underlying competition is fair.[9] Who can disagree with such a reasonable-sounding notion as 'the level playing field'?

I do – when it comes to competition between *unequal* players. And we all should – if we are to build an international system that promotes economic development. A level playing field leads to *unfair* competition *when the players are unequal*. When one team in a football game is, say, the Brazilian national team and the other team is made up of my 11-year-old daughter Yuna's friends, it is only fair that the girls are allowed to attack downhill. In this case, a tilted, rather than a level, playing field is the way to ensure fair competition.

We don't see this kind of tilted playing field only because the Brazilian national team is *never* going to be allowed to compete with a team of 11-year-old girls, and not because the idea of a tilted playing field is wrong in itself. In fact, in most sports, unequal players are not simply allowed to compete against each other – tilted playing field or not – for the obvious reason that it would be unfair.

Football and most other sports have age groups and gender separation, while boxing, wrestling, weightlifting and many other sports have weight classes – the heavyweight, Muhammad Ali, was simply not allowed to box Roberto Duran, the legendary Panamanian with four titles in lighter weight classes. And the classes are divided really finely. For example, in boxing, the lighter weight classes are literally within two-or-three-pound (1–1.5-kilo) bands. How is it that we think a boxing match between people with more than a couple of kilos' difference in weights is unfair, and yet we accept that the US and Honduras should compete on equal terms? In golf, to take another example, we even have an explicit system of 'handicaps' that give players advantages in inverse proportion to their playing skills.

Global economic competition is a game of unequal players. It pits against each other countries that range from, as we development economists like to say, Switzerland to Swaziland. Consequently, it is only fair that we 'tilt the playing field' in favour of the weaker countries. In practice, this means allowing them to protect and subsidize their producers more vigorously and to put stricter regulations on foreign investment.* These countries should also be allowed to protect intellectual property rights less stringently so that they can more actively 'borrow' ideas from more advanced countries. Rich countries can further help by transferring their technologies on favourable terms; this will have the added benefit of making economic growth in poor countries more compatible with the need to fight global warming, as rich country technologies tend to be far more energy efficient.[10]

The Bad Samaritan rich countries may protest that all this is 'special

---

* Quite a few developing countries have chosen *not* to use these tools. Some neo-liberal economists have used this as 'evidence' that these countries do not want policy freedom – which means that the WTO rules are not, in fact, restricting the options for these countries. However, what may look like a voluntary choice is likely to have been shaped by past conditionalities attached to foreign aid and IMF-World Bank programmes, as well as the fear of future punishment by the rich countries. But, even ignoring this problem, it is not right for rich countries to make the choice for developing countries. It is actually quite curious how free-market economists who are so much in favour of choice and autonomy do not hesitate to oppose them when they are by developing countries.

treatment' for developing countries. But to call something special treatment is to say that the person receiving it is also obtaining an unfair advantage. Yet we wouldn't call stair-lifts for wheelchair users or Braille text for the blind 'special treatment'. In the same way, we should not call the higher tariffs and other means of protection additionally made available for the developing countries 'special treatment'. They are just differential – and fair – treatment for countries with differential capabilities and needs.

Last but not least, tilting the playing field in favour of developing nations is not just a matter of fair treatment now. It is also about providing the economically less advanced countries with the tools to acquire new capabilities by sacrificing short-term gains. Indeed, allowing the poor countries to raise their capabilities more easily brings forward the day when the gap between the players is small and thus it becomes no longer necessary to tilt the playing field.

What is right and what is easy

Suppose I am right and that the playing field should be tilted in favour of the developing countries. The reader can still ask: what is the chance of the Bad Samaritans accepting my proposal and changing their ways?

It may seem pointless to try to convert those Bad Samaritans who are acting out of self-interest. But we can still appeal to their enlightened self-interest. Since neo-liberal policies are making developing countries grow more slowly than they would otherwise do, the Bad Samaritans themselves might be better off in the long run if they allowed alternative policies that would let developing countries grow faster. If *per capita* income grows at only 1% a year, as it has in Latin America over the past two decades of neo-liberalism, it will take seven decades to double the income. But if it grows at 3%, as it did in Latin America during the period of import substitution industrialization, income would increase by eight times during the same period of time, providing the Bad Samaritan rich countries with a vastly bigger market to exploit. So it is actually in the long-term interest of even the most selfish Bad Samaritan countries to accept those 'heretical' policies that would generate faster growth in developing countries.

The people who are much harder to persuade are the ideologues – those who believe in Bad Samaritan policies because they think those policies are 'right', not because they personally benefit from them much, if at all. As I said earlier, self-righteousness is often more stubborn than self-interest. But even here there is hope. Once accused of inconsistency, John Maynard Keynes famously responded: 'When the facts change, I change my mind – what do you do, sir?' Many, although, unfortunately, not all, of these ideologues are like Keynes. They can change, and have changed, their minds, if they are confronted with new turns in real world events and new arguments, provided that these are compelling enough to make them overcome their previous convictions. The Harvard economist Martin Feldstein is a good example. He was once the brains behind Reagan's neo-liberal policies, but when the Asian crisis happened, his criticism of the IMF (cited in chapter 1) was more trenchant than those by some 'left-wing' commentators.

What should give us real hope is that the majority of Bad Samaritans are neither greedy nor bigoted. Most of us, including myself, do bad things *not* because we derive great material benefit from them or strongly believe in them, but because they are the easiest thing to do. Many Bad Samaritans go along with wrong policies for the simple reason that it's easier to be a conformist. Why go around looking for 'inconvenient truths' when you can just accept what most politicians and newspapers say? Why bother to find out what is really going on in poor countries when you can easily blame it on corruption, laziness or the profligacy of their people? Why go out of your way to check up on your own country's history when the 'official' version suggests that it has always been the home of all virtues? – free trade, creativity, democracy, prudence, you name it.

It is exactly because most Bad Samaritans are like this that I have hope. They are people who may be willing to change their ways, if they are given a more balanced picture, which I hope this book has provided. This is not just wishful thinking. There *was* a period, between the Marshall Plan (announced sixty years ago, in June 1947) and the rise of neo-liberalism in the 1970s, when the rich countries, led by the US, did *not* behave as Bad Samaritans, as I discussed in chapter 2.[11]

The fact that rich countries did not behave as Bad Samaritans on at least one occasion in the past gives us hope. The fact that that historical episode produced an excellent outcome economically – for the developing world has never done better, either before or since – gives us the moral duty to learn from that experience.

Notes

Prologue

1 The Korean income figure is from H.-C. Lee (1999), *Hankook Gyongje Tongsa* [Economic History of Korea] (Bup-Moon Sa, Seoul) [in Korean], Appendix Table 1. The Ghanaian figure is from C. Kindleberger (1965), *Economic Development* (McGraw-Hill, New York), Table 1–1.

2 http://www.samsung.com/AboutSAMSUNG/SAMSUNGGroup/Time-lineHistory/timeline01.htm

3 Calculated from A. Maddison (2003), *The World Economy: Historical Statistics* (OECD, Paris), Table 1c (UK), Table 2c (USA), and Table 5c (Korea).

4 Korea's *per capita* income in 1972 was $319 (in current dollars). It was $1,647 in 1979. Its exports totaled $1.6 billion in 1972 and grew to $15.1 billion in 1979. The statistics are from Lee (1999), Appendix Table 1 (income) and Appendix Table 7 (exports).

5 In 2004, Korea's *per capita* income was $13,980. In the same year, *per capita* income was $14,350 in Portugal and $14,810 in Slovenia. The figures are from World Bank (2006), *World Development Report 2006 – Equity and Development* (Oxford University Press, New York), Table 1.

6 Life expectancy at birth in Korea in 1960 was 53 years. In 2003, it was 77 years. In the same year, life expectancy was 51.6 years in Haiti and 80.5 years in Switzerland. Infant mortality in Korea was 78 per 1,000 live births in 1960 and 5 per 1,000 live births in 2003. In 2003, infant mortality was 76 in Haiti and 4 in Switzerland. The 1960 Korean figures are from H-J. Chang (2006), *The East Asian Development Experience – the Miracle, the Crisis, and the Future* (Zed Press, London), Tables 4.8 (infant mortality) and 4.9 (life expectancy). All the 2003 figures are from UNDP (2005), *Human Development Report 2005* (United Nations Development Program, New York), Tables 1 (life expectancy) and 10 (infant mortality).

7 The criticisms of the neo-liberal interpretation of the Korean miracle can be found in A. Amsden (1989), *Asia's Next Giant* (Oxford University Press, New York) and H.-J. Chang (2007), *The East Asian Development Experience – The Miracle, the Crisis, and the Future* (Zed Press, London).

8 He continues: 'Any nation which . . . has raised her manufacturing power and her navigation to such a degree of development that no other nation can sustain free competition with her, can do nothing wiser than *to throw away these ladders* of her greatness, to preach to other nations the benefits of free trade, and to declare in penitent tones that she has hitherto wandered in the paths of error, and has now for the first time succeeded in discovering the truth'. Friedrich List (1841), *The National System of Political Economy*, translated from the original German edition published in 1841 by Sampson Lloyd in 1885 (Longmans, Green, and Company, London), pp. 295–6. 'Kicking away the ladder' is also the title of my academic book on the subject, H-J. Chang (2002), *Kicking Away the Ladder – Development Strategy in Historical Perspective* (Anthem Press, London).

Chapter 1

1 T. Friedman (2000), *The Lexus and the Olive Tree* (Anchor Books, New York), p. 31.

2 Friedman (2000), p. 105.

3 Friedman (2000), p. 105.

4 In 1961, Japan's *per capita* income was $402, on a par with those of Chile ($377), Argentina ($378) and South Africa ($396). The data are from C. Kindleberger (1965), *Economic Development* (McGraw-Hill, New York), Table 1.1.

5 This happened when the Japanese prime minister, Hayao Ikeda, visited France in 1964. 'The Undiplomat', *Time*, 4 April 1969.

6 J. Sachs & A. Warner (1995), 'Economic Reform and the Process of Global Integration', *Brookings Papers on Economic Activity*, 1995, no. 1, and M. Wolf (2004), *Why Globalisation Works* (Yale University Press, New Haven and London) are some of the more balanced and better informed, but ultimately flawed, versions of this. J. Bhagwati (1985), *Protectionism* (The MIT Press, Cambridge, Massachusetts) and J. Bhagwati (1998), *A Stream of Windows – Unsettling Reflections on Trade, Immigration, and Democracy* (The MIT Press, Cambridge, Massachusetts) offer a less balanced but probably more representative version.

7 R. Ruggiero (1998), 'Whither the Trade System Next?' in J. Bhagwati & M. Hirsch (eds.), *The Uruguay Round and Beyond – Essays in Honour of Arthur Dunkel* (The University of Michigan Press, Ann Arbor), p. 131.

8 Britain first used unequal treaties in Latin America, starting with Brazil in 1810, as the countries in the continent acquired political independence. Starting with the Nanking Treaty, China was forced to sign a series of unequal treaties over the next couple of decades. These eventually resulted in a complete loss of tariff autonomy, and, very symbolically, a Briton being the head of customs for 55 years – from 1863 to 1908. From 1824 onwards, Thailand (then Siam) signed various unequal treaties, which ended with the most comprehensive one in 1855. Persia signed unequal treaties in 1836 and 1857, and the Ottoman Empire in 1838 and 1861. Japan lost its tariff autonomy following a series of unequal treaties it signed after its opening in 1853, but that did not stop it from forcing an unequal treaty on Korea in 1876. The larger Latin American countries were able to regain tariff autonomy from the 1880s, before Japan did in 1911. Many others regained it only after the First World War, but Turkey had to wait for tariff autonomy until 1923 and China until 1929. See H-J. Chang (2002), *Kicking Away the Ladder – Development Strategy in Historical Perspective* (Anthem Press, London), pp. 53–4.

9 For example, in his controversial study, *In Praise of Empires*, the Indian-born British-American economist Deepak Lal never mentions the role of colonialism and unequal treaties in spreading free trade. See D. Lal (2004), *In Praise of Empires – Globalisation and Order* (Palgrave Macmillan, New York and Basingstoke).

10 See N. Ferguson (2003), *Empire – How Britain Made the Modern World* (Allen Lane, London).

11 After they gained independence, growth accelerated markedly in developing Asian countries. In all 13 Asian countries (Bangladesh, Burma, China, India, Indonesia, Korea, Malaysia, Pakistan, the Philippines, Singapore, Sri Lanka, Taiwan and Thailand) for which data were available, annual *per capita* income growth rates increased after de-colonization. The growth rate jump between the colonial period (1913–1950) and the post-colonial period (1950–99) ranged between 1.1% points (Bangladesh: from -0.2% to 0.9%) to 6.4% points (Korea: from -0.4% to 6.0%). In Africa, *per capita* income growth rate was around 0.6% during the colonial period (1820–1950). In the 1960s and the 1970s, when most countries in the continent became independent, growth rates rose to 2% for the middle-income countries. Even the poorest countries, which usually find it difficult to grow, were growing at 1%, double the rate of the colonial period. H-J. Chang, (2005), *Why Developing Countries Need Tariffs – How WTO NAMA Negotiations Could Deny Developing Countries' Right to a Future* (Oxfam, Oxford, and South Centre, Geneva), downloadable at http://www.southcentre.org/publications/ SouthPerspectiveSeries/WhyDevCountriesNeedTariffsNew.pdf), Tables 5 and 7.

12 Maddison (2003), *The World Economy: Historical Statistics* (OECD, Paris), Table 8b.

13 Average tariffs in Latin America were between 17% (Mexico, 1870–1899) and 47% (Colombia, 1900–1913). See Table 4 in M. Clemens & J. Williamson (2002), 'Closed Jaguar, Open Dragon: Comparing Tariffs in Latin America and Asia before World War II', NBER Working Paper, no. 9401 (National Bureau of Economic Research, Cambridge, Massachusetts). Between 1820 and 1870, when they were subject to unequal treaties, *per capita* income stood still in Latin America (growth rate of -0.03% per year). Annual *per capita* income growth rate in Latin America rose to 1.8% during 1870–1913, when most countries in the region acquired tariff autonomy, but even that was no match for the 3.1% growth rate in *per capita* income that the continent achieved during the 1960s and the 1970s. The Latin American income growth figures are from Maddison (2003), Table 8b.

14 For example, between 1875 and 1913, the average tariff rates on manufactured products rose from 3–5% to 20% in Sweden, from 4–6% to 13% in Germany, from 8–10% to 18% in Italy and from 10–12% to 20% in France. See H-J. Chang (2002), p. 17, Table 2.1.

15 Chang (2005), p. 63, Tables 9 and 10.

16 Sachs and Warner (1995), p. 17. The full quote of the relevant passages: 'Export pessimism combined with the idea of the big push to produce the highly influential view that open trade would condemn developing countries to long-term subservience in the international system as raw materials exporters and manufactured goods importers. Comparative advantage, it was argued by the Economic Commission of [*sic*] Latin America (ECLA) and others, was driven by short-term considerations that would prevent raw materials exporting nations from ever building up an industrial base. The protection of infant industries was therefore vital if the developing countries were to escape from their overdependence on raw materials production. These views spread within the United Nations system (to regional offices of the United Nations Economic Commission), and were adopted largely by the United Nations Conference on Trade and Development (UNCTAD). In 1964 they found international legal sanction in a new part IV of the General Agreement on Tariffs and Trade (GATT), which established that developing countries should enjoy the right to asymmetric trade policies. While the developed countries should open their markets, the developing countries could continue to protect their own markets. Of course, this "right" was the proverbial rope on which to hang one's own economy!'

17 According to an interview in the magazine *Veja*, 15 November 1996, as translated and cited by G. Palma (2003), 'The Latin American Economies During the Second Half of the Twentieth Century – from the Age of ISI to

the Age of The End of History' in H-J. Chang (ed.), *Rethinking Development Economics* (Anthem Press, London), p. 149, endnotes 15 and 16.

18 Chang (2002), p. 132, Table 4.2.

19 A. Singh (1990), 'The State of Industry in the Third World in the 1980s: Analytical and Policy Issues', Working Paper, no. 137, April 1990, Kellogg Institute for International Studies, Notre Dame University.

20 The 1980 and 2000 figures are calculated respectively from the 1997 issue (Table 12) and the 2002 issue (Table 1) of World Bank's *World Development Report* (Oxford University Press, New York).

21 M. Weisbrot, D. Baker and D. Rosnick (2005), 'The Scorecard on Development: 25 Years of Diminished Progress', September 2005, Center for Economic and Policy Research (CEPR), Washington, DC, downloadable from http://www.cepr.net/publications/development_2005_09.pdf

22 Some commentators argue that recent advance in globalization has made the world more equal. This result is highly disputed, but, even if it were true, it has happened because, to put it crudely, a lot of Chinese have become richer, not because income distribution has become more equal within countries. Whatever happened to 'global' inequality, there is little dispute that income inequality has increased in most countries, including China itself, over the past 20–25 years. On this debate, see A. Cornia (2003), 'Globalisation and the Distribution of Income between and within Countries' in H-J. Chang (ed.), *Rethinking Development Economics* (Anthem Press, London) and B. Milanovic (2005), *Worlds Apart – Measuring International and Global Inequality* (Princeton University Press, Princeton and Oxford).

23 For example, see D. Rodrik and A. Subramaniam (2004), 'From "Hindu Growth" to Growth Acceleration: The Mystery of Indian Growth Transition', mimeo., Kennedy School of Government, Harvard University, March 2004. Downloadable from http://ksghome.harvard.edu/~drodrik/Indiapaperdraft March2.pdf

24 Annual *per capita* GDP growth rate between 1975 and 2003 was 4% in Chile, 4.9% in Singapore and 6.1% in Korea. See UNDP (2005), *Human Development Report 2005* (United Nations Development Program, New York).

25 Chile's *per capita* income (in 1990 dollars, as all the following figures are) was $5,293 in 1970, when Salvador Allende, the left-wing president who was subsequently deposed by Pinochet, came to power. Despite the bad press Allende has been getting in the official history of capitalism, *per capita* income in Chile rose quite a lot during his presidency – it was $5,663 in 1971 and $5,492 in 1972. After the coup, Chile's *per capita* income fell, hitting the bottom at $4,323 in 1975. From 1976, it started rising again and peaked at $5,956 in 1981, mainly thanks to the financial bubble. Following the financial crash, it

fell back to $4,898 in 1983 and recovered the pre-coup level only in 1987, at $5,590. The data are from Maddison (2003), Table 4c.

26 Public Citizen's Global Trade Watch (2006), 'The Uses of Chile: How Politics Trumped Truth in the Neo-liberal Revision of Chile's Development', Discussion Paper, September 2006. Downloadable at http://www.citizen.org/documents/chilealternatives.pdf.

27 The output figure is from World Bank (2006). The trade figure is from the WTO (2005), 'World Trade 2004, Prospects for 2005: Developing countries' goods trade share surges to 50-year peak' (Press Release), released on 14 April, 2005. The FDI figures are from various issues of UNCTAD, *World Investment Report*.

28 M. Feldstein (1998), 'Refocusing the IMF', *Foreign Affairs*, March/April 1998, vo. 77, no. 2.

29 The decisions in 18 most important areas at the IMF need a 85% majority. The US happens to own 17.35% of its share. Therefore, it can unilaterally veto any proposal that it does not like. At least three of the next four biggest shareholders are needed in order to block a proposal (Japan with 6.22%; Germany with 6.08%; Britain or France each with 5.02%). There are also 21 issues that require a 70% majority. This means that any proposal regarding these issues can be defeated if the above-mentioned five biggest shareholders band together against it. See A. Buira (2004), 'The Governance of the IMF in a Global Economy', G24 Research Paper, downloadable at http://g24.org/buiragva.pdf

30 Luddites are the early-19th-century English textile workers who tried to reverse the Industrial Revolution by destroying machines. At the World Economic Forum in Davos, Switzerland, in 2003, Mr Richard McCormick, the chairman of the International Chamber of Commerce, called the anti-globalization protesters 'modern-day Luddites who want to make the world safe for stagnation . . . whose hostility to business makes them the enemy of the poor'. As reported by the BBC website on 12 February, 2003.

Chapter 2

1 Richard West (1998), *Daniel Defoe – The Life and Strange, Surprising Adventures* (Carroll & Graf Publishers, Inc., New York) and Paula Back-scheider (1990), *Daniel Defoe – His Life* (Johns Hopkins University Press, Baltimore).

2 However, he was not the first to try it. Earlier English kings, such as Henry III and Edward I, tried to recruit Flemish weavers. In addition to recruiting

Flemish weavers, Edward III centralized trade in raw wool and imposed strict control on wool exports. He banned the import of woollen cloth, thus opening up space for English producers who could not compete with the then dominant Flemish producers. He was also a very good political propagandist who understood the power of symbols. He and his courtiers wore only English cloth to set an example for his 'Buy English' (like Gandhi's *swadeshi*) policy. He ordered the lord chancellor (who presides over the House of Lords) to sit on, of all things, a woolsack – a tradition that has survived until today – to emphasize the importance of wool trade for the country.

3 Henry VII 'set the Manufacture of Wool on Foot in several Parts of his Country, as particularly as *Wakefield, Leeds*, and *Hallifax*, in the West Riding of *Yorkshire*, a Country pitch'd upon for its particular Situation, adapted to the Work, being fill'd with innumerable Springs of Water, Pits of Coal, and other Things proper for carrying on such a Business . . .' (*A Plan*, p. 95, italics original)

4 Henry VII 'secretly procured a great many Foreigners, who were perfectly skill'd in the Manufacture, to come over and instruct his own People here in their Beginnings' (*A Plan*, p. 96).

5 G. Ramsay (1982), *The English Woollen Industry, 1500–1750* (Macmillan, London and Basingstoke), p. 61.

6 Henry VII realized 'that the *Flemings* were old in the business, long experience'd, and turn'd their Hands this Way and that Way, to new Sorts and Kinds of Goods, which the *English* could not presently know, and when known, had not Skill presently to imitate: And that therefore he must proceed gradually'. So he 'knew . . . that it was an Attempt of such a Magnitude, as well deserv'd the utmost Prudence and Caution, that it was not to be attempted rashly; so it was not to be push'd with too much Warmth' (*A Plan*, p. 96, italics original).

7 Henry VII 'did not immediately prohibit the exporting the Wool to the *Flemings*, neither did he, till some Years after, load the Exportation of it with any more Duties than he had before' (*The Plan*, p. 96). As for the ban on raw wool exports, Defoe says Henry VII was 'so far . . . from being able to compleat his Design, that he could never come to a total Prohibition of exporting the Wool in this Reign' (*The Plan*, p. 96). Thus, although Henry VII 'did once pretend to stop the Exportation of the Wool, he conniv'd at the Breach of his Order, and afterwards took off the Prohibition entirely' (*A Plan*, p. 97).

8 *A Plan*, pp. 97–8.

9 Cloth exports (mostly woollen) accounted for around 70% of English

exports in 1700 and was still over 50% of total exports until the 1770s. A. Musson (1978), *The Growth of British Industry* (B.T. Batsford Ltd., London), p. 85.

10 In substance, however, Walpole deserves the title because no previous government head enjoyed such wide-ranging political power as his. Walpole was also the first to take up residence (in 1735) at 10 Downing Street, the famous official residence of the British prime minster.

11 Walpole also attracted vehement criticism, mainly for his corruption, from other important literary personages of his time, such as Dr Samuel Johnson (*A Dictionary of the English Language*), Henry Fielding (*Tom Jones*) and John Gay (*The Beggar's Opera*). It seems as if you did not count in the Georgian literary world unless you had something to say against Walpole. His literary connection does not stop there. His fourth son, Horace Walpole, sometime politician, was a novelist, considered to be a founder of the Gothic novel genre. Horace Walpole is also credited with coining the term 'serendipity', after the Persian story of the mysterious island of Serendip (believed to be Sri Lanka).

12 As cited in F. List (1841), *The National System of Political Economy*, translated from the original German edition published in 1841 by Sampson Lloyd in 1885 (Longmans, Green, and Company, London), p. 40.

13 For details, see: N. Brisco (1907), *The Economic Policy of Robert Walpole* (The Columbia University Press, New York), pp. 131–3, pp. 148–55, pp. 169–71; R. Davis (1966), 'The Rise of Protection in England, 1689–1786', *Economic History Review*, vol. 19, no. 2, pp. 313–4; J., McCusker (1996), 'British Mercantilist Policies and the American Colonies' in S. Engerman & R, Gallman (eds.), *The Cambridge Economic History of the United States, Vol. 1: The Colonial Era* (Cambridge University Press, Cambridge), p. 358; C. Wilson (1984), *England's Apprenticeship, 1603–1763*, 2nd ed. (Longman, London and New York), p. 267.

14 Export subsidies (then called 'bounties') were extended to new export items, like silk products (1722) and gunpowder (1731), while the existing export subsidies to sailcloth and refined sugar were increased in 1731 and 1733 respectively.

15 In Brisco's words, 'Walpole understood that, in order successfully to sell in a strongly competitive market, a high standard of goods was necessary. The manufacturer, being too eager to undersell his rival, would lower the quality of his wares which, in the end, would reflect on other English-made goods. There was only one way to secure goods of a high standard, and that was to regulate their manufacture by governmental supervision' (Brisco, 1907, p. 185).

16 Brisco (1907) points out that the first duty drawback was granted under

William and Mary to the exportation of beer, ale, mum, cider and perry (p. 153).

17 The figures for Germany, Switzerland and the Low Countries (Belgium and the Netherlands were united during 1815–30) are from P. Bairoch (1993), *Economics and World History – Myths and Paradoxes* (Wheatheaf, Brighton), p. 40, table 3.3. Bairoch did not provide the French figure, because of the difficulties involved in the calculation, but John Nye's estimate of the French *overall* (not just manufacturing) tariff rate based on customs receipts puts the figure at 20.3% for the 1821–5 period. Given that the corresponding British figure was 53.1%, which is in line with Bairoch's 45–55%, it may not be unreasonable to say that the average French manufacturing tariff rate was around 20%. See J. Nye (1991), 'The Myth of Free-Trade Britain and Fortress France: Tariffs and Trade in the Nineteenth Century', *Journal of Economic History*, vol. 51. no. 1.

18 Brisco (1907) neatly sums up this aspect of Walpole's policy: 'By commercial and industrial regulations attempts were made to restrict the colonies to the production of raw materials which England was to work up, to discourage any manufactures that would any way compete with the mother country, and to confine their markets to the English trader and manufacturer' (p. 165).

19 Willy de Clercq, the European commissioner for external economic relations during the late 1980s, intones that '[o]nly as a result of the theoretical legitimacy of free trade when measured against widespread mercantilism provided by David Ricardo, John Stuart Mill and David Hume, Adam Smith and others from the Scottish Enlightenment, and as a consequence of the relative stability provided by the UK as the only and relatively benevolent superpower or hegemon during the second half of the nineteenth century, was free trade able to flourish for the first time'. W. de Clercq (1996), 'The End of History for Free Trade?' in J. Bhagwati & M. Hirsch (eds.), *The Uruguay Round and Beyond – Essays in Honour of Arthur Dunkel* (The University of Michigan Press, Ann Arbor), p. 196.

20 J. Bhagwati (1985), *Protectionism* (The MIT Press, Cambridge, Massachusetts), p. 18. Bhagwati, together with other free-trade economists of today, attaches so much importance to this episode that he uses as the cover of the book a 1845 cartoon from the political satire magazine, *Punch*, depicting the prime minister, Robert Peel, as a befuddled boy being firmly led to the righteous path of free trade by the stern, upright figure of Richard Cobden, the leading anti-Corn-Law campaigner.

21 C. Kindleberger (1978), 'Germany's Overtaking of England, 1806 to 1914' (chapter 7) in *Economic Response: Comparative Studies in Trade, Finance, and Growth* (Harvard University Press, Cambridge, Massachusetts), p. 196.

22 The passage is from *The Political Writings of Richard Cobden*, 1868, William Ridgeway, London, vol. 1, p. 150; as cited in E. Reinert (1998), 'Raw Materials in the History of Economic Policy – Or why List (the protectionist) and Cobden (the free trader) both agreed on free trade in corn' in G. Cook (ed.), *The Economics and Politics of International Trade – Freedom and Trade, Volume 2* (Routledge, London), p. 292.

23 See D. Landes (1998), *The Wealth and Poverty of Nations* (W.W. Norton & Company, New York), p. 521.

24 Bairoch (1993), p. 46. One French Commission of Inquiry in the early 19th century also argued that 'England has only arrived at the summit of prosperity by persisting for centuries in the system of protection and prohibition'. Cited in W. Ashworth (2003), *Customs and Excise – Trade, Production, and Consumption in England, 1640–1845* (Oxford University Press, Oxford) p. 379.

25 As cited in List (1841), p. 95. Pitt is cited as the Earl of Chatham, which he was at the time.

26 The full quotation is: 'Were the Americans, either by combination or by any other sort of violence, to stop the importation of European manufactures, and, by thus giving a monopoly to such of their own countrymen as could manufacture the like goods, divert any considerable part of their capital into this employment, they would retard instead of accelerating the further increase in the value of their annual produce, and would obstruct instead of promoting the progress of their country towards real wealth and greatness.' Adam Smith (1776), *The Wealth of Nations*, the 1937 Random House edition, pp. 347–8. Smith's view was later echoed by the respected 19th-century French economist Jean-Baptiste Say, who is reported to have said that, 'like Poland', the US should rely on agriculture and forget about manufacturing. Reported in List (1841), p. 99.

27 Hamilton divided these measures into eleven groups. They are: (i) 'protecting duties' (tariffs, if translated into modern terminology); (ii) 'prohibition of rival articles or duties equivalent to prohibitions' (import bans or prohibitive tariffs); (iii) 'prohibition of the exportation of the materials of manufactures' (export bans on industrial inputs); (iv) 'pecuniary bounties' (subsidies); (v) 'premiums' (special subsidies for key innovation); (vi) 'the exemption of the materials of manufactures from duty' (import liberalization of inputs); (vii) 'drawbacks of the duties which are imposed on the materials of manufactures' (tariff rebate on imported industrial inputs); (viii) 'the encouragement of new inventions and discoveries, at home, and of the introduction into the United States of such as may have been made in other countries; particularly those, which relate to machinery' (prizes and patents for inventions); (ix) 'judicious regulations for the inspection of manufactured commodities' (regulation of product standards); (x) 'the facilitating of pecuniary remittances from place to place' (financial development); and (xi) 'the facilitating of the transportation of commodities' (transport development). Alexander Hamilton (1789), *Report on the Subject of Manufactures*, as reprinted in *Hamilton – Writings* (The Library of the America, New York, 2001), pp. 679–708.

28 Burr and Hamilton were friends in their younger days. However, in 1789, Burr shifted his allegiance and accepted the office of attorney general of the state of New York from Governor George Clinton, despite having campaigned for Hamilton's candidate. In 1791, Burr defeated Philip Schuyler, Hamilton's father-in-law, to become a senator, and then used the office to oppose Hamilton's policies. Hamilton, in turn, opposed Burr's candidacy for the vice presidency in 1792 and his nomination as the minister (ambassador) to France in 1794. To top it all, Hamilton snatched the presidency away from Burr's hands and forced him to become the vice president in the 1800 election. In that election, four candidates ran – John Adams and Charles Pinckney from the Federalist Party and Thomas Jefferson and Aaron Burr from the opposing Democratic Republican Party. In the electoral-college vote, the two Democratic Republican candidates came out ahead, with Burr unexpectedly tying with Jefferson. When the House of Representatives had to choose between the two candidates, Hamilton swung the Federalists towards Jefferson. This was done despite the fact that Hamilton opposed Jefferson almost as much, because he thought Burr was an unprincipled opportunist, whereas Jefferson was at least principled, albeit guided by wrong principles. As a result, Burr had to satisfy himself with the job of vice president. And then, in 1804, when Burr was running for the New York state governorship, Hamilton waged a verbal campaign against Burr, again preventing him from getting the job he wanted. The above details are from J. Ellis (2000), *Founding Brothers – The Revolutionary Generation* (Vintage Books, New York), pp. 40–1 and J. Garraty & M. Carnes (2000), *The American Nation – A History of the United States*, 10th edition (Addison Wesley Longman, New York), pp. 169–70.

29 Similarly, Latin American industrial development was given an important impetus by an unexpected disruption in international trade caused by the Great Depression during the 1930s.

30 Hamilton proposed to issue government bonds to finance public infrastructural investments. The idea of 'borrowing to invest' was suspect to many people at the time, including Thomas Jefferson. It did not help Hamilton's cause that government borrowing in Europe at the time was usually used to finance wars or extravagant life style of rulers. Eventually Hamilton succeeded in persuading Congress, buying Jefferson's consent by agreeing to move the capital to the South – to the newly built Washington, DC. Hamilton also wanted to set up a 'national bank'. The idea was that a bank that was partly owned by the government (20%) and acting as the government's banker could develop and provide stability to the financial system. It could give extra liquidity to the financial system by issuing bank notes, using its special position as a government-backed institution. It was also expected that the bank could finance nationally important industrial projects. This idea, too, was considered dangerous by Jefferson and his supporters, who considered banks to be essentially vehicles of speculation and exploitation. For them, a semi-public bank was even worse, as it is based on an artificially created monopoly. To diffuse such potential resistance, Hamilton asked for a bank with a finite 20-year charter, which was granted, and the Bank of the USA was set up in 1791. When its charter expired in 1811, it was not renewed by Congress. In 1816, another Bank of the USA (the so-called the Second Bank of the USA) was set up under another 20-year charter. When it came up for renewal in 1836, its charter was not renewed (more on this in chapter 4). After that, the US did without even a semi-public bank for nearly 80 years, until the Federal Reserve Board (its central bank) was set up in 1913.

31 The exhibition was called 'Alexander Hamilton: The Man Who Made Modern America' and was held between September 10 2004 and February 28 2005. See the web page at:http//www.alexanderhamiltonexhibition.org.

32 The Whig Party was the main rival to the then dominant Democratic Party (formed in 1828) between the mid-1830s and the early 1850s, and produced two presidents in five elections between 1836 and 1856 – William Harrison (1841–4) and Zachary Taylor (1849–51).

33 Cited in Garraty & Carnes (2000), p. 405.

34 The quote is from R. Luthin (1944), 'Abraham Lincoln and the Tariff', *The American Historical Review*, vol. 49, no. 4, p. 616.

35 One of Lincoln's key economic advisors was Henry Carey, the then leading US economist, who was the son of a leading early American protectionist economist, Mathew Carey, and himself a prominent protectionist economist. Few people have heard of Carey today, but he was regarded as one of the leading American economists of his time. Karl Marx and Friedrich Engels even described him as 'the only American economist of importance' in their letter to Weydemeyer, 5 March 1852, in K. Marx & F. Engels (1953), *Letters to Americans, 1848–95: A Selection* (International Publishers, New York), as cited in O. Frayssé (1994), *Lincoln, Land, and Labour*, translated by S. Neely from the original French edition published in 1988 by Paris, Publications de la Sorbonne (University of Illinois Press, Urbana and Chicago), p. 224, note 46.

36 The consolidation of a protectionist trade policy regime was not the only economic legacy of Lincoln's presidency. In 1862, in addition to the Homestead Act, one of the largest land reform programmes in human history, Lincoln oversaw the passage of the Morill Act. This act established the 'land grant' colleges, which helped boost the country's research and development (R&D) capabilities, which subsequently became the country's most important competitive weapon. Although the US government had supported agricultural research from the 1830s, the Morrill Act was a watershed in the history of government support for R&D in the USA.

37 Bairoch (1993), pp. 37–8.

38 Bhagwati (1985), p. 22, f.n. 10.

39 Bairoch (1993), pp. 51–2.

40 In reviewing my own book, *Kicking Away the Ladder*, the Dartmouth economist Doug Irwin argues that 'the United States started out as a very wealthy country with a high literacy rate, widely distributed land ownership, stable government and competitive political institutions that largely guaranteed the security of private property, a large internal market with free trade in goods and free labor mobility across regions, etc. Given these overwhelmingly favorable conditions, even very inefficient trade policies could not have prevented economic advances from taking place'. D. Irwin (2002), review of H-J. Chang, *Kicking Away the Ladder – Development Strategy in Historical Perspective* (Anthem Press, London, 2002), http://eh.net/bookreviews/library/0777.shtml.

41 These included: 'voluntary' export restraints against successful foreign exporters (e.g., Japanese car companies); quotas on textile and clothing imports (through the Multi-Fibre Agreement); agricultural subsidies (compare this with the repeal of the Corn Laws in Britain); and anti-dumping duties (where 'dumping' is defined by the US government in a way that is biased against foreign companies, as repeated WTO rulings have shown).

42 For further details on the other countries dealt with in this chapter, see Chang (2002), chapter 2, pp. 32–51 and H-J. Chang (2005), *Why Developing Countries Need Tariffs – How WTO NAMA Negotiations Could Deny Developing Countries' Right to a Future*, Oxfam, Oxford, and South Centre, Geneva (http://www.southcentre.org/publications/SouthPerspectiveSeries/WhyDev CountriesNeedTariffsNew.pdf)

43 See the evidence presented in Nye (1991).

44 The average industrial tariff rates were 14% in Belgium (1959), 18% in Japan (1962) and Italy (1959), around 20% in Austria and Finland (1962) and 30% in France (1959). See Chang (2005), Table 5.

45 Chang (2005), Table 5. In 1973, the EEC countries included Belgium, Denmark, France, Italy, Luxemburg, the Netherlands, UK and West Germany.

46 R. Kuisel (1981), *Capitalism and the State in Modern France* (Cambridge Univesity Press, Cambridge), p. 14.

47 Irwin (2002) is an example.

48 In their celebrated article cited in chapter 1, Jeffrey Sachs and Andrew Warner discuss how 'wrong' theories have influenced developing countries to adopt 'wrong' policies. J. Sachs & A. Warner (1995), 'Economic Reform and the Process of Global Integration', *Brookings Papers on Economic Activity*, 1995, no. 1, pp. 11–21.

49 When the Cancún talk of the WTO collapsed, Willem Buiter, the distinguished Dutch economist who was then the chief economist of the EBRD (European Bank for Reconstruction and Development) argued: 'Although the leaders of the developing nations rule countries that are, on average, poor or very poor, it does not follow that these leaders necessarily speak on behalf of the poor and poorest in their countries. Some do; others represent corrupt and repressive élites that feed off the rents created by imposing barriers to trade and other distortions, at the expense of their poorest and most defenceless citizens'. See Willem Buiter, 'If anything is rescued from Cancún, politics must take precedence over economics', letter to the editor, *Financial Times*, September 16 2003.

50 The growth rates in this paragraph are from A. Maddison (2003), *The World Economy: Historical Statistics* (OECD, Paris), Table 8b.

Chapter 3

1 Willem Buiter (2003), 'If anything is rescued from Cancún, politics must take precedence over economics', letter to the editor, *Financial Times*, September 16 2003.

2 Most of the Mexican diaspora are recent immigrants but some of them are the descendants of the former Mexicans who became Americans due to the annexation of large swathes of the Mexican territory – including all or parts of modern California, New Mexico, Arizona, Nevada, Utah, Colorado and Wyoming – after the US-Mexico War (1846–48) under the Treaty of Guadalupe Hidalgo (1848).

3 The numbers are from M. Weisbrot et al. (2005), 'The Scorecard on Development: 25 Years of Diminished Progress', Center for Economic and Policy Research (CEPR), Washington, DC, September, 2005 (http://www.cepr.net/publications/development 2005 09.pdf), Figure 1.

4 Mexican *per capita* income experienced a fall in 2001 (-1.8%), 2002 (-0.8%), and 2003 (-0.1%) and grew only by 2.9% in 2004, which was barely enough to bring the income back to the 2001 level. In 2005, it grew at an estimated rate of 1.6%. This means that Mexico's *per capita* income at the end of 2005 was 1.7% higher than it was in 2001, which translates into an annual growth rate of around 0.3% over the 2001–5 period. The 2001–2004 figures are from the relevant issues of the World Bank annual report, *World Development Report* (World Bank, Washington, DC). The 2005 income growth figure (3%) is from J. C. Moreno-Brid & I. Paunovic (2006), 'Old Wine in New Bottles? – Economic Policymaking in Left-of-center Governments in Latin America', *Revista – Harvard Review of Latin America*, Spring/Summer, 2006, p. 47, Table. The 2005 population growth rate (1.4%) is extrapolated from World Bank (2006), data for 2000–4, found in *World Development Report 2006* (World Bank, Washington, DC), p. 292, Table 1.

5 Mexico's *per capita* income during 1955–82 grew at over 6%, according to J. C. Moreno-Brid et al. (2005), NAFTA and 'The Mexican Economy: A Look Back on a Ten-Year Relationship', *North Carolina International Law and Commerce Register*, vol. 30. As Mexico's population growth rate during this period was 2.9% per annum, this gives us *per capita* income growth rate of around 3.1%. The population growth rate is calculated from A. Maddison (2001), *The World Economy – A Millennial Perspective* (OECD, Paris), p. 280, Table C2-a.

6 For further details, see H-J. Chang (2005), *Why Developing Countries Need Tariffs – How WTO NAMA Negotiations Could Deny Developing Countries' Right to a Future*, Oxfam, Oxford, and South Centre, Geneva (http://www.southcentre.org/publications/SouthPerspectiveSeries/WhyDev CountriesNeedTariffsNew.pdf), pp. 78–81.

7 Tariffs account for 54.7% of government revenue for Swaziland, 53.5% for Madagascar, 50.3% for Uganda and 49.8% for Sierra Leone. See Chang (2005), pp, 16–7.

8 T. Baunsgaard & M. Keen (2005), 'Trade Revenue and (or?) Trade Liberalisation', IMF Working Paper WP/05/112 (The International Monetary Fund, Washington, DC).

9 In this sense, the HOS theory is highly unrealistic in one crucial respect – it assumes that the developing countries can use the same technology as those used by developed countries, but the lack of the capability to use more productive (and naturally more difficult) technologies is exactly what makes those countries poor. Indeed, infant industry protection is exactly aimed at raising such capability, known as 'technological capability' among economists.

10 Remarks at a White House Briefing for Trade Association Representatives on Free and Fair Trade, 17 July 1986.

11 Oxfam (2003), 'Running into the Sand – Why Failure at Cancun Trade Talks Threatens the World's Poorest People', Oxfam Briefing Paper, August 2003, p. 24.

12 The tariff figures are from Oxfam (2003), pp. 25–7. The income figures are from the World Bank data set. In 2002, France and Bangladesh respectively paid around $320 million and $300 million in tariffs to the US. Total income of Bangladesh in the same year was $47 billion, whereas that of France was $1,457 billion. In the same year, the UK paid around $420 million in US tariffs, while India paid about $440 million. UK and Indian incomes in that year were $1,565 billion and $506 billion respectively.

13 According to an estimate by Oxfam in 2002, European citizens are supporting the dairy industry to the tune of £16 billion a year through subsidies and tariffs. This is equivalent to more than $2 per cow per day – half the world's people live on less than this amount. Oxfam (2002), 'Milking the CAP', Oxfam Briefing no. 34 (Oxfam, Oxford). Downloadable at: http://www.oxfam.org.uk/what_ we_ do/issues/trade/downloads/bp34_ cap.pdf

14 T. Fritz (2005), 'Special and Differential Treatment for Developing Countries', Global Issues Paper no. 18, Heinrich Böll Foundation, Berlin.

15 In 1998, a multilateral investment agreement (MIA), which proposed to put severe restrictions on governments' abilities to regulate foreign investment, was proposed in the OECD, the club of rich countries. Ostensibly, it was an agreement only among the rich countries, but the ultimate goal was to make it include the developing countries. By proposing to allow developing countries *voluntarily* sign up to the agreement, the rich countries hoped that all developing countries would eventually feel obliged to sign up to it for fear of being blackballed in the international investors' community. Some developing countries, such as Argentina (a faithful disciple of the IMF and the World Bank at the time), enthusiastically volunteered to sign up to it, putting pressure on other developing countries to do likewise. When the proposal was thwarted in 1998 due to disagreements among the rich countries themselves, the rich countries tried to put the proposal back on the international agenda by bringing it to the WTO. However, in the 2003 Cancún ministerial meeting, it was dropped from the WTO agenda due to resistance from developing countries. On the evolution of these events, see H-J. Chang & D. Green (2003), *The Northern WTO Agenda on Investment: Do as we Say, Not as we Did* (CAFOD [Catholic Agency for Overseas Development], London, and South Centre, Geneva), pp. 1–4.

16 See J. Stiglitz & A. Charlton (2005), *Fair Trade for All – How Trade Can Promote Development* (Oxford University Press, Oxford), pp. 121–2 and Appendix 1. For various numerical estimates of the gains from agricultural liberalization in the rich countries, see F. Ackerman (2005), 'The Shrinking Gains from Trade: A Critical Assessment of Doha Round Projections', Global Development and Environment Institute Working Paper, No. 05–01, October 2005, Tufts University. Two World Bank estimates cited by Ackerman put the share of the developed countries in the total world gain from trade liberalization in agriculture by high-income countries at 75% ($41.6 billion out of $55.7 billion) and 70% ($126 billion out of $182 billion).

Chapter 4

1 Between 1971 and 1985, FDI accounted for only about 0.6% of total fixed capital formation (physical investment) of Finland. Outside the communist bloc, only Japan, at 0.1%, had a lower ratio. The data are from UNCTAD (various years), *World Investment Report* (United Nations Conference on Trade and Development, Geneva).

2 M. Feldstein (2000), 'Aspects of Global Economic Integration: Outlook for the Future', NBER Working Paper, no. 7899, National Bureau of Economic Research, Cambridge, Massachusetts.

3 A. Kose, E. Prasad, K. Rogeff & S-J. Wei (2006), 'Financial Globalisation: A Reappraisal', IMF Working Paper, WP/06/189, International Monetary Fund (IMF), Washington, DC.

4 Bank loans used to be the dominant element of debts until recently, but now bonds account for the lion's share. Between 1975 and 1982, bonds accounted for only about 5% of total net private debts contracted by developing countries. The share rose to about 30% between 1990 and 1998, and to nearly 70% between 1999 and 2005. The data are from World Bank, *Global Development Finance*, the 1999 and the 2005 issues.

5 The distinction between portfolio equity investment and FDI is, in practice, ambiguous. FDI is usually defined as an investor buying up more than a 10% stake in a company in a foreign country, with the intention of getting involved in the management of the company. But there is no economic theory that says that the threshold should be 10%. Moreover, there is a hybrid form emerging that blurs the boundary even more. Traditionally, foreign direct investment has been made by transnational corporations (TNCs), which are defined as productive corporations with operations in more than one country. But recently what the UN calls 'collective invest-ment funds' (such as private equity funds, mutual funds or hedge funds) have become active in foreign direct investment. FDI by these funds differs from traditional FDI by TNCs because it does not have the potentially infi-nite commitments of TNCs. These funds typically buy up firms with a view to selling them off after 5–10 years, or even earlier – without improving their productive capabilities, if they can get away with it. On this phenomenon, see UNCTAD (2006), *World Investment Report, 2006* (United Nations Conference on Trade and Development, Geneva).

6 For an up-to-date literature review on the aid issue, see S. Reddy & C. Minoiu (2006), 'Development Aid and Economic Growth: A Positive Long-Run Relation', DESA Working Paper, no. 29, September 2006, Department of Economic and Social Affairs (DESA), United Nations, New York.

7 The data on capital flows in this paragraph are from World Bank (2006), *Global Development Finance 2006*, (World Bank, Washington, DC.), Table A.1.

8 Foreigners bought $38 billion worth of developing country bonds in 1997, but, during 1998–2002, the sum fell to $23 billion per year. During 2003–2005, the amount went up to $44 billion per year. This means that, compared to 1997, bond purchases during 1998–2002 was 40% lower, while the 2003–5 purchase was double that of the 'dry' period and 15% higher than in 1997.

9 Portfolio equity investment into developing countries fell from $31 billion in 1997 to $9 billion per year during 1998–2002. In 2003–5, it averaged $41 billion per year. This means that, during 1998–2002, the average annual port-folio equity investment inflow into developing countries was less than 30% of what it was in 1997. In 2003–5, it was 30% higher than in 1997 and 4.5 times more than in the 'dry' period of 1998–2002.

10 The Asian crises are well documented and analysed by J. Stiglitz (2002), *Globalization and Its Discontents* (Allen Lane, London). Also see the chap-ters in H-J. Chang, G. Palma and H. Whittaker (eds.) (2001), *Financial Liberalisation and the Asian Crisis*, (Palgrave, Basingstoke and New York).

11 In 2005, the US stock market was worth $15,517 billion. The Indian market was $506 billion. http://www.diehardindian.com/overview/stockmkt.htm.

12 In 1999, the Nigerian stock market was worth a mere $2.94 billion, whereas that of Ghana was a mere $0.91 billion. http://www.un.org/ecosocdev/geninfo/afrec/subjindx/143stock.htm

13 B. Eichengreen & M. Bordo (2002), 'Crises Now and Then: What Lessons from the Last Era of Financial Globalisation', NBER Working Paper, no. 8716, National Bureau of Economic Research (NBER), Cambridge, Massachusetts.

14 This is the title of chapter 13 of J. Bhagwati (2004), *In Defense of Globalization* (Oxford University Press, New York).

15 The new, more nuanced view of the IMF is set out in detail in two papers written by Kenneth Rogoff, a former chief economist of the IMF (2001–2003), and three IMF economists. E. Prasad, K. Rogoff, S-J. Wei & A. Kose (2003), 'Effects of Financial Globalisation on Developing Countries: Some Empirical Evidence', IMF Occasional Paper, no. 220, International Monetary Fund (IMF), Washington, DC, and Kose et al. (2006).

16 Kose et al. (2006), pp. 34–5. The full quote is: 'premature opening of the capital account without having in place well-developed and well-supervised financial sectors, good institutions, and sound macroeconomic policies can hurt a country by making the structure of the inflows unfavourable and by making the country vulnerable to sudden stops or reversals of flows'.

17 World Bank (2003), *Global Development Finance, 2003* (World Bank, Washington, DC.), Table 1.1.

18 World Bank (2006), Table A.1.

19 L. Brittan (1995), 'Investment Liberalisation: The Next Great Boost to the World Economy', *Transnational Corporations*, vol. 4, no. 1. p. 2.

20 For example, one study by a group of IMF economists shows that, for a sample of 30 poorer developing countries during 1985–2004, FDI inflows turned out to be *more* volatile than equity flows or debt flows. See Kose et al. (2006), Table 3. The 30 countries are Algeria, Bangladesh, Bolivia, Cameroon, Costa Rica, the Dominican Republic, Ecuador, EI Salvador, Fiji, Ghana, Guatemala, Honduras, Iran, Jamaica, Kenya, Malawi, Mauritius, Nepal, Niger, Papua New Guinea, Paraguay, Senegal, Sri Lanka, Tanzania, Togo, Trinidad and Tobago, Tunisia, Uruguay, Zambia and Zimbabwe. FDI inflows were less volatile than equity or debt flows for the sample of 'emerging market' economies, which include Argentina, Brazil, Chile, China, Colombia, Egypt, India, Indonesia, Israel, Korea, Malaysia, Mexico, Pakistan, Peru, the Philippines, Singapore, South Africa, Thailand, Turkey and Venezuela.

21 P. Loungani & A. Razin (2001), 'How Beneficial is Foreign Direct Investment for Developing Countries?', *Finance and Development*, vol.. 28, no. 2.

22 In addition, with the increasing importance of collective investment funds that I discussed previously (note 5), there is also shortening of time horizons for FDI, which makes such 'liquidizing' of FDI more likely.

23 These include local content requirements (where TNCs are required to buy more than a certain share of inputs from local producers), export requirements (where they are forced to export more than a certain proportion of their output) and foreign exchange balancing requirements (where they are required to export at least as much as they import).

24 Christian Aid (2005), 'The Shirts off Their Backs – How Tax Policies Fleece the Poor', September 2005.

25 Kose et al. (2006), pp. 29.

26 Moreover, brownfield investment can magnify the negative impact of transfer pricing. If a TNC that has bought up, rather than newly created, a company is practising transfer pricing, the firm that has now become a TNC subsidiary could be paying less tax than it used to when it was a domestic firm.

27 The data are from UNCTAD (United Nations Conference on Trade and Development).

28 Especially when it comes to FDI by collective investment funds (see notes 5 and 22), this may be the sensible strategy, as they do not have the industry-specific knowhow to improve the productive capabilities of the firms they buy up.

29 R. Kozul-Wright & P. Rayment (2007), *The Resistible Rise of Market Fundamentalism: Rethinking Development Policy in an Unbalanced World* (Zed Books, London), chapter 4. Also, see Kose et al. (2006), pp. 27–30.

30 The measures include: requirements for joint ventures, which increases the chance of technology transfer to the local partner; explicit conditions concerning technology transfer; local contents requirements, which forces the TNC to transfer some technology to the supplier; and export require-ments, which force the TNC to use up-to-date technology in order to be competitive in the world market.

31 Sanjaya Lall, the late Oxford economist and one of the leading scholars on TNCs, once put this point well: 'while having more FDI, on the margin, may usually (if not always) bring net benefits to the host country, there still is a question of choosing between different strategies regarding the role of FDI in long-term development'. See S. Lall (1993), Introduction, in S. Lall (ed.), *Transnational Corporations and Economic Development* (Routledge, London).

32 The quote is from *Bankers' Magazine*, no. 38, January 1884, as cited in Wilkins (1989), *The History of Foreign Investment in the United States to 1914* (Harvard University Press, Cambridge, Mass), p. 566. The full quote is: 'It will be a happy day for us when not a single good American security is owned abroad and when the United States shall cease to be an exploiting ground for European bankers and money lenders. The tribute paid to foreigners is . . . odious . . . We have outgrown the necessity of submitting to the humiliation of going to London, Paris or Frankfort [*sic*] for capital has become amply abundant for all home demands.'

33 Foreign lenders were also badly treated. In 1842, the US became a pariah in the international capital market when 11 state governments defaulted on foreign (mainly British) loans. Later that year, when the US federal government tried to raise a loan in the City of London, *The Times* hit back, saying: '[t]he people of the United States may be fully persuaded that there is a certain class of securities to which no abundance of money, however great, can give value; and that in this class their own securities stand pre-eminent'. As cited in T. Cochran & W. Miller (1942), *The Age of Enterprise: A Social History of Industrial America* (The Macmillan Company, New York), p. 48.

34 The second Bank of USA, set up in 1816 under a 20-year charter, was 20% owned by the government and federal tax revenue was deposited there, but it did not have note issue monopoly, so it could not be considered a proper central bank.

35 As cited in Wilkins (1989), p. 84.

36 Even until as late as 1914, when it had become as rich as the UK, the US was one of the largest net borrowers in the international capital market. The authoritative estimate by the US historian Mira Wilkins puts the level of US foreign debt at that time at $7.1 billion, with Russia ($3.8 billion) and Canada ($3.7 billion) trailing far behind (p. 145, Table, 5.3). Of course, at that point, the US, with its estimated lending at $3.5 billion, was also the fourth largest lending country, after the UK ($18 billion), France ($9 billion) and Germany ($7.3 billion). However, even after subtracting its lending, the US still had a net borrowing position of $3.6 billion, which was basically the same as the Russian and the Canadian figures. See Wilkins (1989).

37 Wilkins (1989), p. 563

38 Cited in Wilkins (1989), p. 85.

39 Wilkins (1989), p. 583.

40 Wilkins (1989), p. 83, and p. 583

41 At the time, the territories were North Dakota, South Dakota, Idaho, Montana, New Mexico, Utah, Washington, Wyoming, Oklahoma and Alaska. The Dakotas, Montana and Washington in 1889, Idaho and Wyoming in 1890, and Utah in 1896 became states, and thus were no longer subject to this Act. See Wilkins (1989), p. 241.

42 Wilkins (1989), p. 579.

43 Wilkins (1989), p. 580.

44 Wilkins (1989), p. 456.

45 For further details, see M. Yoshino (1970), 'Japan as Host to the International Corporation' in C. Kindleberger (ed.), *The International Corporation – A Symposium* (The MIT Press, Cambridge, MA).

46 Between 1971 and 1990, FDI accounted for less than 0.1% of total fixed capital formation (physical investment) of Japan, as opposed to 3.4% average for the developed countries as a whole (for 1981–1990). The data are from UNCTAD, *World Investment Report* (various years).

47 Government of Japan (2002), 'Communication to the Working Group on Trade and Investment', 27 June 2002, WT/WGTI/W/125.

48 Between 1971–95, FDI accounted for less than 1% of total fixed capital formation in Korea, while the developing country average for the 1981–95 period (pre-1980 figures are not available) was 4.3%. Data from UNCTAD (various years).

49 In Taiwan, between 1971–95, FDI accounted around 2.5% of total fixed capital formation, as against the developing country average of 4.3% (for 1981–95). Data from UNCTAD (various years).

50 S. Young, N. Hood, and J. Hamill (1988), *Foreign Multinationals and the British Economy – Impact and Policy* (Croom Helm, London), p. 223.

51 Young et al. (1988), p. 225

52 According to the US Department of Commerce 1981 survey, *The Use of Investment Incentives and Performance Requirements by Foreign Governments*, 20% of US TNC affiliates operating in Ireland reported the imposition of performance requirement, in contrast to the 2–7% in other advanced countries – 8% in Australia and Japan, 7% in Belgium, Canada, France and Switzerland, 6% in Italy, 3% in the UK and 2% in Germany and the Netherlands. See Young et al. (1988), pp. 199–200. For further discussions on the Irish FDI strategy, see H-J. Chang & D. Green (2003), *The Northern WTO Agenda on Investment: Do as we Say, Not as we Did* (CAFOD [Catholic Agency for Overseas Development], London, and South Centre, Geneva), pp. 19–23.

53 Particularly notorious in this regard is the so-called Chapter 11 in NAFTA (North American Free Trade Agreement), which the US has managed to include in all its bilateral free trade agreements (except in the one with Australia). Chapter 11 gives foreign investors the right to take the host country government to special international arbitration bodies of the World Bank and the United Nations if they think the value of their investment has been reduced due to government action, ranging from nationalization to environmental regulation. Despite involving the government, these arbitration procedures are closed to public participation, observation and input.

54 Kozul-Wright & Rayment (2007), ch. 4.

55 P. Hirst & G. Thompson (1999), *Globalization in Question*, 2nd edition (Polity Press, Cambridge), chapter 3, provides detailed information on this.

56 World Bank (1985), *World Development Report, 1985* (Oxford University Press, New York), p. 130.

57 Nokia was founded as a logging company in 1865. The shape of the modern Nokia group started emerging when Finnish Rubber Works Ltd (founded in 1898) bought the majority shares in Nokia in 1918 and in Finnish Cable Works (founded in 1912) in 1922. Finally, in 1967, the three companies were merged to form Nokia Corporation. Some Finnish observers summarize the nature of the merger by saying that the name of the merged company (Oy Nokia Ab) came from wood processing, the management from the cable factory and the money from the rubber industry. Nokia's electronic business, whose mobile phone business forms the core of the company's business today, was set up in 1960. Even until 1967, when the merger between Nokia, FRW and FCW happened, electronics generated only 3% of Nokia group's net sales. The electronics arm lost money for the first 17 years, making its first profit only in 1977. The world's first international cellular mobile telephone network, NMT, was introduced in Scandinavia in 1981 and Nokia made the first car phones for it. Nokia produced the original hand-portable phone in 1987. Riding on this wave, Nokia rapidly expanded during the 1980s by acquiring a series of electronics and telecommunications companies in Finland, Germany, Sweden and France. Since the 1990s, Nokia's leading business has been mobile phones. By the 1990s, Nokia became the leader in mobile telecommunications revolution. For further details, see H-J. Chang (2006), 'Public Investment Management', National Development Strategy Policy Guidance Note, United Nations DESA (Department of Economic and Social Affairs) and UNDP (United Nations Development Program), Box 15.

Chapter 5

1 Property rights need not be *private* property rights, as is implicitly assumed by many people who emphasize the role of property rights. There are many *communal* property rights that work well. Many rural communities from all over the world have communal property rights that effectively regulate the use of common resources (e.g., forest, fishery) to prevent their over-exploitation. A more modern example is open-source computer software, such as Linux, where users are encouraged to improve the product but are banned from using the improved product for their personal benefit.

2 Strictly speaking, the soft budget constraint is not a problem due to ownership *per se*. All that is needed to 'harden' it is to punish lax management, which can be done even under state ownership. Moreover, soft budget constraints alone do not make the managers of the enterprises lazy. Why?

If professional managers (whether they are running an SOE or a private enterprise) know they will be severely punished for poor management (say, have their salaries cut or even lose their jobs), they will not have the incentive to mismanage their firms (allowing for, of course, the usual principal-agent problem). If they are punished for poor management, the fact that their company survives thanks to government bail-out is neither here nor there for them. Therefore, even though soft budget constraints are more likely for SOEs due to their ownership status, the key cause of the problem is the incentives for the SOE managers, rather than soft budget constraints. If that is the case, privatization is unlikely to change the performances of the enterprises involved. For further discussion, see H-J. Chang (2000), 'The Hazard of Moral Hazard – Untangling the Asian Crisis', *World Development*, vol. 28, no. 4.

3 T. Georgakopolous, K. Prodromidis, & J. Loizides (1987), 'Public Enterprises in Greece', *Annals of Public and Cooperative Economics*, vol. 58, no. 4.

4 *The Wall Street Journal*, May 24 1985, as quoted in J. Roddick (1988), *The Dance of the Millions: Latin America and the Debt Crisis* (Latin America Bureau, London), p109.

5 Temasek Holdings owns majority shares in the following enterprises: 100% of Singapore Power (electricity and gas) and of PSA International (ports), 67% of Neptune Orient Lines (shipping), 60% of Chartered Semiconductor Manufacturing (semiconductor), 56% of SingTel (telecommunications), 55% of SMRT (rail, bus and taxi services), 55% of Singapore Technologies Engineering (engineering) and 51% of SembCorp Industries (engineering). It also owns a controlling stake in the following enterprises: 32% of SembCorp Marine (shipbuilding) and 28% of DBS (the largest bank in Singapore). See H-J. Chang (2006), 'Public Investment Management', National Development Strategy Policy Guidance Note, United Nations DESA (Department of Economic and Social Affairs) and UNDP (United Nations Development Program), Box 1.

6 According to a well-known World Bank report on SOEs, the average share of the SOE sector in GDP in the 40 developing countries it studied was 10.7% during 1978–91. The corresponding figure for Korea was 9.9%. See World Bank (1995), *Bureaucrats in Business* (Oxford University Press, New York), Table A.1. Unfortunately, the World Bank report did not provide the data on Singapore. However, the Singapore Government's Department of Statistics estimated that GLCs accounted for 12.9% of GDP in 1998, with the non-GLC public sector (such as Statutory Boards) accounting for another 8.9%, giving a total of 21.8%. The Department of Statistics defined GLC as those companies in which the government has an effective ownership of 20% or more. For the sources, see Chang (2006), Box 1.

7 According to World Bank (1995), Table A.1, the share of the SOE sector in GDP during 1978–91 were 4.7% in Argentina and 1.9% in the Philippines.

8 For further details on POSCO, see Chang, (2006), Box 2.

9 Chang (2006), Box 3.

10 The three principles are those of *minzu* (nationalism) *minquan* (people's power or democracy) and *minsheng* (people's livelihood).

11 www.economywatch.com/world_economy/china/structure-of economy.html.

12 J. Willner (2003), 'Privatisation and State Onwership in Finland', CESifo Working Paper, no. 1012, August 2003, Ifo Institute for Economic Research, Munich.

13 M. Berne & G Pogorel (2003), 'Privatisation Experiences in France', paper presented at the CESifo Conference on Privatisation Experiences in the EU, Cadenabbia, Italy, November 2003.

14 The story of Renault's privatization is typical of the French privatization process. Renault was first established as a private company in 1898. It was nationalized in 1945 for having been 'an instrument of the enemy' – its owner, Louis Renault, was a Nazi collaborator. In 1994, the French state started selling the shares, but kept a 53% share. In 1996, it relinquished its majority share, reducing its holdings to 46%. However, 11% of the shares was sold to what the company website calls 'a stable core of major shareholders', many of them financial institutions partly controlled by the French state. Since then, the French government has gradually reduced its share to 15.3% (as of 2005), but still remains the largest single shareholder. Moreover, an important part of this reduction in the French government's share is explained by the acquisition in 2002 of 15% of Renault shares by Nissan, which had formed an alliance with Renault in 1999. Since Renault has owned the controlling stake (first 35%, now 44%) in Nissan since 1999, the French state effectively controls 30% of Renault's shares, making it the dominant force in Renault. See Chang (2006), Box 2.

15 Chang (2006), Box 2.

16 W. Henderson (1963), *Studies in the Economic Policy of Frederick the Great* (Frank Cass, London), pp. 136–152.

17 See T. Smith (1955), *Political Change and Industrial Development in Japan: Government Enterprise, 1868–1880* (Stanford University Press, Stanford) and G. C. Allen (1981), *A Short Economic History of Modern Japan*, 4th edition (Macmillan, London and Basingstoke), for further details.

18 See H-J. Chang (2002), *Kicking Away the Ladder – Development Strategy in Historical Perspective* (Anthem Press, London), p. 101.

19 T. Kessler & N. Alexander (2003), 'Assessing the Risks in the Private Provision of Essential Services', Discussion Paper for G-24 Technical Group, Geneva, Switzerland, September 15–6, 2003, available at the website, http://www.unctad.org/en/docs/gdsmdpbg2420047_en.pdf,

20 Indeed, there is evidence that gains in productivity in privatized enterprises usually occur *before* privatization through anticipatory restructuring, suggesting that restructuring is more important than privatization. See Chang (2006).

21 D. Green (2003), *Silent Revolution – The Rise and Crisis of Market Economics in Latin America* (Monthly Review Press, New York, and Latin American Bureau, London), p. 109.

22 *Miami Herald*, 3 March 1991. As cited in Green (2003), p. 107.

23 P. Tandon (1992), *World Bank Conference on the Welfare Consequences of Selling Public Enterprises: Case Studies from Chile, Malaysia, Mexico and the U.K.*, Vol. 1: Mexico, Background, TELMEX, World Bank Country Economics Department, June 7 1992, p. 6.

24 Kessler & Alexander (2003).

25 Many academic studies have shown that competition is usually more important than ownership status in determining SOE performance. For a review of these studies, see H-J. Chang & A. Singh (1993), 'Public Enterprise in Developing Countries and Economic Efficiency', *UNCTAD Review*, 1993, no. 4.

26 Some economists argue that competition may be 'simulated' in a natural-monopoly industry by artificially dividing it up into smaller (say, regional) units and rewarding/punishing them according to their relative performances. Unfortunately, this method, known as 'yardstick competition', is difficult to manage even for well-resourced developed country regulators, as it involves administering complicated performance-measurement formulas. It is highly unlikely that the regulators in developing countries can cope with them. Moreover, in the case of network industries (e.g., railways), the potential benefit from simulated competition among regional units should be set against the increased costs of co-ordination failure due to the fragmentation of a network. The British railway privatization of 1993 created dozens of regional operators that compete with each other very little (due to geographically-based franchising) while providing poor connections with trains run by other operators.

27 For example, during the 1980s, the state-owned railway of Britain faced quite intense (partial) competition from privately-owned bus companies in some market segments.

Chapter 6

1 It is estimated that, in 2005, 6.1% of the adult population (15–49 years) in sub-Saharan African carry the HIV virus, as opposed to 1% for the world as a whole. The epidemic has taken on apocalyptic proportions in Botswana, Lesotho and South Africa, but is also very serious in Uganda, Tanzania and Cameroon. It is estimated by the United Nations that Botswana has the most serious epidemic, with 24.1% of the adult population having HIV virus in 2005. Lesotho (23.2%) and South Africa (18.8%) follow closely. The problem is also very serious in Uganda (6.7%), Tanzania (6.5%) and Cameroon (5.4%). All the statistics are from UNAIDS (United Nations Program on HIV/AIDS) (2006), *2006 Report on the Global AIDS Epidemic*, downloadable at http://data.unaids.org/pub/GlobalReport/2006/2006_GR_CH02_en.pdf.

2 *Per capita* income in 2004 was $4,340 in Botswana, $3,630 in South Africa, $800 in Cameroon, $740 in Lesotho, $330 in Tanzania and $270 in Uganda. The figures are from World Bank (2006), *World Development Report 2006*, Tables 1 and 5.

3 When the US government announced its intention to stockpile the anti-anthrax drug, Cipro, Bayer volunteered to give a substantial discount to the US government (it offered $1.89 per tablet instead of the drugstore price of $4.50 per tablet). But the US government considered even this insufficient, given the fact that a copy drug produced in India cost less than ¢20. The US government got another 50% discount from Bayer by threatening to impose compulsory licensing. For further details, see A. Jaffe & J. Lerner (2004), *Innovation and Its Discontents – How Our Broken Patent System Is Endangering Innovation and Progress, and What to do about It* (Princeton University Press, Princeton), p. 17.

4 H. Bale, 'Access to Essential Drugs in Poor Countries – Key Issues', downloadable from http://www.ifpma.org/News/SpeechDetail.aspx?nID=4

5 'Strong global patent rules increase the cost of medicines', *The Financial Times*, February 14 2001.

6 See the website of the US pharmaceutical industry association, http://www.phrma.org/publications/profile00/chap2.phtm#growth.

7 For example, a major survey conducted in the mid-1980s asked the chief R&D executives of US firms what proportion of the inventions they developed would not have been developed without patent protection. Among the 12 industry groups surveyed, there were only three industries where the answer was 'high' (60% for pharmaceutical and 38% for other chemicals and 25% for petroleum). And there were six others where the answer was basically 'none' (0% for office equipment, motor vehicles, rubber products and textiles,

1% for primary metals and instruments). In the remaining three industries, the answer was 'low' (17% for machinery, 12% for fabricated metal products and 11% for electrical equipment). See E. Mansfield (1986), 'Patents and Innovation: An Empirical Study', *Management Science*, vol. 32, February. The result of this study is confirmed by a number of other studies conducted in the UK and Germany, cited in F. Scherer & D. Ross (1990), *Industrial Market Structure and Economic Performance* (Houghton Mifflin Company, Boston), p. 629, footnote 46.

8 A study based on a survey of 650 high-level R&D managers of listed companies in the US found that patents are considered much *less* important in preserving an innovator's advantage than these 'natural advantages'. See R. Levin, A., Klevorick, R., Nelson, S. & Winter (1987), 'Appropriating the Returns form Industrial Research and Development', *Brookings Papers on Economic Activity*, 1987, no. 3.

9 F. Machlup & E. Penrose (1950) 'The Patent Controversy in the Nineteenth Century', *Journal of Economic History*, vol. 10, no. 1, p. 18.

10 See J. Schumpeter (1987), *Capitalism, Socialism and Democracy*, 6th edition (Unwin Paperbacks, London). According to the authoritative British historian of economic thought, Mark Blaug, Schumpeter mentions patents only a few times in the thousands of the pages he wrote.

11 For further details on the anti-patent movement, see Machlup & Penrose (1950).

12 J. Gleeson (2000), *The Moneymaker* (Bantam, London). A more scholarly biography and a systematic discussion of Law's economic theories is A. Murphy (1997), *John Law – Economic Theorist and Policy-maker* (Clarendon Press, Oxford).

13 According to the eminent economic historian, Charles Kindleberger, Law argued that 'if the money supply were increased by bank notes issued for productive loans, employment and output would rise proportionately, and the value of money would remain stable'. See C. Kindleberger (1984), *A Financial History of Western Europe* (George Allen & Unwin, London). For further details, see Murphy (1997).

14 According to a contemporary account, around 900 British workers – watchmakers, weavers, metal-workers and others – were recruited by Law's brother William and settled in Versailles (Gleeson, 2000, p. 121). The historian John Harris gives a samller estimate: 'About 70 watchmakers were recruited and established in Versailles and Paris, at least 14 glass makers and over 30 metal workers emigrated. The last group included lock- and file-makers, hinge-makers, girders, and an important group of foundry workers who were established at Chaillot in Paris. Most of the other workers in metals and glass were in Normandy, at Harfleur and Honfleur. A substantial colony of woollen workers was set up at Charlaval and on Law's recently acquired Norman estate, Tancarville. The main groups listed certainly do not include all the skilled workers involved … The total number of workers who emigrated through the Law scheme was probably over 150 …' J. Harris (1991), 'Movement of Technology between Britain and Europe in the Eighteenth Century' in D. Jeremy (ed.), *International Technology Transfer – Europe, Japan, and the USA, 1700–1914* (Edward Elgar, Aldershot).

15 For further details on the British ban on the emigration of skilled workers, see D. Jeremy (1977), 'Damming the Flood: British Government Efforts to Check the Outflow of Technicians and Machinery, 1780–1843', *Business History Review*, vol. LI, no. 1, and J. Harris (1998), *Industrial Espionage and Technology Transfer – Britain and France in the Eighteenth Century* (Ashgate, Aldershot), ch. 18.

16 For further details, see Jeremy (1977) and Harris (1998)

17 Technologies were relatively simple at the time so that a person with the right skills background could learn a lot about its technology from a tour of a factory.

18 For further details, see Harris (1998), D. Landes (1969), *The Unbound Prometheus – Technological Change and Industrial Development in Western Europe from 1750 to the Present* (Cambridge University Press, Cambridge) and K. Bruland (ed.) (1991), *Technology Transfer and Scandinavian Industrialisation*, (Berg, New York).

19 The British patent law came into being in 1623 with the Statute of Monopolies, although some argue that it did not really deserve the name of a 'patent law' until its reform in 1852, For example, see C. McLeod (1988), *Inventing the Industrial Revolution: the English Patent System, 1660–1800* (Cambridge University Press, Cambridge).

20 Russia (1812), Prussia (1815), Belgium and the Netherlands (1817), Spain (1820), Bavaria (1825), Sardinia (1826), the Vatican state (1833), Sweden (1834), Württemberg (1836), Portugal (1837) and Saxony (1843). See E. Penrose (1951), *The Economics of the International Patent System* (The Johns Hopkins Press, Baltimore), p. 13.

21 The original signatories were 11 countries: Belgium, Brazil, France, Guatemala, Italy, the Netherlands, Portugal, El Salvador, Serbia, Spain and Switzerland. The inclusion of trademarks in the agreement enabled patent-less Switzerland and Netherlands to sign up to the Convention. Before the Convention went into effect in July 1884, Britain, Ecuador and Tunisia signed up, bringing the number of original member countries to 14. Subsequently, Ecuador, El Salvador and Guatemala denounced the Convention, and did

not re-join it until the 1990s. The information is from the WIPO (World Intellectual Property Organization) website: http://www.wipo.int/about-ip/en/iprm/pdf/ch5.pdf#paris.

22 They were on the Brownian motion, the photoelectric effect and, most importantly, special relativity.

23 It was only in 1911, six years after he finished his Ph.D., that he was made a professor of physics in the University of Zürich.

24 For further details on the history of Swiss patent system, see Schiff (1971), *Industrialisation without National Patents – the Netherlands, 1869–1912 and Switzerland, 1850–1907* (Princeton University Press, Princeton).

25 Moreover, the 1817 Dutch patent law was rather deficient even by the standards of the time. It did not require a disclosure of the details of patents, it allowed the patenting of imported inventions, it nullified national patents of inventions that acquired foreign patents and there was no penalty on others using patented products without permission as far as it was for their own business. See Schiff (1971), pp. 19–20.

26 Although Edison made some critical contributions to the development of the filament-based light bulb, he did not single-handedly invent it, as is commonly believed. However, he owned all the relevant patents.

27 According to T. Cochran & W. Miller (1942), *The Age of Enterprise: A Social History of Industrial America* (New York, The Macmillan Company), the fact that, between 1820 and 1830, the US produced 535 patents per year against 145 for Great Britain was mainly due to the difference in 'scruples' (p. 14). Contrast this to the argument by K. Sokoloff & Z. Khan (2000) that it was thanks to a 'good' patent system that the US far exceeded Britain in patenting *per capita* by 1810, expressed in their paper, 'Intellectual Property Institutions in the United States: Early Development and Comparative Perspective', prepared for World Bank Summer Research Workshop on Market Institutions, July 17–19, 2000, Washington, DC, (p. 5). The truth probably lies somewhere in between.

28 Durand made the same statement regarding his 1811 patent of an oil lamp. See S. Shephard (2000), *Pickled, Potted & Canned – How the Preservation of Food Changed Civilization* (Headline, London), p. 228.

29 According to this Act, 'it [was] a penal offence to sell an article made abroad which has upon it any word or mark leading the purchaser to believe that it is made in England, in the absence of other words denoting the real place of origin' As cited in E. Williams (1896), '*Made in Germany*' (William Henemann, London), p. 137. The edition consulted is the 1973 edition with an introduction by Austen Albu (The Harvester Press, Brighton).

30 For further details, see Williams (1896), p. 138.

31 Williams (1896), p. 138.

32 The prominent business economist John Kay makes this point brilliantly in a satire featuring Virginia Woolf and her time-travelling literary agent. See J. Kay (2002), 'Copyright law's duty to creativity', *The Financial Times*, October 23 2002.

33 Jaffe & Lerner (2004), p.94. The average was not quite 20 years at that time because some poor countries were yet to fully comply with TRIPS.

34 Chemical (including pharmaceutical) substances remained unpatentable until 1967 in West Germany, 1968 in the Nordic countries, 1976 in Japan, 1978 in Switzerland and 1992 in Spain. Pharmaceutical products remained unpatentable until 1959 in France, 1979 in Italy and 1992 in Spain. The information is from S. Patel (1989), 'Intellectual Property Rights in the Uruguay Round – A Disaster for the South?', *Economic and Political Weekly*, 6 May 1989, p. 980, and G. Dutfield & U. Suthersanen (2004), 'Harmonisation or Differentiation in Intellectual Property Protection? – The Lessons of History', Occasional Paper 15 (Quaker United Nations Office, Geneva), pp. 5–6.

35 With TRIPS, developing countries have been compelled to introduce pharmaceutical product patents, at the latest by 2013 in the case of the poorest countries. When the TRIPS agreement came into effect in 1995, developing countries were to comply to it by 2001. The poorest countries (the Least Developed Countries, or LDCs) were given until 2006, but, at the end of 2005, this was extended to 2013.

36 Dutfield & Suthersanen (2004), p. 6.

37 Jaffe & Lerner (2004), pp. 25–6, p. 34, pp. 74–5.

38 Both cases were eventually settled outside the court.

39 Jaffe & Lerner (2004), pp. 34–5.

40 Jaffe & Lerner (2004), p. 12.

41 The two professors also show that the number of patent suits initiated in the US were around 1,000 per year until the mid-1980s, but are now over 2,500 per year (Jaffe & Lerner, 2004, p. 14, figure 1.2). Given that patent suits are notoriously expensive to fight, this means that resource is diverted from generating new ideas to defending existing ones.

42 In a letter to Robert Hooke, dated February 5 1676.

43 Thus, Jefferson's view of what we can and cannot own was the exact opposite of what we have today – he may have thought nothing of owning other people, but he found it absurd that people should be allowed to own ideas and have their rights protected through an artificial monopoly created by the government called patents.

44 Especially with 'golden rice 2', developed in 2005 by Syngenta, which now owns the technology, the benefits could be even greater. Golden rice 2 produces 23 times more beta carotene than the original golden rice.

45 See http://en.wikipedia.org/wiki/Golden_ rice. Xerophthalmia (Greek for dry eyes) is an inflammation of the conjunctiva of the eye with abnormal dryness and corrugation (*Oxford English Dictionary*).

46 On the golden rice controversy, see RAFI (Rural Advancement Foundation International) (2000), *RAFI Communique*, September/October 2000, Issue #66. Also see Portykus's own account in 'The "Golden Rice" Tale' at http://www.biotech-info.net/GR_tale.html+golden+rice&hl=ko&gl=kr&ct=clnk&cd=4.

47 The IPR expenditure is cited in M. Wolf (2004), *Why Globalisation Works* (Yale University Press, New Haven), p. 217. The foreign aid figure is from the OECD.

48 Wolf (2004), p. 217.

49 As Joseph Stiglitz proposes, a public fund could also be set up to guarantee purchase of valuable inventions, such as life-saving drugs. J. Stiglitz (2006), *Making Globalization Work – The Next Steps to Global Justice* (Allen Lane, London), p. 124.

50 Allowing easier parallel imports may result in some reverse inflow of cheap copies from developing countries before the end of IPR life in developed countries, but there are ways to control them; copy drugs can be manufactured in different shapes and sizes from the originals, while special identification microchips may be implanted in the packaging for the originals to distinguish them from copies. For further discussion of issues related to making IPRs weaker in poor countries, see H-J. Chang (2001), 'Intellectual Property Rights and Economic Development – Historical Lessons and Emerging Issues', *Journal of Human Development*, 2001, vol. 2, no. 2. The article is reprinted in H-J. Chang (2003), *Globalization, Economic Development and The Role of the State* (Zed Press, London).

Chapter 7

1 Of course, the boundary between macroeconomic policy and microeconomic policy (policy that affects particular agents in the economy) is not always clear. For example, regulation regarding the kinds of assets that financial firms (e.g., banks, pension funds) can hold is typically classified as a microeconomic policy, but this can have macroeconomic impacts, if the amount of assets concerned is large.

2 Domingo Cavallo, 'Argentina must grow up', *Financial Times*, 27 July, 2001.

3 *The Los Angeles Times*, October 20 1978.

4 S. Fischer (1996), 'Maintaining Price Stability', *Finance and Development*, December 1996.

5 Interview with *Playboy*, February 1973.

6 For further discussion, see H-J. Chang & I. Grabel (2004), *Reclaiming Development – An Alternative Economic Policy Manual* (Zed Press, London), pp. 181–2 and 185–6.

7 Fischer (1996), p. 35.

8 Moreover, neo-liberals believe that government spending is, by nature, less efficient than private spending. Martin Feldstein, the economic advisor to Ronald Reagan, once put it: 'Increased government spending can provide a temporary stimulus to demand and output but in the longer run higher levels of government spending crowd out private investment or require higher taxes that weaken growth by reducing incentives to save, invest, innovate, and work.' The quote is from: http://www.brainyquote.com/quotes/quotes/m/martinfeld333347.html

9 A. Singh (1995), 'How did East Asia grow so fast? – Slow Progress towards an Analytical Consensus', UNCTAD Discussion Paper, no. 97, Table 8. The other statistics in the paragraph are from the IMF database.

10 The average annual inflation rates (defined as the average annual percentage growth of consumer price index) for the 1960s were 1.3% in Venezuela, 3.5% in Bolivia, 3.6% in Mexico, 10.4% in Peru and 11.9% in Colombia. The rate in Argentina was 21.7%. The information is from Singh (1995), Table 8.

11 The average inflation rates were 12.1% in Venezuela, 14.4% in Ecuador and 19.3% in Mexico. The rates were 22% in Colombia and 22.3% in Bolivia. The data are from Singh (1995), Table 8.

12 The details are from F. Alvarez & S. Zeldes (2001), 'Reducing Inflation in Argentina: Mission Impossible?' http://www2.gsb.columbia.edu/faculty/szeldes/Cases/Argentina/

13 Moreover, in the neo-liberal argument, economic stability is wrongly equated with price stability. Price stability is, of course, an important part of overall economic stability, but the stabilities in output and employment are also important. If we define economic stability more broadly, we cannot say that neo-liberal macroeconomic policy has succeeded even in its self-proclaimed goal of achieving economic stability over the past two and a half decades, as output and employment instabilities have actually increased during this period. For a full discussion of this issue, see J. A. Ocampo (2005),

'A Broad View of Macroeconomic Stability', DESA Working Paper, no. 1, October, 2005, DESA (Department of Economic and Social Affairs), United Nations, New York.

14 A study by Robert Barro, a leading neo-liberal economist, concludes that moderate inflation (inflation rate of 10–20%) has low negative effects on growth, and that, below 10%, inflation has no effect at all. See R. Barro (1996), 'Inflation and Growth', *Review of Federal Reserve Bank of St Louis*, vol. 78, no. 3. A study by Michael Sarel, an IMF economist, concurs. It estimates that, below 8%, inflation has little impact on growth – if anything, he points out, the relationship is positive below that level – that is, inflation helps rather than hinders growth. See M. Sarel (1996), 'Non-linear Effects of Inflation on Economic Growth', *IMF Staff Papers*, Vol., 43, March.

15 M. Bruno (1995), 'Does Inflation Really Lower Growth?', *Finance and Development* pp. 35–38; M. Bruno & W. Easterly (1995), 'Inflation Crises and Long-run Economic Growth', National Bureau of Economic Research (NBER) Working Paper, no. 5209, NBER, Cambridge, Massachusetts.; M. Bruno, and W. Easterly (1996), 'Inflation and Growth: In Search of a Stable Relationship' *Review of Federal Reserve Bank of St Louis*, vol. 78, no. 3.

16 PBS (Public Broadcasting System) interview: http://www.pbs.org/fmc/interviews/volcker.htm.

17 Calculated from the IMF dataset.

18 On the profit rate data, see S. Claessens, S. Djankov & L. Lang (1998), 'Corporate Growth, Financing, and Risks in the Decades before East Asia's Financial Crisis', Policy Research Working Paper, no. 2017, World Bank, Washington, DC, figure 1.

19 T. Harjes & L. Ricci (2005), 'What Drives Saving in South Africa?' In M. Nowak & L. Ricci, *Post-Apartheid South Africa: The First Ten Years* (IMF, Washington, DC), p. 49, figure 4.1.

20 There are many different ways to calculate profit rates, but the relevant concept here is returns on assets. According to Claessens et al. (1998), figure 1, the returns on assets in 46 developed and developing countries during 1988–96 ranged between 3.3% (Austria) and 9.8% (Thailand). The ratio ranged between 4% and 7% in 40 of the 46 countries; it was below 4% in three countries and above 7% in three countries. Another World Bank study puts the average profit rate for non-financial firms in 'emerging market' economies (middle-income countries) during the 1990s (1992–2001) at a lower level of 3.1% (net income/assets). See S. Mohapatra, D. Ratha & P. Suttle (2003), 'Corporate Financing Patterns and Performance in Emerging Markets', mimeo., March, 2003, World Bank, Washington, DC.

21 *OECD Historical Statistics* (OECD, Paris), Table 10.10.

22 There is no evidence that greater central bank independence has any association with lower inflation, higher growth, higher employment, better budget balance or even greater financial stability in developing countries. See the evidence presented in S. Eijffinger & J. de Haan (1996), 'The Political Economy of Central-bank Independence', 'Special Papers in International Economics', No. 19, Princeton University and B. Sikken & J. de Haan (1998), 'Budget Deficits, Monetization, and Central-bank Independence in Developing Countries', *Oxford Economic Papers*, vol. 50, no. 3.

23 http://en.wikipedia.org/wiki/Federal_Reserve_Board

24 On the evolution of IMF policy in Korea following the 1997 crisis, see S-J. Shin & H-J. Chang (2003), *Restructuring Korea Inc.* (Routledge Curzon, London), chapter 3.

25 J. Stiglitz (2001), *Globalization and Its Discontents* (Allen Lane, London), chapter 3.

26 H-J. Chang & I. Grabel (2004), p. 194.

27 It is for this reason that Ocampo (2005) argues that 'fiscal policies cannot be expected to serve by themselves as the major instrument of counter-cyclical management' (p. 11).

28 The remark was made in the documentary movie, *Gore Vidal: The Man Who Said No*, made when Vidal campaigned in 1982 for a California senator seat against Jerry Brown. The full quote is: 'In public services, we lag behind all the industrialized nations of the West, preferring that the public money go not to the people but to big business. The result is a unique society in which we have free enterprise for the poor and socialism for the rich.'

29 John Burton, the *Financial Times* correspondent in Seoul in the early days of Korean financial crisis in 1997, wrote: 'The public has reacted as it has done in previous economic downturns by obeying calls to tighten their belts in the belief that spending less will somehow save the nation from its debt crisis'. Unfortunately, in his view, 'no economist has warned that some austerity measures, such as promises by housewives to serve smaller meals at home, could deepen the country's plunge into recession since it would further reduce the demand needed to bolster growth'. J. Burton, 'Koreans resist the economic facts – With a presidential election near, foreign plots are blamed for national ills', *Financial Times*, December 12 1997.

Chapter 8

1 Press Conference, October 15 2006.

2 As of April 2006, these included Chad, Kenya and Congo in Africa, India, Bangladesh and Uzbekistan in Asia, Yemen in the Middle East, and Argentina

in Latin America. See the website of the NGO, Brettonwoods Project, dedicated to monitoring the IMF and the World Bank. http://www.brettonwoodsproject.org/article.shtml?cmd%5B126%5D=x126–531789.

3 This point was eloquently made by Hilary Benn, the British international development secretary, at the 2006 annual meeting of the World Bank, as he was refusing to give unconditional support to Mr Wolfowitz's anti-corruption drive.

4 G. Hodgson & S. Jiang (2006), 'The Economics of Corruption and the Corruption of Economics: An Institutionalist Perspective', a paper presented at the Annual Meeting of the European Association for Evolutionary Political Economy, November 3–4 2006, Istanbul.

5 See C. Kindleberger (1984), *A Financial History of Western Europe* (Oxford University Press, Oxford), pp. 160–1, for England and pp. 168–9 for France. Also see R. Nield (2002), *Public Corruption – The Dark Side of Social Evolution* (Anthem Press, London), chapter 4 for France, and chapter 6 for Britain. Even in Prussia, arguably the least corrupt European country in the 18th century, offices were not openly for sale but effectively sold to the highest bidder, as the government very often gave jobs to those willing to pay the highest amount for the tax that was customarily imposed on the first year's salary. See R. Dorwart (1953), *The Administrative Reforms of Frederick William I of Prussia* (Harvard University Press, Cambridge, Massachusetts), p. 192.

6 Nield (2002), p. 62.

7 He was supposed to induce the members of his party to support the government by offering them the gifts of offices in the civil service. See Nield (2002), p. 72.

8 The Pendleton Act required the most important jobs (about 10% of total) to be competitively filled. This ratio rose to 50% only by 1897. G. Benson (1978), *Political Corruption in America* (Lexington Books, Lexington, Massachusetts), pp. 80–5.

9 As cited in T. Cochran & W. Miller (1942), *The Age of Enterprise: A Social History of Industrial America* (The Macmillan Company, New York), p. 159.

10 As cited in J. Garraty & M. Carnes (2000), *The American Nation – A History of the United States*, 10th edition (Addison Wesley Longman, New York), p. 472. Open sales of votes by them were especially widespread in the 1860s and 1870s. The group of corrupt assemblymen from both parties, called 'Black Horse Cavalry', demanded $1,000 per vote on railroad bills and vigorous bidding drove prices up to $5,000 per vote. The group also introduced 'strike bills', which, if passed, would greatly hinder some wealthy interests or corporation,

and would then demand payment to drop the bill. As a result, some companies created lobbying organizations that bought legislation, sparing themselves from blackmail. See Benson (1978), pp. 59–60.

11 The information is from World Bank (2005), *World Development Report 2005 – A Better Investment Climate for Everyone* (World Bank, Washington, DC), p. 101, Box 5.4.

12 S. Huntington (1968), *Political Order in Changing Societies* (Yale University Press, New Haven), p. 386.

13 One crucial action to take is making elections cheaper by limiting electoral expenditure by *both* the candidates *and* the political parties; if you ban only one category, spending will simply shift from one part of the other. A ban on political advertising is also important in making elections cheaper in today's media-heavy world. Strengthening of the welfare state (which, of course, requires an improvement in government revenue) will also help reduce electoral corruption by making the poor less vulnerable to vote-buying. Higher taxes will also enable the government to improve the salaries of its officials, making them less tempted by venality. Of course, there is a bit of a chicken-and-egg problem; without first recruiting good people, to whom you have to pay good salaries, it may not be possible to increase the tax collection capacity. Thus the first place to clean up is the revenue-collection services. The best example is the British excise service in the 17th century (collecting indirect taxes). Meritocracy, unheralded inspections and clear rules were introduced to great effect in the excise service before other parts of the British government. It not only increased government revenue but also later served as a template for improving the customs service and other departments. On the issue of government tax capability in general, see J. di John (2007), 'The Political Economy of Taxation and Tax Reform in Developing Countries' in H-J. Chang (ed.), *Institutional Change and Economic Development* (United Nations University Press, Tokyo, and Anthem Press, London). For further details on the reform of the British excise service, see Nield (2002), pp. 61–2.

14 See chapter 3 for the effect of trade liberalization on government finance in developing countries.

15 This point is made very well by Hodgson & Jiang (2006).

16 J. Stiglitz (2003), *The Roaring Nineties* (W. W. Norton, New York and London) provides detailed discussions of these cases.

17 See the articles in the special issue on 'Liberalisation and the New Corruption' in *IDS Bulletin*, vol. 27, no. 2, April 1996 (Institute of Development Studies, University of Sussex). On the Russian case, see J. Wedel (1998), *Collision and Collusion: The Strange Case of Western Aid to Eastern Europe* (St Martin's Press, New York).

18 http://www.usaid.gov/our_ work/democracy_ and_ governance/.

19 http://www.brainyquote.com/quotes/authors/f/franklin_d_roosevelt.html.

20 M. Wolf (2004), *Why Globalisation Works* (Yale University Press, New Haven and London), p. 30.

21 As cited in J. Bhagwati, *In Defense of Globalisation* (Oxford University Press, New York, 2004), p. 94.

22 N. Bobbio (1990), *Liberalism and Democracy*, translated by Martin Ryle and Kate Soper (Verso, London).

23 M. Daunton (1998), *Progress and Poverty* (Oxford University Press, Oxford), pp. 477–8.

24 S. Kent (1939), *Electoral Procedure under Louis Philippe* (Yale University Press, New Haven).

25 M. Clark (1996), *Modern Italy, 1871–1995*, 2nd ed. (Longman, London and New York), p. 64.

26 On the record of ARA in Uganda and Peru, see Di John (2007).

27 More recent examples include the right to a clean environment, the right to equal treatments across sexes or ethnicities, and consumer rights. Being more recent, the debates surrounding these rights are more controversial and, therefore, their 'political' nature easier to see. But, as these rights are becoming more widely accepted, they look increasingly less political – especially witness the way in which environmental rights, which were only supported by the radical fringe a few decades ago, have become so widely accepted in the last decade or so that they do not look like a political issue any more.

28 For example, when a law regulating child labour was proposed in the British Parliament in 1819, some members of the House of Lords objected to the law on the grounds that 'labour ought to be free', despite the fact that it was an extremely mild law by the standards of our time – the proposed law was supposed to apply only to cotton factories that were considered most hazardous, while banning only the employment of children under the age of nine. See M. Blaug (1958), 'The Classical Economists and the Factory Acts: A Re-examination', *Quarterly Journal of Economics*, 1958, vol. 72, no. 2. For the 'economic' argument against ownership of ideas, see chapter 6.

29 Daron Acemoglu, the MIT economist, and James Robinson, the Harvard political scientist, put the same point in more academic language. They predict that democracy will become more widespread with globalization, as it will make democracy more innocuous. In their view, globalization is likely to make 'the elites and conservative parties to become more powerful and democracy to become less redistributive in the future, especially if new forms of representation for the majority – in both the political sphere and the workplace – do not emerge. Thus, democracy will become more consolidated: however, for those who expect democracy to transform society in the same way as British democracy did in the first half of the twentieth century, it may be a disappointing form of democracy'. J. Robinson & D. Acemoglu (2006), *Economic Origins of Dictatorship and Democracy* (Cambridge University Press, Cambridge), p. 360.

30 A telling example in this regard is an opinion poll before the 2000 US presidential election which revealed that the most important reason cited by the respondents against either of the candidates was that he was 'too political'. So many people rejecting someone who is seeking the biggest political office in the world on the ground that he is 'too political' is a testimony to the extent which the neo-liberals have succeeded in demonizing politics.

31 However, extension of franchise to poor people in European countries in the late 19th and the early 20th centuries did *not* lead to an increase in income transfer, contrary to what the old liberals had feared, although it led to reallocation of spending (especially towards infrastructure and internal security). Income transfer expanded only after the Second World War. For further information, see T. Aidt, J. Dutta, and E. Loukoianova (2004), 'Democracy Comes to Europe: Franchise Extension and Fiscal Outcomes, 1830–1938', *European Economic Review*, vol. 50, pp. 249–283.

32 See the literature reviews in A. Przeworski & F. Limongi (1993), 'Political Regimes and Economic Growth', *Journal of Economic Perspectives*, vol. 7, no. 3 and Robinson & Acemoglu (2006), chapter 3.

33 A. Sen, 'Democracy as a Universal Value', *Journal of Democracy*, vol. 10, no. 3, 1999.

34 One important dimension that we need to bear in mind when understanding the struggle for democracy in today's developing countries is that universal suffrage now enjoys an unprecedented legitimacy. Since the end of the Second World War, selective franchising – once so 'natural' – has become simply unacceptable. Rulers now only have a binary choice – full democracy or no election. An army general who has come to power through a military *coup d'état* may easily suspend elections, but he cannot declare that only rich people or only men can vote. Such heightened legitimacy has made it possible for today's developing countries to introduce and sustain democracy at much lower levels of development than was the case with today's rich countries in the past.

35 Technically speaking, the blacks in the southern states were disenfranchised *not* on the basis of their race, but on the basis of property and literacy qualifications. This was because the Fifth Amendment to the US Constitution introduced after the Civil War banned racial restrictions on voting. But they

were effectively racial restrictions, as, for example, the literacy test was conducted extremely leniently for the whites. See H-J. Chang (2002), *Kicking Away the Ladder – Development Strategy in Historical Perspective* (Anthem Press, London), p. 74.

Chapter 9

1 The quote is from *Japan Times*, 18 August 1915.

2 S. Gulick (1903), *Evolution of the Japanese* (Fleming H. Revell, New York), p. 117.

3 Gulick (1903), p. 82.

4 D. Etounga-Manguelle (2000), 'Does Africa Need a Cultural Adjustment Program?' in L. Harrison & S. Huntington (eds.), *Culture Matters – How Values Shape Human Progress* (Basic Books, New York), p. 69.

5 B. Webb (1984), *The Diary of Beatrice Webb: The Power to Alter Things*, vol. 3, edited by N. MacKenzie and J. MacKenzie (Virago/LSE, London), p. 160.

6 Webb (1984), p. 166.

7 S. Webb & B. Webb (1978), *The Letters of Sidney and Beatrice Webb*, edited by N. MacKenzie and J. MacKenzie (Cambridge University Press, Cambridge), p. 375.

8 Webb & Webb (1978), p. 375. When Webb visited Korea, it had been just annexed by Japan in 1910.

9 T. Hodgskin (1820), *Travels in the North of Germany: describing the present state of the social and political institutions, the agriculture, manufactures, commerce, education, arts and manners in that country, particularly in the kingdom of Hannover*, vol, I (Archbald, Edinburgh), p.50, n. 2.

10 For example, Hodgskin (1820) has a section entitled 'the causes of German indolence' in p.59.

11 M. Shelly (1843), *Rambles in Germany and Italy*, vol. 1 (Edward Monkton, London), p. 276.

12 D. Landes (1998), *The Wealth and Poverty of Nations* (Abacus, London), p. 281.

13 John Russell (1828), *A Tour in Germany*, vol. 1 (Archibald Constable & Co, Edinburgh), p. 394.

14 John Buckingham (1841), *Belgium, the Rhine, Switzerland and Holland: The Autumnal Tour*, vol. I (Peter Jackson, London), p. 290.

15 S. Whitman (1898), *Teuton Studies* (Chapman, London), p. 39, no. 20, quoting John McPherson.

16 Etounga-Manguelle (2000), p. 75.

17 Sir Arthur Brooke Faulkner (1833), *Visit to Germany and the Low Countries*, vol. 2 (Richard Bentley, London), p. 57.

18 Faulkner (1833), p. 155.

19 S. Huntington (2000), 'Foreword: Cultures Count' in L. Harrison & S. Huntington (eds.), *Culture Matters – How Values Shape Human Progress* (Basic Books, New York), p. xi. In fact, Korea's *per capita* income in the early 1960s was less than half that of Ghana, as I point out in the Prologue to this book.

20 Representative works include the following. F. Fukuyama (1995), *Trust: The Social Virtues and the Creation of Prosperity* (Hamish Hamilton, London); Landes (1998); L. Harrison & S. Huntington (eds.) (2000), *Culture Matters – How Values Shape Human Progress* (Basic Books, New York); the articles in the 'Symposium on "Cultural Economics"', *Journal of Economic Perspectives*, Spring 2006, vol. 20, no. 2.

21 Landes (1998), p. 516.

22 M. Morishima (1982), *Why Has Japan Succeeded? – Western Technology and the Japanese Ethos* (Cambridge University Press, Cambridge). This argument has been popularized by Fukuyama (1995).

23 Based on their analysis of the World Value Survey data, Rachel McCleary and Robert Barro argue that Muslims (together with 'other Christians', that is, Christians that do not belong to the Catholic, the Orthodox or the mainstream Protestant churches) have exceptionally strong beliefs in hell and after life. See their article, 'Religion and Economy', *Journal of Economic Perspectives*, Spring 2006, vol. 20, no. 2.

24 It is said that, of the nine names of Allah, two mean the 'just one'. I thank Elias Khalil for relaying this point to me.

25 Gulick (1903), p. 117.

26 Landes (2000), 'Culture Makes Almost All the Difference' in L. Harrison & S. Huntington (2000), p. 8.

27 Fukuyama (1995), p. 183.

28 This is the position taken by a number of authors in Harrison & Huntington (2000), especially the concluding chapters by Fairbanks, Lindsay and Harrison.

29 This term refers to the fact that the Indian economic growth rate was stuck at a relatively low 3.5% (around 1% in *per capita* terms) during 1950–80. It is supposed to have been coined by the Indian economist, Raj Krishna, and was popularized by Robert McNamara, the former president of the World Bank.

30 L. Harrison, 'Promoting Progressive Cultural Change' in L. Harrison & S. Huntington (eds.) (2000), p. 303.

31 Authorities on Japan, like the American political scientist Chalmers Johnson and the British sociologist Ronald Dore, also provide evidence showing that the Japanese were much more individualistic and 'independent-minded' than they are today. See C. Johnson (1982), *The MITI and the Japanese Miracle* (Stanford University Press, Stanford) and R. Dore (1987), *Taking Japan Seriously* (Athlone Press, London).

32 K. Koike (1987), 'Human Resource Development' in K. Yamamura & Y. Tasuba (eds.), *The Political Economy of Japan*, vol. 1 (Stanford University Press, Stanford).

33 J. You & H-J. Chang (1993), 'The Myth of Free Labour Market in Korea', *Contributions to Political Economy*, vol. 12.

Epilogue

1 The 2002 US proposal argued for a radical reduction in industrial tariffs to 5–7% by 2010 and their total abolition by 2015. Since it did not envisage any exception, it is more potent than what happens in my Tallinn Round. The current EU proposal is slightly milder than my Tallinn proposal in that it calls for a reduction to 5–15%. But even that is going to bring tariffs in developing countries to the lowest level since the days of colonialism and unequal treaties – and, more importantly, a level that was not seen in most of today's developed countries before the 1970s. For further details on the US and EU proposals, see H-J. Chang (2005), *Why Developing Countries Need Tariffs – How WTO NAMA Negotiations Could Deny Developing Countries' Right to a Future* (Oxfam, Oxford, and South Centre, Geneva) http://www.southcentre.org/publications/SouthPerspectiveSeries/WhyDevCo untriesNeedTariffsNew.pdf

2 Welles says these lines, which he wrote himself, as Harry Lime, the villain of the movie. This script for *The Third Man* was written by the famous British novelist, Graham Greene, who later turned it into a novel of the same name, except for these lines.

3 In 2002, manufacturing value-added *per capita* in 1995 US dollars was $12,191 in Switzerland. $9,851 in Japan, $5,567 in the USA, $359 in China and $78 in India. See UNIDO (2005), *Industrial Development Report 2005* (United Nations Industrial Development Organisation, Vienna), Table A2.1.

4 The figure for Korea in 2002 was $4,589 and that for Singapore was $6,583. UNIDO (2005), Table A2.1. Thus the Singapore figure is 18 times that of China and 84 times that of India

5 World Bank (1993), *The East Asian Miracle – Economic Growth and Public Policy* (Oxford University Press, Oxford), p. 102.

6 A. Winters (2003), 'Trade Policy as Development Policy' in J. Toye (ed.), *Trade and Development – Directions for the Twenty-first Century*, (Edward Elgar, Cheltenham). As cited in J. Stiglitz and A. Charlton (2005), *Fair Trade for All – How Trade Can Promote Development* (Oxford, Oxford University Press), p. 37.

7 For further details on Taiwan, see R. Wade (1990), *Governing the Market – Economic Theory and the Role of Government in East Asian Industrialisation* (Princeton University Press, Princeton), pp. 219–220. Moreover, the Nationalist Party, which ruled Taiwan during the 'miracle' years, was heavily influenced, through its Comintern membership in the 1920s, by the Soviet Communist Party. Its party constitution was apparently a copy of the latter's. There lies the explanation for the sight of the professional hand-raisers for the geriatric members of the Nationalist Party Politburo that amused the rest of the world so much in the 1980s. Taiwan's second president, Chiang Ching-Kuo, who succeeded his father, Chiang Kai-Shek, as the leader of the party and the head of the state, was a communist as a young man and studied in Moscow with future leaders of the Chinese Communist Party, including Deng Xiao-ping. He met his Russian wife when he was studying in Moscow.

8 Korea also had its share of Marxist influence. General Park Chung-Hee, who masterminded the Korean economic miracle, was a communist in his young days, not least because of the influence of his brother, who was an influential local communist leader in their native province. In 1949, he was sentenced to death for his involvement in a communist mutiny in the South Korean army, but earned an amnesty by publicly denouncing communism. Many of his lieutenants were also communist in their young days.

9 Some left-wing development campaigners have unwittingly contributed to legitimizing the notion of the 'level playing field' by throwing the argument back at the developed countries. They point out that the playing field is tilted the other way when it comes to areas where developing countries are often (although not always) stronger (e.g., agriculture, textiles). If we are going to have free competition, they argue, we have to have it everywhere, and not just where the more powerful countries find it more convenient.

10 The plain fact is that poor countries have low energy efficiency and thus emit much more carbon for each unit of output than do rich countries. For

example, in 2003, China produced $1,471 billion worth of output while emitting 1,131 million tonnes of CO_2. This means that, for every tonne of CO_2, it produced $1,253. Japan produced $4,390 billion, while emitting 336 million tonnes of CO_2, which translates into $13,065 per tonne of CO_2. This means that Japan produced more than 10 times the Chinese output per each tonne of CO_2. Admittedly, Japan is one of the most energy efficient economies, but even the notoriously energy-inefficient (for a rich country) US produced more than five times the Chinese output per tonne of CO_2 – it produced $6,928 for every tonne of CO_2 that it emitted (it produced $10,946 billion worth of output and emitted 1,580 tonnes of CO_2). The carbon emission data are from the US government source. G. Marland, T. Boden, and R. Andres (2006) *Global, Regional, and National CO_2 Emissions. In Trends: A Compendium of Data on Global Change*, Carbon Dioxide Information Analysis Center, Oak Ridge National Laboratory, U.S. Department of Energy (available online at http://cdiac.esd.ornl.gov/trends/emis/tre_tp20.htm). The output figures are from World Bank (2005), *World Development Report 2005* (World Bank, Washington, DC).

11 Some people argue that this Good Samaritanism was partly motivated by the Cold War, which demanded that rich capitalist countries behave nicely to poor countries lest the latter should 'go over to the other side'. But international competition has always been there. If the international competition for influence was the only thing that made the rich countries 'do the right thing' in the third quarter of the 20th century, why did the European empires not do the same in the 19th century when they were in even more fierce competition with each other?

Index